D0878872

THE DIPLOMA DISEASE
Education, Qualification and Development

By the same author
British Factory—Japanese Factory

The Diploma Disease

Education, Qualification and Development

RONALD DORE

UNIVERSITY OF CALIFORNIA PRESS
Berkeley and Los Angeles

First published in 1976

University of California Press
Berkeley and Los Angeles

© George Allen & Unwin Ltd 1975

ISBN 0-520-03107-5
LC 75-22653

Printed in Great Britain

For Sally and Johnny
the only children who actually have
to put up with my views on education

Preface

Nowadays we are supposed to smile at the naive optimism of the Victorians who believed so unquestioningly in the inevitability of 'progress'. 'Civilisation', as they saw it, was continually advancing to ever greater degrees of perfection and refinement. From its metropolitan centres it was reaching out to illuminate the darkest corners of the earth. Macaulay looked forward to the day when India would be a cultural outpost of Europe, its inhabitants not a whit 'lower' in their level of civilisation than those of the metropolis. Oh, the ineffable simplicity — and arrogance — of it all!

Yet, under the skin, most of us are still children of the Enlightenment; we still believe that learning, knowing, understanding, thinking 'civilise'; that education, the cultivation of human minds and spirits, is the foundation of a good and economically productive society; that the improvement of education is a means to a better society.

I, at least, certainly believe that. I also believe, unlike our trendy deschoolers, that there is a lot to be said for doing the educating in special places called schools and universities. Unfortunately, not all schooling is education. Much of it is mere qualification-earning. And more and more of it becomes so. Everywhere, in Britain as in India, in Russia as in Venezuela, schooling is more often qualification-earning schooling than it was in 1920, or even in 1950. And more qualification-earning is *mere* qualification-earning — ritualistic, tedious, suffused with anxiety and boredom, destructive of curiosity and imagination; in short, anti-educational.

We, perhaps, can live with that problem for a while longer before it becomes desperate. There is still a certain amount of educational vitality in our school systems capable of resisting the ritualising disease of qualificationism. But for the much more fragile school systems of the countries of the Third World, where all the stresses of a dualistic development pattern enhance the virulence of the ritualising disease, what for us is a worrying problem becomes a disaster. Primary schools which serve chiefly to give the majority of their pupils the label 'failed drop-out'; secondary schools and universities which seem designed to squeeze every ounce of curiosity and imagination out of a man before he is discharged into the bureaucracy to take responsibility for his country's destinies; growing armies of secondary and university graduates for whom *no* slots can be found in the bureaucracy, and — despite these growing numbers of educated unemployed — relentless and growing pressure for more secondary schools and universities in order to 'widen opportunity': such, in the developing countries of the Third World, are the consequences of using schools as the chief means of sifting each generation into those who get the prize jobs and those who don't, and of letting that sifting function dominate — even it seems, obliterate — the schools' ancient function of providing *education*.

That, together with some modest suggestions as to what might be done about it, is the burden of this book. The first chapter surveys the dimensions of the problem. The five which follow chart the progress of the qualification disease through the histories of Britain, Japan, Sri Lanka and Kenya, sorting out the forces responsible for the 'late development effect' — the tendency for qualificationism to be (a) more deeply entrenched and (b) more disastrous in its consequences, the later in world history a country's development drive starts. Chapter 7 takes a look at the state of theory — the fluctuations over the last twenty years in academic opinion concerning what education is supposed to be able to do to improve men and societies. It also, I trust, serves to expose error and to advance the truth. The next four chapters look at some of the more conventional attempts to tackle the problems of overblown qualification-ridden school systems, especially in those countries where the will to reform has been strongest — Cuba, Tanzania, Sri Lanka — and suggests why they are unlikely to succeed. Chapter 12 is a digression (but an irresistible one) to examine the more radical, but alas not more sensible and probably, indeed, rather less honest, recipes of the deschoolers. Having shown that they simply evade the question — how does society decide who gets what job? — and having concluded that Tanzania and Cuba are over-optimistic in believing that one can go on letting schools combine this social selection function with their educational function without the former over-whelming and distorting the latter, Chapter 13 goes on to consider ways in which the schools can be *entirely relieved* of the social selection function — selection by aptitude tests (or other forms of lottery) rather than achievement tests; apprenticeship and mid-career, rather than pre-career, education and training. The next chapter looks at the hard-to-assess experience of the one country which has moved in that direction, namely China, and the last mulls over some of the ethical and political implications such a change would entail; what it would mean for the value a society places on 'effort'; how it would accord with a sense of justice; how it would affect those fictions by which societies reconcile the lip service they pay to equality with the facts of inequality, and how a solution which most educationists would denounce as 'élitist' might in fact alter the distribution of income and power and respect in society.

My thesis may not be entirely popular. It rests on the assumption that *good* (as opposed to merely qualified) administrators and doctors and teachers are, if not exactly born rather than made, at least pretty well made by their early teens, and that in the process of perfecting them after that, formal schooling may be as much a hindrance as a help. No one would expect educators to be happy with *that* thesis. Even less will members of the international educational establishment like the implication that the little replicas of our school systems which they have been helping to build in developing countries serve those societies even worse than they serve ours. And they will be supported in their objections by the generous indignation of that large, indeed in Britain, dominant, body of social scientists whose pronouncements generally imply (though rarely argue) that all differences in capacity between adults are the consequences of unequal social opportunities rather than of differences in innate potential. In a world in which the words 'pool of ability' evoke ribald jeers, and plans are made for universal college education, a world in which the training mystique leads to a proliferation of courses guaranteed to turn anybody into a dynamic manager or a sympathetic social worker or an imaginative teacher, any attempt to draw attention to the ineluctable differences of human talent and suggest that social arrangements should be based on an explicit recognition of those differences can hardly expect the warmest of welcomes.

Since I am not much practised in polemical writing, readers may notice a somewhat less than synchromesh smoothness at the points where I shift from my more accustomed low-geared scholarly attempts to sort, classify and explain into a less familiar denouncing-and-urging mode. I am told, too, that I romanticise and exaggerate. Perhaps. If I do lay on the colouring a bit thick at times it is not just novitiate's awkwardness which is responsible, however. For a thesis of this kind to have a chance of penetrating the defences of the educational establishment, its barbs must be sharpened and launched with conviction. I derive that conviction, on the days when I possess it, from the reflection that among those of my acquaintance who have developed the habit of thinking sociologically about education systems, nobody else has had the luck to see at fairly close hand how schools work in three societies as different as Britain, Japan and Sri Lanka. I would like to believe that anyone who has would be forced to conclusions very similar to mine.

Another good reason for painting the picture in strong primary colours is to provoke — not just to argument but to research, for this is a field in which research is sadly lacking. What I have called my 'conclusions' should, more modestly, be described as hypotheses for the evidence is at some points sketchy. This is particularly so for three crucial parts of the thesis: concerning the mechanisms of the qualification spiral (there are too few empirical surveys of actual recruiting and promoting practices); concerning parents', pupils' and teachers' perceptions of the purpose of schooling in developing countries and how these shape educational experience and aspirations; and thirdly, concerning the link between the motivational patterns established in school and the way people perform their jobs subsequently — between qualification-orientation on the one hand and lack of initiative and a sense of social responsibility on the other. Some research now being done by colleagues at the Institute of Development Studies should illuminate the first two issues, but these are, by and large, topics to which educational sociologists, economists and psychologists have shown a singular indifference. Perhaps my jeremiad will provoke some of them into research and experiment to prove that I am wrong and the situation is nothing like as bad as I paint it. I hope so. I shall, of course — for my modesty does not stretch that far — be surprised (and suspicious) if further evidence does not in fact confirm my views. But either way, further evidence on these, what seem to me most crucial issues would be welcome. If this book does nothing more than to evoke that evidence, it will have served a purpose.

Acknowledgements

It is always hard to know how many and which of one's ideas one has stolen from whom, but I am sure I must owe most to my colleagues at the Institute of Development Studies. To them many thanks for much stimulation, much tolerance. A number of people have read all or part of the typescript — Manfred Bienefeld, Mark Blaug, Alison Chapman, Emanuel de Kadt, Nancy Dore, John Hajnal, Paul Isenman, Richard Jolly, Angela Little, Keith Lewin, John Oxenham, Miguel Sanchez Padron, Philip Stewart, Jonathan Unger, Wije Wijemanne and Peter Williams. They have all done something to improve it. To them many thanks and the usual absolution from all responsibility etc. Angela Little, Francine Duclerc and Caryl Evans ferretted things out of libraries for me and Jonathan Unger other things out of the Chinese press. I am grateful to them — as also to my wife, Nancy, for sharing and enlivening the job of making the index, and to Ethel Royston for not only typing and retyping, but also remaining cheerful throughout it all.

Contents

Chapter 1

The Problem Elaborated

> The destiny of India is now being shaped in her classrooms. This, we
> believe, is no mere rhetoric . . . it is education that determines the
> level of prosperity, welfare and security of the people.

That opening sentence of the Report of the Indian Education
Commission sums up the assumptions of most writers on education and
development in the early sixties.

Those years, the honeymoon period of African independence, the
years which saw the launching of the UN's First Development Decade,
were the optimistic years. The Addis Ababa Conference organised by
UNESCO laid down a grand plan for the achievement of universal,
compulsory and free primary education by 1980. A conference in
Karachi did the same for Asia. The manpower planners were fanning
out from the foundations and the aid-giving agencies. They were to
devise the strategies whereby the new states could, in the shortest
possible time, amass the human capital necessary for take-off into
modernity.

The economists had just 'discovered' education. In the first decade of
development thinking — the decade which followed the Asian wave of
independence — the emphasis had been all on the lack of physical
capital. Capital was the missing factor which outside aid donors could
supply to create the impetus for self-sustained development. But soon it
was apparent that physical capital was not enough. Capital given to
Europe under the Marshall Plan, capital given to Japan to restore its
devastated industries, proved productive because those countries had
people with the knowledge necessary to make it productive. Similar
investment in an Indonesia or Burma, which lacked the engineers and
managers and technicians of the richer countries, failed to produce the
same results. And so economists discovered — or actually rediscovered,
because Adam Smith had never overlooked the point — the importance
of complementary human factors, of 'investment in human resources'.

Some of these economists were most concerned to demonstrate the
importance of education, to estimate, by various forms of calculation,
the 'social rate of return' — the balance of the costs and benefits it

1

brought to society. They argued, for example, that 'expenditure on education . . . is to be thought of as an investment — investment in mankind. . . . The returns on education, both individually and socially, are at least as high as those in physical capital (Vaizey and Debeauvais, 1961, p. 38).

Others devised means of estimating what *kinds* of skills poor countries should concentrate on producing. They were less concerned with the question of how to teach farmers and fishermen and petty traders to be better farmers and fishermen and petty traders. Their concern was with producing, in the shortest possible time, men to meet the demands for *modern* expertise — civil engineers, factory managers, architects, doctors, accountants, teachers. Afritania, they would say, now, in 1963, has twenty Afritanian engineers. There are another twenty-five expatriate engineers and about twenty unfilled vacancies. If industry grows at 12 per cent a year, the present sixty-five 'slots' for engineers will have grown to 253 in twelve years time. And to make sure that we have replaced all expatriates and built a corps of 253 Afritanian engineers by 1975, and to allow for the likelihood that 20 per cent will brain-drain away, we need to build a university department to come 'on stream' in 1967 and produce thirty-six Afritanian engineers a year thereafter.

Dualism and the education explosion
It was all very bold and brave and planned with impeccable rationality. And the emphasis of the manpower planners on 'middle and higher level manpower' coincided roughly with what people in the poor countries wanted to hear. They too saw development as primarily a matter of building, and then expanding, a 'modern sector'. There were to be factories and government offices, hospitals and marriage guidance clinics modelled on the factories and offices and clinics of the rich countries, staffed by people with the same skills, the same outlooks, the same qualifications, the same sort of clothes and tastes and manners as their counterparts in the rich countries. The factories and offices and clinics would at first be limited in number: tiny bridge-heads of modernity in a sea of 'traditional society'. Development consisted of expanding that bridge-head until the invading forces of modernity had dominated and permeated the whole of the once traditional society.

The secondary schools and universities ran, as it were, the immigration service for the modern sector bridge-head. They decided who was to be let into the modern sector bridge-head and provided the necessary orientation for a productive life within it. There was still a role outside the bridge-head for the primary schools; they were means of mobilising the people behind support for the government's policies; they could improve farm productivity perhaps, even within the constraints imposed by the nature of traditional society; above all they provided the necessary recruits for the secondary schools. Primary schools were the only place one could go to get the necessary application forms for entry into the bridge-head zone, the only place one could go to learn how to fill them out.

The world's bureaucracies are littered with development plans gone awry, with targets unfulfilled. But not many educational plans fall in that category. Their targets — at least the targets for secondary expansion — are much more likely to be overfulfilled than underfulfilled. Much more public pressure is mobilised to support them — and not surprisingly, for life in the modern sector has very considerable attractions. In the ex-colonies the patterns of the modern sector were set by the colonial administration; the style of life which they established — and the income levels that sustain them — have tended to persist beyond independence. In the late sixties, the Ugandan graduate just entering the civil service could expect his income to be fifty times the average income per head in Uganda. Even in India, after a much longer period of independence under governments with a much more explicitly egalitarian philosophy, the ratio was twelve to one. Who would not want a visa into the bridge-head zone? What parent, if he could afford it and felt his son had a chance, would not want to send his child to primary school to get him into the visa queue? What politician could resist the demands of parents for more secondary schools, for a bigger queuing area? Even if the number of visas eventually to be issued is fixed and already vastly oversubscribed for, no one likes his child to be told already at the end of primary school that he has been ruled out of consideration, that he cannot even stay in the queue.

Even at much more modest levels of employment the modern sector is still desirable. The *minimum* wage in government employment in Tanzania — for a labouring job in the public works department which a few lucky people can get with a primary graduation certificate — was still in 1973 $420 a year — about five times the estimated average income per head in Tanzania. The job provides a security which the farmer, dependent on the vagaries of the rains, may well envy; it provides access to medical care and pensions; the rights and dignity of the worker are protected by labour laws and recognised trade unions — the fruits of the victories of European workers in their struggles with their employers, embodied in world norms by the ILO and exported to the developing country as models of how a modern state ought to be — of how the modern sector, the bridge-head zone of modernity in the developing country, ought to be constructed.

Who would not want a visa into the bridge-head zone, when the alternative is so starkly different?

And so the educational explosion. Enrolments throughout the developing world have shown a rapid increase. Crash courses for teacher training, supplementation by untrained teachers, double shift use of schools, grants and subsidies to self-help schools, increases in class size, occasionally, in the more boldly experimental countries, the use of student monitors to help teach — numerous are the devices that have been resorted to in order to meet the rising level of demand for schooling.

The onset of disillusion
There are murmurs of the dangers of a 'decline in quality' resulting from all these makeshift measures. But it is not that which is responsible for the doubts and disillusionment of the seventies which have followed the educational optimism of the sixties. Two other consequences of the educational explosion weigh much more heavily on the minds of politicians and administrators. The first is the endless escalation of costs as rising enrolment ratios are compounded by the consequences of high birth rates and falling infant mortality. Each cohort of children coming to school age is bigger than the last, and a bigger proportion of them want schooling. In many countries education was taking 10—15 per cent of government expenditure at the beginning of the sixties, 20—25 per cent by the end of the decade. According to UNESCO public expenditure on education equalled 2.4 per cent of GNP in the average developing country in 1960, 3.4 per cent in 1970 (UNESCO, 1973, Table 2.6).

The second overt, acknowledged, worried-about problem is the problem of the 'educated unemployed'; of those who have got what used to be considered valid visas into the modern sector, but have not found a suitable niche to settle in. People's ideas as to what qualifications fit what jobs tend to change over time (as we shall see in more detail later), but most Ceylonese would still agree that eight years of education ought to be about right for a manual job, ten years — and a secondary certificate — for a clerical job. At the beginning of the seventies, the schools were producing annually about 70,000 children with eight years education, nearly 100,000 with the first 'Ordinary level' secondary certificate and another 12,000 with higher level certificates. At the same time the total number of wage and salary jobs coming available was *altogether* probably no more than 70,000 — *and* there were all the disappointed aspirants of previous years joining them in the competition.

The paradox of the situation is that the worse the educated unemployment situation gets and the more useless educational certificates become, the *stronger* grows the pressure for an expansion of educational facilities. If you have set sights — or if your parents have set your sights for you — on a modern sector 'job', and if you find that your junior secondary certificate does not get you one, there is nothing to be done except to press on and try to get a senior secondary certificate, and if that doesn't work to press on to the university. The chances are that this will in fact prove to be a sensible decision. The mechanism of 'qualification escalation' ensures that once one is in the modern-sector-qualification range, the higher the educational qualification one gets the better one's chances of getting *some* job.

Educational inflation
The way the qualification-escalation ratchet works is roughly like this. A bus company may 'normally' require a junior secondary leaving certificate for £5-a-week bus conductors and a senior secondary leaving certificate for its £7-a-week clerks. But as the number of senior certificate leavers grows far larger than the number of clerkships that are available, some of them decide that £5 a week as a bus conductor is better than nothing at all. The bus company gives them preference. Soon all the available conductor slots are filled by senior certificate holders: a senior certificate has become a necessary qualification for the job.

It is not entirely clear why employers allow qualifications to escalate in this way. The chief reason seems to be that they are simply unquestioning victims of the widespread myth that education 'improves' people, and that they are therefore getting more for their money if they get a senior certificate for £5 a week rather than a junior certificate. Some who have made their decision more wittingly might defend it on the grounds that those who go on to senior secondary must at least have shown more persistence. And in a country which rations entrance into senior secondary by academic tests rather than by the purse, they might be right in concluding that those who have got through to senior secondary are brighter and less likely to miscount the change. Even if the rationing of secondary education is wholly by the purse — as in those countries like the Philippines or India where almost any smart entrepreneur can set up a secondary school — the bus owners well might still find that these senior secondary pupils, since they come from the better-off homes, are more nicely spoken and reliable. Or it might just be that, faced with fifty applicants for five bus conducting jobs, all of whom could do the job equally well, it just simplifies the whole process to consider only the ten people with senior certificates — and provides a clear objective and legitimate reason for saying no to the other forty. (The last, the legitimation aspect of it, may be particularly helpful if that forty includes a known ne'er-do-well whom some pestiferous relative is trying to push upon you.)

Whatever the reason, it happens. Senior certificates get the bus conducting jobs: BAs preempt the clerkships. The pressure to get on higher up the school ladder is intensified: so is the pressure on the government to build more schools to *allow* more children to get higher up. And it is hard to see a limit to the process. It may be some time before the bus company begins to accept BAs for its bus conducting jobs. The first applicant might well be rejected as dangerously over-educated, likely to be resentful at having sunk so low and to have too fine a conception of himself to work hard. But in countries where free enterprise operates in higher education, eventually it is likely to happen. As more and more of the superfluous BAs are the product of gimcrack local colleges set up on a shoe-string, using the cheap services of unemployed MAs and PhDs, so it becomes more and more obvious that they are not in any real sense more intellectually sophisticated than junior certificate holders. And as the BA job threshold moves slowly down the occupational prestige scale the acceptability of lower paid jobs to BAs slowly increases. Once it has been established for some years that there is nothing unusual or particularly demeaning in a BA accepting a job as a £7-a-week typist, it becomes easier for the BAs who fail in that particular competition to settle for £6 a week as a store clerk. And once store clerkships at £6 a week are accepted as BA jobs, it becomes easier for a BA to accept the £5-a-week bus conductor job without feeling so degraded that he is impelled to take his resentment out on his customers.

The rapidity of this process of qualification escalation — or certificate devaluation, and hence the shape of the educated unemployed problem, varies from one developing country to another, for reasons which will be considered in Chapter 6, and different countries are at different stages in the process. All the countries of South Asia are at an advanced stage; those of West Africa farther along than those of East Africa, and so on, but all seem to be moving in the same direction.

But so what? the reader may say. Why should that be a problem? Surely all this education is still a good thing. What if the executive clerk doing a routine job does have a BA? Surely he will do the job the better for it? Surely he will be a better, more culturally enriched person. And if the vast majority of junior secondary school leavers never get a job in the modern sector, surely, when they eventually recognise their fate and settle down to their ancestral occupations as farmers, as fishermen, as petty traders, they will be better, more productive farmers and traders; they will lead a richer cultural and intellectual life; they will be more effective and responsible political animals, better fathers and mothers to their children?

Ministry of Education officials in many countries would agree. But officials of the Treasury or of Ministries of the Interior would give two very short answers to those arguments. First, the cost of these marginal improvements in the performance of clerks and farmers is just too high. In Ghana, in 1971 the education of each university graduate was costing the state over ₵4,000 per annum, more than twelve times the per capita national income (and 160 times the annual cost of keeping a child in primary school; Williams, 1974, p. 335). Secondly, they would say, it may be true that *eventually* the educated unemployed will settle down to their fate in the traditional sector, but the process of 'cooling them out' is a tricky and potentially dangerous one. It takes time for people to realise that because a junior secondary certificate got such and such a job five years ago, that is no good reason for expecting it to do so now. And even if the reality is appreciated, the sense of being wronged — the sense of having a *right* to a job which the system, i.e. the government, refuses to honour — persists. And the concentration of disaffected resentful job-seekers in the towns can be a politically dangerous one. Even more dangerous, because they have a more effective framework for organisation, can be the anticipatory frustration of university and high school students who see unemployment as the only thing they have to look forward to. The 'revolt of youth' in Sri Lanka in April 1971 is a lesson which is not lost on political leaders elsewhere.

Education and qualification

But there is another, more fundamentally challenging answer to the 'surely the more education the better' argument. The trouble is, this second argument runs, that the so-called educated unemployed have not, in fact, been educated. Nor indeed have the educated employed. They have certainly been schooled but they are the victims of a system of schooling without education.

A much-quoted book on the subject is Cyril Beeby's *Quality of Education in Developing Areas*. An Australian educator with a wide acquaintance with developing countries, Beeby suggests that all societies' educational systems go through a regular process of evolution. They begin with the classroom-drilled rote-learning beloved of Victorian schoolmasters in England; they progress, as the teachers gain a little more confidence and are prepared to answer questions which are 'outside the curriculum', to the freer, child-centred, more autonomous patterns of learning characteristic of acknowledged 'best practice' in the classrooms of the rich countries today. Most of the developing countries are still at the Victorian rote-learning stage, but gradually they will grow out of it.

It is a comforting thesis, particularly since Beeby has some suggestions to make about accelerating the process. Developing countries don't actually have to make the Dewey revolution all over again, all by themselves. Unfortunately, the odds are that it is wrong. In this, as in so many other ways, the process of development in a country which starts deliberately modernising in the mid-twentieth century is very different from the process of less deliberate development the rich countries experienced in the nineteenth century. Marx couldn't have been more wrong, as Trotsky long ago pointed out, when he said 'the industrial countries show the less developed countries the image of their own future'.

The effect of schooling, the way it alters a man's capacity *and will* to do things, depends not only on what he learns, or the way he learns it, but also on *why* he learns it. That is at the basis of the distinction between schooling which is education, and schooling which is only qualification, a mere process of certificating — or 'credentialling', as American sociologists have recently started to call it.

Most people, when they speak of 'education', have in mind a process of learning — be it by disciplined training or by freer more enjoyable methods of experiment — which has mastery as its object. Knowledge may be sought for its own sake, for the sheer play delight of using the mind. It may be sought to meet some criterion for self-respect: the boy who persists with his reading practice so that he, too, can have his turn reading the lesson in church; the older social scientist who settles down to learn about computers to keep up with his younger colleagues. It may be sought for profitable use: the merchant's son learns accountancy in order to become a better and richer merchant. It may be sought out of respect for some conception of a professional calling — as when the doctor reads reports of the latest discoveries about kidneys in order to be a better, more conscientiously self-respecting doctor. In any case, whether the mastery is an end in itself, or whether the knowledge is mastered for use, and whether that use is a practical one or mere self-indulgent pleasure, it is mastery of the knowledge itself which counts.

In the process of qualification, by contrast, the pupil is concerned not with mastery, but with being certified as having mastered. The knowledge that he gains, he gains not for its own sake and not for constant later use in a real life situation — but for the once-and-for-all purpose of reproducing it in an examination. And the learning and reproducing is all just a means to an end — the end of getting a certificate which is a passport to a coveted job, a status, an income. If education is learning to *do* a job, qualification is a matter of learning in order to *get* a job.

The difference is a difference in what is now fashionably called the 'hidden curriculum'. What the educator is saying implicitly — and sometimes explicitly — to his pupils is: 'learn this or you will not become a good doctor, a skilful carpenter, a fully-developed human being, a good useful citizen; you will not know how to *earn* your living, you will not be able to appreciate the higher pleasures of art or poetry'. What the qualifier says to his pupils is: 'learn this or you will not get the chance to be a doctor or a carpenter; nobody will *give* you a living'. The first appeals to the inner standards of conscience and promises self-achieved fulfilment; the second invokes external arbiters, threatens exclusion, evokes anxiety. The first preserves the teacher-pupil relation as complete in itself; the second makes both dependent on the tyranny of the examiners.

Maslow, one of the most eloquent and humane of psychologists, has expressed the difference well in his characterisation of the contrast between self-actualising activity and activity which merely fulfils lower level deficiency needs. In self-actualising activity,

> . . . gratification breeds increased rather than decreased motivation, heightened rather than lessened excitement. The appetites become intensified and heightened. They grow upon themselves and instead of wanting less and less, such a person wants more and more of, for instance, education . . . Growth is, *in itself,* a rewarding and exciting process, e.g. the fulfilling of yearnings and ambitions, like that of being a good doctor, the acquisition of admired skills, like playing the violin or being a good carpenter; the steady increase of understanding about people, or about the universe, or about oneself: the development of creativeness in whatever field or, most important, simply the ambition to be a good human being.

Whereas deficiency-motivated man, whose need (e.g. for a certificate) can only be satisfied from outside,

> . . . cannot be said to be governing himself, or in control of his own fate. He *must* be beholden to the sources of supply of needed gratifications . . . he must adapt and adjust by being flexible and responsive and by changing himself to fit the external situation. He is the dependent variable: the environment is the fixed independent variable. (Maslow 1973, pp. 241, 243.)

The distinction is a familiar one. The extent to which the pressure of examinations cramps and distorts the educational process is a familiar problem. British grammar schools have their qualifiers in plenty, like this young PhD teacher:

> I reckon I can do A level chem. in four terms. Four terms flat out, mind. We have to go really fast. We have tests twice a week, but we get the results. For instance, last year I got an open to Pembroke, Cambridge, and an exhibition at Trinity Hall, Cambridge, and then

I got half-a-dozen places. I've got fourteen places in the last two years and then these opens. I do pretty well; my results are all right. The way we teach, we teach for results. I want the passes, the schols, and all those things. Tests all the time, and scrub the teaching methods, forget about the educational side . . . let me give you an instance: if a boy asks a question it might raise some interesting matters. Now [you could] waste a whole period and follow up those matters and that's all right. But that's not our way. (Jackson and Marsden, 1966, p. 51.)

This single-minded young man at least shows a certain zest and confident panache as he sets out to outwit the examiners at their own game — and doubtless some of this rubs off on to his pupils to their advantage. Even this saving grace is lacking in most schools of developing countries. To its less confident teachers the examiners are as remotely awesome and authoritative as to the pupils. More important, perhaps, is the fact that so much is at stake when only the very best examination results hold the promise of a job. In such an anxiety-ridden atmosphere (and for a number of other reasons to be discussed later) the need to qualify much more effectively kills any nascent desire to educate or to get educated, and makes the examination-backwash effect a good deal worse than in most richer countries. During a conversation with a very intelligent civics teacher in Sri Lanka, she was asked about the civics course she was teaching to her 16-year-old charges:

What sort of topics do you discuss in the classroom?

Well, there are four parts to it really. You have to do six questions, one from each part. The first is about the departments of government; then the second is about democracy and feudalism and totalitarianism; the third is the government of Ceylon — Parliament, local government and so on. And the fourth is about British government, the Commonwealth and the United Nations. The United Nations is practically compulsory. There is a question on it every year.

No, I didn't mean the examination; I meant: do you discuss practical questions of current affairs in the classes? For example the new constitution? There was a lot of news in the paper yesterday about the abolition of the Senate. Would you discuss that?

The Senate, yes. Last year, for instance, there was a question about whether the Senate had fulfilled its role as envisaged by the Soulbury Commission.

No, I meant whether you ever go outside the actual teaching for the examination and talk about things that are going on in the country.

Oh no, with students of that age I don't think it would be possible. You see they have no clear picture.

This was a Grade 10 class, the class most conscious of the fact that the future of each individual was going to be set by the secondary certificate exam at the end of that year. Earlier on in their school careers, at the beginning of primary school, teachers still have some time for education. But less and less so, as the backwash of examinations reaches farther and farther back into the primary school. The Grade 8 selection exam effectively decides who will get the coveted science places. In many African countries exams at the end of the sixth year determine who shall and who shall not have a chance of secondary education; from the third year on everything is subordinated to preparation for those tests. Well-meaning educational administrators, having at last observed that the majority of the children who get to Grade 5 are destined, by the ineluctable facts of the labour market situation, to a farming future, put agriculture and practical subjects into the curriculum. But what teacher, intent on coaching the maximum number of his pupils through the hard subjects like mathematics and English, can give much time to agriculture? What child would wish to acknowledge himself in advance as a drop-out failure in the race to the modern sector by showing an interest in such a subject?

The qualified and the educated
Is it any wonder, then, that the products of this kind of schooling are not, when cooled out of their modern sector hopes and settled back on their farms, notably more innovative and successful farmers than those who have not been to school? Is it surprising that the frustrations of unemployed school leavers and university graduates have not proved to be that fructifying kind of tension that breeds the successful entrepreneurs? The whole of their schooling has conditioned them to become employees. The whole of the modern sector is an employee sector; its employee teacher, the representative of the modern sector in the village, demonstrates the employee model in himself. The would-be employee has learned to take orders, not initiatives.

At least those who *get* the certificates and the jobs will have been well prepared, then. At least the employee-orientation of the schools will have prepared *them* well for their subsequent careers. In a limited way, yes. They will have learned the virtues of punctuality, regularity, hard work, conformity to regulation, obedience to the instructions of superiors. These are not insignificant qualities, perhaps. But are they the qualities *most* required in the members of administrative and managerial bureaucracies given the task of modernising their society? What of imagination, creativity, honesty, curiosity and the determination to get to the bottom of things, the desire to do a good job for its own sake? These are not the qualities likely to be bred by a prolonged dose of qualification-oriented schooling — most prolonged in those highest up in the hierarchy on whose initiatives the most depends. If a man has got his civil service job by dint of eighteen or twenty years of joyless conformity to the imposed rituals of qualification-oriented schooling, who can blame him if he turns into the cautious official, joylessly performing the rituals of office? If he has never had a chance to discover the satisfaction of learning for its own sake, who can blame him for not being able to enjoy working for its own sake? If he has been denied the chance to experience the disinterested altruism of which Maslow's self-actualiser is capable, if all his training has been in the self-regarding exercise of securing his own success, who can blame him if he attaches more importance to his own subsequent bureaucratic advancement than to the actual job of transforming his country? Those who have visited Third World ministries and noticed that it is often the expatriate advisors who carry on working after hours when their local colleagues have packed up and gone home should not give the advisors themselves too much credit. They are the lucky ones, coming from those privileged strata in privileged societies where children are still given an education, still made capable of zestful self-initiated and self-directed work which provides its own satisfaction — a privileged experience which the schools of developing countries rarely offer to their pupils.

But let us beware of assuming any much greater virtue in our own educational systems, for it was in the schools and universities of the advanced countries that the qualification rot started. The trouble is that the later the point in world history that a country begins its deliberate modernisation[1] process, the more definitively the disease takes hold — as I trust the next five chapters, dealing with Britain, Japan, Sri Lanka and Kenya, will show.

---

[1] I should make clear that when I use 'modernise', 'modernising' or 'modernisation' I do not subscribe to any one of the theories about the 'essential character' of modernisation as a process of transformation which all societies must somehow go through — a process, according to taste, of rationalisation, disenchantment, bureaucratisation, differentiation and re-integration, increasing use of inanimate power, increasing homelessness of consciousness or whatever. I use the verb 'modernise' in a strictly transitive sense. It is

what somebody does to something. I say 'modernise' rather than 'change', when the person doing the changing explicitly sees the changes as towards a more 'advanced' state in some scale of what he sees as progress. Third World leaders are trying to modernise their countries largely by transforming them in the image of other countries which they consider more advanced; sometimes according to even more 'advanced' prescriptions of what the richer countries themselves will or ought to become. When, as for example with Nyerere's ideal of Ujamaa organisation, they see the transformation as towards something not necessarily more advanced but just different and uniquely national, I would not call that 'modernisation'. I do, most of the time, however, assume that the long-term aims of most of the conscientious leaders of the Third World are shaped by their image of the industrial countries; that if they defined those long-term goals explicitly they would turn out to be an amalgam of such stereotypical elements as America's productive power, Japan's low crime rate, Sweden's social cohesion, France's artistic vitality, etc.

Chapter 2

England

It would be hard to make out a case for believing that the economic growth of Britain was a consequence of improved or expanded education.

> The industrial revolution was accomplished by hard heads and clever fingers. Men like Bramah and Maudslay, Arkwright and Crompton, the Darbys of Coalbrookdale and Neilson of Glasgow, had no systematic education in science and technology. Britain's industrial strength lay in its amateurs and self-made men: the craftsman-inventor, the mill-owner, the iron-master . . . In this rise of British industry the British universities played no part; indeed formal education of any sort was a negligible factor in its success. The schools attended scarcely changed since the schooldays of John Milton two centuries earlier. For the working classes there was no systematic schooling. Illiteracy was widespread: even as late as 1841 a third of the men and nearly half the women who were married in England and Wales signed the register with a mark. (Ashby, 1961, p. 466.)

One can, to be sure, overstress this point. The basic general education which some of the entrepreneurs and inventors of the late eighteenth and early nineteenth centuries received was probably not irrelevant to their later careers. Significantly a higher proportion of them were former pupils of the dissenting academies than can be explained by mere chance (Flinn, 1967, p. 25) which, given the state of the public schools patronised by the orthodox Anglican gentry, is perhaps not surprising.

There are also reasonable grounds for saying that the *relevant* statistic is that two-thirds of the men *could* write their names when they got married, rather than that one-third couldn't. Anderson's '40% threshold', his thesis that for all the major historical cases of economic growth an overall 40 per cent school enrolment rate seems to have been a precondition (Anderson, 1965, p. 34), has a certain plausibility. Economic growth in Britain was not just a matter of a few inventions in the textile industry and in engineering; it depended on numerous rationalising initiatives of farmers and merchants and craftsmen and small entrepreneurs. And eighteenth-century Britain did have institutionalised means of teaching enough of the young to read and write and calculate — even, sometimes, to think — to provide a sizeable number of men capable of such initiatives.

But — to summarise the argument of the following brief and perhaps idiosyncratic (but at least purposefully so) history of British education:

1. There was no spurt in educational provision preceding or accompanying the acceleration of economic growth known as the industrial revolution.

2. The effect of early industrialisation was, if anything, to harden the divisions between the schools of different social strata, rather than to provide channels for social mobility.

3. It was not until industrialisation was well under way that the state began to play a role of any importance in the direction of the educational system.

4. It took even longer before the state's management of the educational system became much affected by the intention to stimulate or sustain economic growth — to meet national training needs, etc.

5. And it was even later still that the national training needs were seen to require the 'sponsored mobility' of bright children from the poorer classes through the educational system to man the expanding middle-class occupations.

6. Meanwhile, until this happened, the occupation of a man depended chiefly on family connections which secured entry into different kinds of craft and professional apprenticeships, and on his ability to develop the necessary competence during his apprenticeship, and afterwards on the job. It also depended in part on what he had *learned* in school, but not much on any certificates or qualifications he might have got from school.

7. The standards of competence required by various crafts and professions gradually became more precisely defined — at first by the practitioners who established their own means of testing and certifying skills.

8. But gradually public authorities took an increasing hand in the definition of competence, beginning with the professions of most direct public concern such as medicine.

9. And (as a related, but not identical trend) general educational qualifications granted by the core educational system of elementary and secondary schools, colleges and universities, have played an increasing role in the control over access to occupations.

10. With the result that the social definition of the purpose of schooling has changed, and with it the motivation of students and the quality of learning.

The beginnings

England, at the end of the eighteenth century, had many schools (if fewer in proportion to population than in the sixteenth century; Anderson, 1965, p. 359) but it was far from having a school system. There was just a haphazard array of schools sustained for a multiplicity of private profit-making or religious purposes. They ranged from dame-schools unashamedly concerned primarily with child-minding, through elementary schools which sought seriously to teach the basic three Rs, and ancient grammar schools which drilled the conventional rudiments of a classical education into the heads of recalcitrant children for reasons which had long since been forgotten, to dissenting academies with a fairly clear conception of the moral character and intellectual attitudes which they sought to produce.

Those schools were not intended as channels of social mobility (it was even less common than in Chaucer's day for orphans to become 'poor clerks at Oxford' and eventually princes of the church). They were there to prepare children for a place in society which their parentage determined with more or less certainty. Gentlemen students went to Oxford to learn to be gentlemen — so that 'their reason, fancy and carriage be improved by lighter institutions and exercises, that they might become rational and graceful speakers, and be of an acceptable behaviour in their counties' (Seth Ward — a seventeenth-century author admittedly — quoted in Hill, 1965, p. 302). And so it was for those born into lower orders of society. There were certain things a merchant should know to be a self-respecting merchant; certain things a weaver might wish his children to know so that they could aspire like him to the position of church deacon, and certain useful things they needed to know in order to be successful merchants and weavers.

The class stratification of England's schools sharpened in the nineteenth century as the more-or-less culturally cohesive rural and small town communities which in the Elizabethan period had supported grammar schools of very mixed social composition receded into the historical distance. As the agricultural revolution and then the industrial revolution concentrated and separated the two nations of nineteenth-century England, creating the great industrial towns in which the 'masters' living on the hill and the 'men' in the valley hardly met outside of the mill, so, too, the bifurcation of the educational system proceeded apace. Whether capitalism strengthened the Protestant Ethic or vice versa, a new serious-mindedness spreading from the dissenters to the Anglican community began to affect the public schools. But Dr Arnold's brand of moral regeneration was one which reflected the fact that these schools were now pretty exclusively schools for an upper class conscious of its responsibilities as rulers. The Christian gentlemen whom Arnold sought to breed were to be the leaders, the 'prefects' in Wilkinson's phrase, of English society (Wilkinson, 1964).

Civilising the lower orders

The same religiously-based sense of social responsibility, refracted through a sense of class self-interest, prompted the new concern with the education of the poor which gradually developed in the first half of the nineteenth century. The new system of schools which was slowly built up into the state elementary education system was entirely separate from the schools of the middle class. Its primary aim was to instruct the lower orders in the elementary virtues of diligence, thrift, hygiene, sobriety and proper deference to superiors, while simultaneously imparting a certain minimum of cognitively useful knowledge.

The fact that deference to superiors could no longer be taken for granted was apparent in the Gordon Riots, in Peterloo, in the Luddite movement, in the popular agitations of 1832; and later in the growth of trade unions and Chartism. The world's ruling classes can be placed on a continuum. At one end are those who see their authority as resting on coercive power supported by ignorance — like the landlords in West Pakistan who told a researcher in 1961 that the last thing they wanted were schools which would surely have no effect other than to breed communists (Abbott, 1966, p. 296). At the other end are the Confucian rulers of Tokugawae Japan or of the golden age of the Ch'ing dynasty who are so certain of the truth and persuasiveness of the ideology which justifies their power that they see every interest in building schools to diffuse it among the people.

The middle and upper classes of early nineteenth-century Britain were spread all the way along this continuum. The debate about the education of the poor in the first half of the century was largely a debate between the majority who were said to 'dread the consequences of teaching the poor more than they dread the effects of their ignorance' (Simon, 1960, p. 169), and the minority who thought, like the Rev. Andrew Bell, that it would improve 'the subordination and orderly conduct' of children (Hurst, 1972, p. 14), or like Kay-Shuttleworth, that it would help the poor to understand — and so come happily to accept — 'the true causes which determine their physical condition and regulate the distribution of wealth among the several classes of society', (ibid., p. 23).

By the 1840s, however, new concerns began to appear. A parliamentary committee looked into the effects of education on work-efficiency and was told that educated Saxon workmen were a good deal more versatile than their unlettered English counterparts (Bowman, 1965, p. 105). Forster's 1870 Bill to make elementary education universally available was avowedly prompted in part by a concern with Britain's industrial competitiveness (Wickwar, 1949, p. 59).

Training for Work

It was, indeed, almost entirely in the factories and mines, the workshops and mills, not in the schools, that the skills which fed Britain's industrial advance were both accumulated and transmitted. The continuity of traditional apprenticeship systems, only gradually altering in form from the eighteenth century to the present day, is proof of that. In the pioneer industrialiser (unlike, as we shall see, the situation in late-developing countries) progress was by invention or by the importation of inventions which made marginal incremental advances. Skilled workmen were able to absorb them on the job and add them to their repertoire, transmitting to the next generation a larger reservoir of skills than they themselves had inherited. Only occasionally did engineers who made the bigger leaps find it necessary to introduce deliberate training schemes — as did Boulton and Watt, who found the millwrights available to be recruited to their steam engine plant incapable of learning to work to the fine tolerances their plans required. Only towards the end of the century did technical institutes begin on any substantial scale to provide some skilled workmen with a general basic understanding of mechanical and metallurgical principles which helped them to absorb new techniques.

So it was, too, with the higher level — what eventually became to be recognised as the professional — skills of the engineer. The engineers fully emerged to self-consciousness as a profession, distinguishing themselves from the millwrights and clockmakers who had been their forerunners, with the foundation of the Royal Institution of Civil Engineers in 1818. Their purpose in coming together and founding their society was partly to exchange knowledge and ideas, partly to define and to protect the status and good name of the engineer by control over admission. Training was by apprenticeship and self-study; proof of competence was provided by work performance vouched for by one's peers.

And so, in the engineering profession, it remained until 1897. In other professions the resort to theoretical written examinations came sooner: the solicitors in 1835, the accountants in 1880. But the process of which this was a symptom — the systemisation of the body of principles on which the work of the profession was based; its rationalisation into a form which made it partly susceptible to teaching and learning in the classroom — proceeded steadily. Engineering became a proper university subject taught by chaired professors at Glasgow and London in the 1840s. Formal university training thus became, for members of the middle class, a short cut on the road to competence as an engineer. But still it was a short cut only in so far as one genuinely learned more quickly that which one would otherwise have had to learn in apprenticeship. The formal qualification in itself gained no recognition; it was to be several decades before the possession of a university degree helped by gaining formal exemption from the normal training requirements of the engineering institutions.

The growth of pre-career qualification

But once *that* process had begun, its acceleration in the twentieth century was rapid. It had two aspects: on the one hand the increasing willingness of professional groups to entrust to secondary schools and universities the business of training and selecting their recruits; and on the other, the gradual systematisation and re-orientation of the school and university system towards serving this function.

This latter involved three related changes. First was the slow, reluctant evolution of the universities' curricula, making more of the content of their courses plausibly relevant to the occupational destinations of their students. The second was the growth and systematisation of secondary education parallel to, but following, the gradual systemisation of elementary education. The third element was the integration of the elementary and secondary schools and universities into a single pyramidical structure, opening channels of merit competition for passage from one stratum to the next to supplement the more traditional methods of rationing educational opportunity — by fee charges and the constraints of social convention.

The story of how the universities gradually ceased to be 'comfortably monastic establishments for clerical sinecurists with a tinge of letters' (G. M. Trevelyan in Glass, 1961, p. 393) is a long and complex one. The growth of medical education and introduction of engineering technology was one aspect; the latter a particularly slow, hard-fought process, even in Glasgow (Ashby, 1961, pp. 466-75). The shocking discovery at the Paris exhibition of 1867 that Britain's technical supremacy was rapidly being lost helped to turn the tide, but it was not until the establishment of the new wave of civic universities at the turn of the century that the place of engineering in university education was fully established.

More generally important was the pressure to introduce 'modern studies' in the humanities and social sciences which might have some relevance to the administrative, managerial and political careers for which a large proportion of university graduates were destined. Most influential in this respect were the competitive examinations for the civil service which followed the Northcote-Trevelyan report. The standards they set had a powerful influence on the standards of university teaching. The more or less simultaneous ending of patronage in the civil service, the army and the church (leaving finance and industry (!) as the two major fields in which patronage prevailed) altered the whole significance of learning for the upper-middle class and was perhaps the most important influence tending — though in a very covert way — to 'vocationalise' university education. At the same time the expansion of secondary schools employing graduate teachers and the continuous growth of the universities themselves made the production of teachers a major vocational function of universities.

However, many professions — law, accountancy, architecture, for instance — still rely only half-heartedly on university training.

As for secondary education, the state's concern begins effectively with the establishment of a Department of Science and Art in 1858 to encourage secondary science teaching by monetary grants, and the Endowed Schools Act a decade later. By then those of the older endowed grammar schools which had not been transformed into exclusive boarding establishments for the upper class had been supplemented by large numbers of new foundations: Wesleyan and other religious schools and the so-called proprietary schools organised on the joint stock principle. These catered primarily for the middle class. The Taunton Commission of 1868, which was appointed to inquire into the health of the schools, nicely reflects the increasing extent to which education was becoming, for sections of the middle class, the major determinant of occupation and social status. The mercantile and industrial middle class, it pointed out, had property in an ongoing business to bequeath to their children; it was to other groups that the schools were of particular concern: to 'the great body of professional men, especially the clergy, medicine men and lawyers', who 'have nothing to look to but education to keep their sons on a high social level'.

It was not however until more than three decades later, with the 1902 Act, that public authorities were squarely given the responsibility of providing secondary education. Thereafter numbers in secondary schools rapidly increased: from 100,000 in 1895 to double that number at the beginning of the First World War and to well over half a million by the mid-thirties (Glass, 1961, p. 392).

The third and last element of the re-orientation of the educational system for occupational selection — the hierarchical integration of the three layers — was also a long time maturing. The linking of the secondary and university layers occurred first. Preparation for university entrance became increasingly recognised as an objective of secondary education. Already in 1868 the Taunton Commission had judged the quality of schools by their success in sending pupils to the universities, but only after the establishment of the civic universities did the majority of grammar schools acquire university preparatory sixth forms, and not, perhaps, until the 1960s did the importance of the sixth form in the grammar school scheme of things reach the point at which the Ordinary level General Certificate of Education, taken at the age of 15 or 16, became predominantly defined in most schools as the selection hurdle for sixth-form/university entry, rather than as a terminal secondary leaving certificate.

The integration of elementary and secondary education was an even slower development. It was a long time before the argument that the national need to maximise the use of its reserve of talent combined with a nascent egalitarianism to call forth public funds. State scholarships to allow children to move from the elementary to the grammar schools which could lead on to the university started in 1907, but for a long time the flow was little more than a trickle. Still, less than 50 per cent of the pupils in grammar schools were scholarship holders in 1938. The elementary schools for the working class were allowed to add secondary-level forms, parallel to the predominantly middle-class grammar schools, and such vocational technical training as developed was concentrated in this elementary-extension sector, separate from and of lower prestige than the clerkly/university-preparatory secondary grammar school sector (ibid., p. 399).

Eventually, the 1944 Act planned, and largely brought about, the final integration of the system, but although it removed most of the economic obstacles to full working-class participation in educational pyramid-climbing, it could not as quickly remove some of the cultural obstacles — the lack of interest of many working-class parents in seeing their sons enter an educational and occupational career which they viewed either with hostility as alienating or with humility as not for the likes of them — something to aspire to which would lead only to disappointment. What proportion of the nation's parents were fully *in* the race by 1960, awaiting the results of the 11-plus grammar school entrance tests with open or concealed anxiety, is hard to guess. It was certainly a larger proportion than in 1940; the change in aspirations and expectations had been considerable. So, consequently, was the net increase in the volume of human disappointment which each annual round of selection occasioned. And as the working class began to add its anxieties to the more intense neuroses of the middle class (for the middle-class parent, failure in the 11-plus forbode actual *loss* of status, not just loss of the chance to better oneself) public pressure slowly built up for the ending of selection and the establishment of comprehensive secondary education.

Today not even that issue is fully settled, while the next stage of educational evolution — the attempt to postpone even further the point of invidious selection by developing comprehensive (or at least *more* comprehensive) university education on the American model — is as yet only foreshadowed in vague hints in Labour Party documents. But (cataclysms apart) come it certainly will, for the more definitively important educational qualifications become in determining occupation and social status, and the more deeply rooted the ideology of equality of opportunity, and the more nationally homogeneous are Britain's parents in their aspirations to seize opportunity, the stronger will grow the pressure to have second chances and third and fourth chances — to ensure that no one has his child ruled definitively out of the race for top jobs until the last possible moment.

The inflation of qualifications
But what is the proof that academic attainment in the formal educational system *has* become more definitely important in determining career destinations? Evidence is not hard to find. Trends emerge fairly clearly if one looks at the various career guides which have been produced for ambitious young Englishmen since the end of the last century.[1]

Take civil engineering, for example. Between 1897 and 1971 the transition from apprenticeship and mid-career qualification to *pre-career* qualification has been almost complete. Until 1897 there was no written examination of any kind. An apprenticeship, the ability to learn on the job by observation and deliberate self-study, evidence of personal work accomplishments confirmed by the grilling of a professional interview were what got one membership in the institutions and hence the right to give oneself the title of engineer. By 1897, however, the importance of basic theoretical knowledge was too obvious to be wholly denied. Soon the civil engineers had, like most of the other professions, the full three-stage range of qualifying examinations: preliminary, intermediate and final. Technical institutes oriented their courses to these, or to the higher national certificates and diplomas which were accepted as their equivalents. From the very beginning a university degree was an acceptable alternative to the institutions' own examinations; the graduate had only to acquire three years' practical experience and submit to a professional interview in order to become a full member. But in the first decades of this century the majority of entrants to the profession got there by part-time study whilst serving a practical apprenticeship — often as a 'premium-

---

[1]E. H. Coombe, *What Shall I Be: A Guide to Occupations* (London, 1900); G. H. Williams, *Careers for Our Sons* (Carlisle, 1908); D. Cross, *Choosing a Career: A Guide to Success* (London, 1908); H. E. Morgan, *Careers for Boys and Girls* (London, 1926); K. H. Edwards, *A Guide to Employment for Boys and Girls* (Middlesbrough, 1930); L. H. Turner, *Dictionary of Careers* (3rd edn, London, 1946); Ministry of Labour, *Careers Guide* (London, 1950); H. R. Jackson, *Careers Encyclopaedia* (7th edn, London, 1970); G. Brown, *The Careers Handbook for Boys* (London, 1971).

paying' pupil with special claims to be allowed to work in a variety of departments in the factory. The author of the 1926 careers guide was still advising that 'a degree of B.Sc. Engineering is a valuable supplementary qualification . . . But it can never be a substitute for practical training . . . Apprenticeship is still the best way of entering the engineering profession.' But he was fighting for a losing cause. The trend towards pre-career qualification throughout the century has proved inexorable. In 1935, for the first time, the number of graduate entrants into civil engineering exceeded the number of mid-career qualifiers. By 1950 the latter were becoming more and more a rarity. By 1970 they were so few in number that together with the other members of the Council of Engineering Institutions, the civil engineers closed off the part-time qualification route altogether. Henceforth a formal degree from a university or college of technology was a necessary pre-condition for a professional career as an engineer.

Other professions have not gone quite so far in their reliance on university training. Brown's 1971 guide estimates that 60 per cent of newly qualified solicitors are graduates, but advises that 'while a degree is an asset, no-one should be deterred from entering the profession because he cannot or does not wish to go to a university'. The accountants were until recently much less predisposed to encourage university study. Three years at a university gained exemption from only two of the five years required as an articled clerk — and carried the disadvantage, as the 1908 guide remarked, that the transition from the 'brightness and movement of the university to the drudgery of a first year's accountant clerk is a severe strain and may very well disgust a man'. They were recently forced to relent, however, and grant three years' exemption for a university degree.

Thus, even the professions which are most jealous to preserve their own qualification system and to stress *practical* training have been moving in the same general direction as the civil engineers. There are three parts to the trend. First, increasing reliance on certificates of general education. By 1970 the special preliminary examinations of all the major professions had been replaced by the requirement of a certain minimum cluster of passes or credits in various subjects in the General Certificate of Education, either at the Ordinary (O) or at the Ordinary and Advanced (A) levels. Secondly, that minimum level showed a steady tendency to increase, and thirdly, the requirements for on-the-job pupillage before full professional status is achieved have tended to contract.

Librarians are a good example. At the beginning of the century a librarian had to have only a 'love of books and the capacity to advise the managers as to purchases, and inquirers as to suitable works' — he had, in other words, actually to be able to do his job. By the 1930s, intending librarians were told that a school certificate was a 'useful possession'. By 1950 it was the minimal requirement. No one could be a librarian who had not continued his education to the age of (usually) 15 or 16. By 1970 two A levels — an extra two years of study for the average child — were the minimum requirement, and the Library Association looks forward to the day when 'the possession of a university or CNAA degree becomes as common as possession of a G.C.E. with A levels today' (*Library Association Research,* October 1972, p. 196). Meanwhile the minimum apprenticeship period of three years was reduced to one (after a special two-year training in librarianship) in the 1950s and was waived altogether for university graduates in the 1970s, by which time three universities and six polytechnics were offering degree courses in librarianship (*The Times,* 18 June 1972).

Perhaps nothing better epitomises the slow change in Britain's mechanisms and criteria for job selection than the terminology of these guides, with the emphasis slowly shifting from personal aptitude to quantitatively measurable educational achievement. The 1900 guide talks of the 'ingredients of success' (journalists need 'plenty of adaptability, energy, tact and a good constitution'). In 1910 it is still 'qualities required'. But by 1950 the comparable heading is 'educational requirements', and the 'candidates must have obtained at least . . .' sort of lists rarely leave the realm of bureaucratic formality. To be sure, the system seems to be saying, two people both with Bs in history and French at A level might certainly differ in their interests and personal capacities, as personalities and as human beings. But so what? *De minimis non curat lex* — nor the bureaucratic regulations of a credential-constipated society either.

Why the qualification spiral?

Having documented this trend, the next thing to do is first to explain it, and then to analyse its consequences. First, to explain. There is, of course, a standard explanation which suits very well all those — in both the educational and other professions — who connive at the steady progress towards ever higher levels of pre-career qualifications for every profession. We live, runs this explanation, in the age of the knowledge explosion. The range of information and ideas to be mastered by any profession increases at an exponential rate. It is only natural that every profession requires individuals of greater general educational maturity than used to be the case, and a longer period of purely professional preparation before starting a career.

This is not a negligible argument. The range of general basic techniques which a civil engineer could usefully learn has increased enormously over the last century. But is that an argument why it is best to do that learning in a concentrated period of three or four years between the ages of 18 and 22 rather than over ten years of part-time study combined with practical training between the ages of 18 and 28? Who is in the best position to assess the *relevance* of what he learns: the undergraduate familiar only with laboratories and not with factories, or the factory apprentice? Why should it be that the polytechnics at least (even if not yet all the universities) have resorted to sandwich courses as a means of putting *back* into the pre-career qualification pattern the practical experience which apprenticeship used to provide? Does the man who does all his learning by the age of 22 really remember what he once learned when, after specialising for ten years in one branch, he runs at the age of 30 up against a problem in another field? And is it not odd that the argument about escalating knowledge requirements should be made to justify a system which ends formal teaching in the early twenties and then allows a man to practise for *forty years* without any obligation to learn all the exploding knowledge which has been generated since he left the university?

The case begins to look fishy. Is there no other explanation of the trend? There is, and it seems a plausible one. It runs as follows. The ability and desire to learn all that a professional engineer needs to know through apprenticeship and prolonged part-time study are rare qualities. The particular necessary combination of qualities which was needed to carry a man through that route to an engineering career — the intellectual ability, the capacity for persistence, the interest in things mechanical, the ambition for a professional career and the social assurance necessary to assume that one has a right to such a career — was perhaps found in only 2 per cent, say, or 3 or 5 per cent of the population. In 1910, when less than 1 per cent of each age group was getting into a university, the majority of that 2 or 5 per cent had no choice but to choose the apprenticeship route.

But what happens as the society gets more affluent and the university population expands to embrace, say, 5—8 per cent of each age group? Our 2—5 per cent of potential engineering apprentices are likely to be among the children who show enough talent to be encouraged by teachers and parents to aim at a university education; more of them have parents who could afford to send them to a university, more of those from poorer homes have access to scholarships. And if a man has a realistic choice between spending three or four amiable, gentlemanly, and perhaps even intellectually exciting years in a university with the assurance of coasting thereafter to full professional status and a full professional salary at the age of 25, or alternatively submitting to the discipline of factory life at the age of 16 or 17 and sacrificing most of his leisure to part-time study for ten years, eventually to struggle through to full professional status near the age of 30 — if a man is offered that choice, which is he likely to choose? And as more and more of those with the ability and motivation to become engineers are *able* to choose the pre-career qualification route, the number whom circumstances deprive of that opportunity and who yet have the ability and drive to succeed in following the apprenticeship route gradually dwindles. So much so that that route may be closed off without danger of arousing public outcry.

And from the point of view of the officials of these professional associations, a good thing too. University graduation carries prestige, if for no other reason than because of its early association with the upper-middle classes. A profession which achieves the status of a graduate profession thereby achieves higher social prestige relative to other professions which do not — and with higher prestige goes the ability to claim higher fees for one's services.

One can give a similar account of the rise in minimum entry qualifications to, say, the library profession. Put briefly it is as follows. Fifty years ago, large numbers of people who were bright enough to be good librarians left school before the age of 15, and most of those who continued their education beyond the age of 15 had access to better paid or more prestigeful jobs than librarianship. Nowadays, by contrast, most of the children who have the required level of librarian potential stay on at school until they are 18. (Moreover the big expansion of numbers staying at school until the age of 18 means that they cannot all, as perhaps they could fifty years ago, expect *more* rewarding jobs than librarianship.) Hence libraries *can get* people with higher level certificates; and they *need to* recruit such people if they are to go on recruiting men and women with the same degree of librarian potential as those they were recruiting fifty years earlier. Or in other words:

> the O level requirements were originally laid down by the professions — as the A level requirements are now being laid down — less because there was any precision about what they were measuring than in order to ensure access to what it was fashionable in the late 1950s and early 1960s, to call 'the pool of ability'. (Briggs, 1973.)

There are several assumptions implicit in this explanation.

1. That good librarians are, if not exactly born rather than made, at least already made by the age of 15, and not much re-made later. That is to say that one could take a population of 15 year olds and rank them according to their *ability to learn* how to be good librarians, from the first to the hundredth percentile.

2. That the education which the new A-level entrants to the libraries receive after, say, the age of 15 does little of itself to enhance their potential to learn to become good librarians once they have entered a

library. Likewise, that a rise in the *general* level of education does little to alter the shape of the hypothetical 'distribution of librarian potential' in society. When the school leaving age is raised in 1990 to the age of 22, there will still be, if not exactly the same bottom 40 per cent, or whatever it is, at least some not much smaller proportion of people who 'do not have it in them' to become good librarians.

3. But that the qualities which make people good librarians do *correlate* quite highly with the qualities measured by general education achievement tests — O levels and A levels — both types of performance being a function of intelligence and effort. That is to say that the 'distribution of potential for librarianship' coincides roughly with a 'distribution of general ability'.

4. If the bottom limit of the *effective recruitment range* for librarianship is relatively fixed by ability constraints, irrespective of educational changes, the *top* limit may change with the occupational structure and the relative attractiveness of different occupations. Thus the occupations generally considered more attractive than librarianship recruit a larger proportion of each age group today than in 1920. Similarly the chairman of the training committee of the Engineering Industries Association complains in 1973 that 'where we used to get A and B stream boys [for apprenticeships], we are now getting C and D streams, with the banks, solicitors and offices attracting the better qualified' (*The Times* Business News, 24 March 1973).

5. The responsible officials of all professional bodies seek to protect their professions from slippage of their effective recruitment range down the ability distribution. One way of doing so is to raise entry requirements. That way you are taken more seriously; if you are taken more seriously you attract higher levels of ability, and your qualificational requirements exclude lower levels of ability; thus you maintain average ability levels which in turn ensures that you are taken seriously, and the whole circular process enables you to sustain the prestige which justifies higher salaries or professional fees. After a famous local government scandal involving a public relations consultant, the President of the Institute of Public Relations wrote to *The Times* in an attempt to repair the damage. The Institute had, he claimed, a detailed code of conduct, 'a standard of ethical behaviour as high as those of the long established professions'. His clinching argument was that 'qualification by examination is making rapid headway; although optional at present I expect it to become compulsory' (*The Times,* 30 April 1974).

In short, it is not a belief in the saving virtues of education in itself which explains why the Institute of Brewing required one A level and four O levels in 1973 compared with only five O levels in 1953, or why the Worshipful Company of Spectacle Makers should have gone from four O levels to two As and three Os over the same period (Briggs,

1973). The explanation lies in the fact that educational qualifications are seen as an ability-filtering device and (precisely *because* they are so seen) as a prestige-conferring device. Perhaps the clearest evidence of this can be seen in the entrance regulations of those colleges of nursing which will not count as acceptable an O level pass in such (one would have thought) an eminently relevant subject as domestic science, but require would-be nurses to show their paces in properly difficult subjects like English or maths, which better indicate whether they have the level of ability thought necessary to follow the training courses and to sustain the good name of the profession (ibid., p. 83).

The process of qualification inflation described here as taking place slowly in Britain over the course of this century is, of course, the same as that which was described in the last chapter as taking place much more rapidly in developing countries and bidding fair, in many of them, soon to produce BA bus conductors. There is a slight difference, however. The simpler picture given in the previous chapter was of a supply-led spiral. A surplus of graduates at one level induces them to *apply for* jobs one notch below what they have hitherto conventionally been entitled to. In Britain there is evidence that the spiral, though sometimes supply-led (compare the recent concern with graduate unemployment), is in part demand-led. That is to say that competitive bidding for the 'pool of ability' between professions can lead to anticipatory raising of entrance standards and a demand for, say, A-level leavers, greater than the numbers who *would anyway* have gone on to A level; hence many 'would-be entrants to particular professions or would-be professions, many of them highly motivated for personal or family reasons, having to struggle for a further year or two in school' (ibid., p. 102) beyond the point at which (until the careers master told them what they had to do) their appetite for general education was satisfied. Either way, the essence of a qualification *spiral* is that both demand and supply factors contribute and interact to exacerbate each other. The contributions from the demand side are likely to be greater when there is a high level of competition either between professional groups for status (the situation in Britain where professional group autonomy is greater than in any·other industrial country; Burrage, 1972) or between private employing organisations for both status and competitive efficiency (the situation, as we shall see in the next chapter, in Japan). Generally speaking, however, supply factors have been dominant both historically and in developing countries today. A brave OECD study designed to explain differences in the educational compositions of different occupational groups in fifty-three countries concluded that about 70 per cent of the variation could be attributed to 'variations in the supply of the educational system' (OECD, 1971b, p. 167).

Rational?
The five assumptions listed above *explain* the process of qualification inflation in Britain. Do they justify it?

It all depends on how far higher education *creates* as well as measures talents. When the navy advertises in the Sunday newspaper its intention to recruit graduates, it is clearly not the cognitive knowledge pumped into them at the university which counts; the navy 'is interested in any graduate who's interested in us, with a degree in either Science or the Humanities'. The reason is because 'we see your time spent at a University as time spent making up your own mind, thinking for yourself. And we know that you don't get a degree without a good deal of intelligence and concentration'. Which is the more important? The thinking which you have to go to a university to do? Or the intelligence and concentration which the degree test only measures, having presumably been there already? (See Little and Oxenham, 1975, p. 12.)

If it is chiefly the latter; if it is true that educational achievements chiefly *measure* and do little to *create* talent, that it is his first-class mind which makes an efficient Treasury mandarin or diplomat, irrespective of whether his golden youth at Oxbridge was spent getting his first-class degree in economics or in classics, then one wonders whether it *is* sensible for the British taxpayer to spend some £3,000 pumping a man full of Greek hexameters for three years merely in order to *assess* his likely capacity to write pithy diplomatic telegrams. Surely there must be means of making the diagnosis at an earlier stage — and other means of giving people a chance of learning to think for themselves, if it is *that* which universities add to their stature.

Many private employers do, indeed, believe that there are other means. Some of them would much prefer to get hold of highly intelligent young men and start training them at 18. Many of the senior officials of the Bank of England, recruited at 18 in the days of Montague Norman when there was, as a matter of policy, no graduate recruitment, would rather like to revert to that practice. But that option is simply not open to an individual employer. As long as most employers who are bidding for the 5 or 10 per cent most able people in each age group continue to recruit in the graduate market, no single employer could persuade a young man who was in that group *not* to go on and demonstrate that he belongs to it by getting a degree. Any young man who accepted a job at 18 would be tying his future to that particular employer and closing off other options (apart from re-nouncing three years' dolce vita at a university). Hence (particularly since the state, not the employer, pays for it), it becomes only sensible even for employers sceptical about the real value of university education to recruit only from graduates. Attempts to alter market-established education/occupation links from the employer's side *can* only be made collectively. Hence the full-page *Times* advertisement of recent months urging would-be managers to go into the army rather than the university was demonstratively signed by the chairmen or directors of twenty-five leading companies (*The Times,* 11 January 1974).

So there is a gap between private and social rationality. That gap may be wide enough in Britain. It becomes, as will be argued later, far greater, disastrously greater, in the later developing countries.

The *Times* advertisement just mentioned brings us, next, to the empirical assumptions about abilities which are involved in using educational qualifications as a screening device. Is it in fact true that educational achievements do correlate with, and can be used as a proxy measure for, the sort of abilities which most employers seek and value? For accountants, computer programmers, engineers and clerks the answer is probably yes, in any country. For managers, however, the answer might vary. In Japan, where intelligence and persuasiveness and zeal have traditionally been seen as the qualities which evoke consent from subordinates, the answer might well, again, be yes. In Britain, however (as in Sri Lanka), it has been (and still, in the age of the social contract, remains) 'character' which is thought to ensure the effective subordination of the lower orders — those qualities of calm and self-assurance and judgement which were bred in men in certain *kinds* of (private) schools (not certain *levels* of schooling) or in the officer ranks of the army. Hence, in the *Times* advertisement, the chairmen of Beaverbrook Newspapers and the Ford Motor Company, the personnel directors of Whitbread and Spillers Dog Foods, proclaim their concurrence in the view that:

> Of course, we don't expect a young man from the Army to be fluent in Mediaeval French Literature or a master of Micro-Biology.
> But in our experience as employers, we've found that a Short-Service Commission in the Army equips a man to make the change to business management very easily.
> For both jobs are concerned with the handling of people and getting the best out of them, often in trying situations.
> (Anyone who has had to keep twenty soldiers calm when a crowd are hurling bricks at them will readily agree.)

Whether they will succeed in reversing — or changing the direction of — the qualification spiral remains to be seen. Note, however, that it is still not necessarily the formative, educative role, even of the army, which these employers value. It might still be that the army too is seen as a tester, rather than as a creator, of talent. As the chairman of a national bank is reported to have told the 18-year-old son of a friend who came looking for a job: 'Come back in three years' time with a good degree from a good Oxbridge college or a good chit from the colonel of a good regiment.' Note the 'good's. The reference to the 'good Oxbridge college' is also a reminder that educational records can in Britain (less so in Japan, say, or Nigeria) have other significance than as a proxy test of intelligence and effort. Ability to get into a 'good' Oxbridge college indicates the right background and manner; having been there promises possession of the right connections.

And the consequences for education?
The rationality of the system has so far been questioned from the point of view of employers and job applicants and society's collective concern with getting people into the right jobs; round pegs into round holes.

But what of the implications of the qualification inflation for the education system? It means, in effect, that over the last century in which educational certificates have come into increasing use for job selection the significance of education for those being educated has changed. In nineteenth-century England the various classes of English society went to their own schools to prepare themselves for a career to which it had pleased, if not God, at least the class system to call them. The East India Company official sent his son to Haileybury in order that he should become a good, self-respecting, effective East India Company official — should fill the place which *patronage* would give him with distinction and aplomb. The merchant's son went to school to become a better merchant. The working man's son went to elementary school to become a better — more diligent and sober and intelligent — working man.

Now, whether the knowledge one gets from schools is useful or exciting, whether the values and attitudes one picks up there are appropriate, has become of secondary importance. Schools are places where one gets certificates; O levels and A levels, passports to such and such jobs, hurdles over which one leaps to go on to more schools for more certificates as passports to even better jobs. And all are in the race. Even for the middle-class child, patronage now cuts less ice. The City and the major companies have adopted rationalised managerial recruiting procedures. Even if one goes to the army one needs that 'good chit', and if one takes the other, Oxbridge, route, one needs the 'good' degree (as well as good A levels to get there). Only the very rich who do not *need* a job, or the unambitious content with the backwater jobs which patronage can still buy (running charitable foundations for distressed gentlefolk, say) can afford to spend their time at Oxbridge *merely* pursuing truth and intellectual excitement without concern for certificates (assuming that it *is* truth and not the champagne breakfasts that they have come to Oxford for). Add to this the presence of a higher proportion of working-class students at the universities whose families could not mobilise even the most modest form of patronage. They, having faced tougher difficulties, are likely to have had even more intensive coaching at O and A level in the art of hurdle jumping, developing as a reflex action the tendency with every idea they meet to size it up for jumping height.

And if the objective significance of education for individual life chances has changed, would it be surprising that subjective perceptions of that process and attitudes to it have also changed? Is there any evidence that they have? At least one university teacher thinks there is.

Pelican books [thirty years ago] were aimed unambiguously and enthusiastically at general adult education and the general educated reader, at people who wanted simply to inform themselves, reading on their own, or perhaps hand in hand, those who liked classes on important topics but who were not pursuing (indeed the right word) a degree or diploma. But now apparently the market is shifting with wonderfully so many more people in university or polytechnic. Most paperback publishers now aim their shotguns at the students. . . .

What I find utterly terrible about this kind of publication is the further assumption that the student is solely 'course-oriented' (only the jargon expresses the enormity), that he is not likely to be a general reader. I fear that they are right statistically. Most students do not, will not and perhaps — some kind excusing soul may prove — cannot read outside their ruddy subject. For we are not now talking about intellectuals or general readers. Most — not all, but most — are simply at university to get a degree. To adapt Dr. Johnson's famous description of politics, 'reading is nothing but a rising in the world'. (Bernard Crick, *New Statesman,* 6 October 1972.)

So much for a political scientist's view. Similar sentiments were expressed by a chemist who described on the BBC how he rated the production of young scientists along with the production of inventions as a major objective of his research laboratory:

It is reasonable to ask how we are adding to the process of further education already carried out — with about £10,000 to £15,000 (exclusive of lost earnings) per Ph.D. — by the universities. The answer is startling. We are undoing the effects of partial brain-washing, restoring the natural curiosity so evident in children, encouraging and purging from the system of our young lions the tranquillisers administered to them over the previous fifteen years by our educational system — tranquillisers that have made the young lions behave like young lambs. (Davies, 1967, p. 577.)

To suggest that there is a steady process of decline in the quality of British education may seem contrary to common sense. Surely, it might be objected, with every year bringing exciting new materials and methods, the child-centred education of today, with its emphasis on problem solving, and on encouraging the child's own learning initiatives, is infinitely more imaginative and genuinely educative than schooling in Britain thirty or forty years ago. That is undoubtedly true, and at the primary level these trends, associated with declining authoritarianism and a more liberal regard for individuality, and for co-operation rather than competition, have indeed made British schools a better place. It is at the secondary and higher levels that trends in this direction are blunted, overwhelmed, by backwash from the competition to qualify. There is reason to believe that the situation at the crucial secondary level is a good deal worse in Britain than in the United States, for two reasons. First because, with a much larger proportion of the American age groups going to university and getting their more definitive labels there, secondary level qualifications are less important. Secondly, entrance to American universities, where it is competitive and not open, is determined not by the achievement tests for the high school diploma (the equivalent of Britain's GCE/CSE) but by the separate (and much harder to cram for) Scholastic Aptitude Tests. Whether or not these are the reasons for it, that the difference exists is certainly the impression of one schoolteacher writing to *The Times:*

Having taught history and social science in both British and American schools, it has been my experience that the exam-bound curriculum in Britain limits pupil-teacher efforts to those that are immediately measurable in some pseudo-objective sense — to readily forgettable stuffing. There is far greater opportunity in U.S. secondary schools, at least in those I have taught in, to deal with historical and cross-cultural comparison, analysis of political, social, economic and psychological factors and interpretations of the 'whys' and consequences of events — problem solving activities. (*The Times,* 22 April 1975.)

Some would argue that the situation in Britain has reached a point at which drastic measures are required. Lord Ashby is one of these. He would draw a careful distinction between genuinely vocational higher education in such subjects as medicine and non-vocational higher education (in the humanities and social and natural sciences), certification of which is, however, commonly used and pursued for vocational purposes.

The motive which must be resisted is the pursuit of non-vocational higher education solely in order to get certification for a job. It is of course the employers who must be reformed first. They are doing a great disservice to higher education by using degrees and diplomas, which are quite irrelevant to the jobs they are filling, as filters for selecting candidates . . . If non-vocational higher education is to serve its real purpose (which is to civilise people) it ought not to attract people who only want to be certified, not civilised. I can see only one way in which higher education systems can promote this, and it would be an unpopular way: namely *not* to certify non-vocational education. (Ashby, 1972.)

To this admirable suggestion, we shall return in Chapter 13.

Chapter 3

Japan

The argument of this chapter can be stated in three brief sentences. Japan's educational system has grown in a way very different from Britain's. Some of the differences can be ascribed to differences in the two countries' cultural traditions and the nature of their social structures. Some — the more interesting ones for the argument of this book — can be attributed to the fact that Japan started industrialisation *later* than Britain as part of a deliberate, state-directed, policy of 'catching-up' modernisation.

Let us first list, schematically, some of the major differences.

Britain experienced a slow growth in the provision of primary education; Japan, a much more rapid growth.

That growth, in Britain's case, started when industrialisation was well under way; and in Japan was almost completed by the time industrialisation began in earnest.

The state's role in this growth of primary education was minimal at first, increasing slowly; whereas in Japan it was dominant from the beginning.

And this weak role of the state reflected uncertainty in the dominant classes concerning the desirability of mass primary education; whereas Japan's leaders had little doubt, from the very beginning, that education would contribute to both the loyalty and the productiveness of the masses.

Many of the individual schools, and the educational traditions of all the schools, were the product of a con- whereas Japan's 'modern' schools started from scratch, based largely on

35

tinuous evolution over centuries, only accelerated, not broken, in modern times;

imported models, breaking continuity with the (far from insignificant) educational traditions of pre-1860 Japan.

One important element of that continuity was the two-nation pattern of parallel school systems, only slowly merging, after 1902, into a (partial) pyramid;

whereas Japan's new school system was designed as an integrated pyramid structure from the beginning.

And one implication of the diversity of the schools was that the political/cultural effects of schools were very different for different social classes;

whereas the ideology propagated by the much more integrated Japanese system was homogenising and less class-divisive.

Technical education only slowly received state support and was generally relegated to second-class citizen status;

whereas it was fostered much earlier in Japan as an integral part of the system.

British universities existed largely by the inertia of their endowments; their social function was unclear and much questioned; they were only gradually 'nationalised' and only partially subordinated to public policy;

whereas the Japanese university system was established by the state with the primary role, from the beginning, of serving the state's manpower needs.

The role of education in allocating people to jobs — as a channel of social mobility — did not predominate over heredity and apprenticeship until the mid-twentieth century;

whereas in Japan educational qualifications played a large part in determining career opportunities from a very early stage.

And, largely because of the last difference mentioned, the increase in demand for secondary and higher education has been relatively slow in Britain.

whereas in Japan it has been more rapid and has already reached much higher levels.

The traditional system
Before Japan was wrenched into the modern world — brought suddenly

to the realisation that unless she modernised her polity and her technology she would be colonised by the Western powers — she had already a fairly sophisticated pattern of traditional education.

One set of schools was for the boys of the samurai class — that 6—7 per cent of the population who had the hereditary status of warriors but who, after 250 years of peace, were primarily civil administrators, a gentry no longer rural but concentrated in the 260-odd castle towns which dominated the 260-odd fiefs into which Japan was divided.

These schools had a remarkable similarity to the grammar schools of Europe. (For more detail see Dore, 1963.) Education centred on learning to read a classical language — ancient Chinese rather than Latin and Greek. The purpose of mastering that language was to read the Chinese classics, for the historical, literary and philosophical writing of the Chinese sages, like the Greek and Latin classics, were seen as the chief repository of experienced wisdom, of aesthetic values, of philosophical sophistication and nobility, and even of ontology and morality (much more so than in England, since Buddhism was much less effective than Christianity in claiming parity of esteem with the classical tradition).

There was no formalised distinction of school/university levels in this system; indeed, only in an emergent way a 'system' at all. Some pupils, particularly apt, continued their studies into their late twenties as disciples/junior colleagues of their teachers rather than as mere pupils.

These schools, a rarity in 1750, were found in almost every fief a century later, and many of them had already begun to introduce 'modern studies' based on translations of Dutch books — Western medicine to supplement the Chinese medical classics; Western mathematics to supplement the Chinese (and Japanese — though written by Japanese in Chinese just as Newton wrote in Latin) mathematical treatises; Western metallurgy to support experiments in the founding of cannons; Western navigation and shipbuilding; and finally, in a small way, Western political economy.

With the education of the sons of the hereditary class of samurai soldier-officials, the fief governments generally considered their responsibility for education to be at an end. A few of them gave small prizes to outstanding pupils in the commoner schools, or distributed free copies of copybooks which expressed especially meritorious sentiments. Beyond that they let the commoners take care of their own education. And on the whole they took care of it reasonably well. Whatever base one uses to estimate, it seems reasonable to assume that by 1870 some 40—45 per cent of boys and some 15 per cent of the girls of each age group were getting enough formal education to give them basic Japanese literacy, basic numeracy and a smattering of their country's history and geography.

Most of these schools were run as a private business; some by doctors and village elders and other benevolent retired old men as a charity, and sometimes from motives very similar to those which made the Scottish Presbyterians encourage education — because literacy, the key to the moral classics, was the road to goodness. Goodness, of course, included all the typical lower-class virtues; thrift, diligence, honesty, filial piety, acceptance of place. The only difference was that Japanese Confucianists had little interest in the supernatural, and no church. Hence there was no charitable school *movement* led by religious bodies; only individual initiatives. The schools were small affairs, usually centring on an individual teacher with one or two helpers, likely to disappear when that teacher died.

So Japan, when it entered the modern era, had a two-nation system of schools even more sharply divided than contemporary Britain's — an inequality and an insulated separateness which reflected an inequality of citizenship rights as between samurai gentry and commoners greater than that of France's *ancien régime*.

Total transformation
But Japan experienced between 1868 and 1875 what Britain has never experienced even in the days of the Protectorate — a period of wholesale reform which altered the structure of society in a very basic way. The fiefs were denied their autonomy and made prefectures of the central government; the feudal barons were ordered to leave their fiefs and turned into a palely ineffective metropolitan aristocracy, compensated for their feudal revenues by government bonds of declining value; the samurai gentry became central government bureaucrats, policemen, schoolteachers, soldiers and pioneer businessmen; the peasants were confirmed as the legal owners of the land to which they had previously been bound; freedom of occupation was roundly declared, and equality before the law.

The justification for all these changes, the arguments by which the small group of young lower-samurai leaders persuaded their feudal superiors gracefully to give up their fiefs and walk off the stage of history, was that Japan *had* to do all these things if she were to acquire the 'civilisation' (in those days the word 'modernisation' had not been invented) which would make her wealthy and strong and fully capable of resisting the threat of colonisation by the Western powers. And the development of a modern educational system was to be an essential element of that policy.

In the early years of the reform period the first tentative efforts at state regulation of schools preserved the existing dichotomy between the popular schools for commoners and the middle-class schools for higher learning. But all this was swept away by the decree of 1872 which announced a plan for a unified state educational system on the French model — with eight regional universities, each directing the activities of 32 middle schools and 210 primary schools. 'Learning is the key to success in life . . . there shall, in the future, be no community with an illiterate family; nor a family with an illiterate person'. The actual blueprint was changed long before any effective measures could be taken to implement it, but the belief in the saving virtues of education remained constant; so did the determination (a) to bring the whole nation within the scope of the elementary system and (b) to make the national school system a unitary pyramid of graded layers in which all children started from the same place, moving as far up the ladder as, in the words of the 1872 decree, their 'ability and their means' permitted.

The bases for a unitary system
Several factors made possible this leap towards a unified school system, such as Britain never accomplished. The most important was the discontinuity in both the composition and the culture of the ruling class. In Britain there has been a steady continuity from the aristocratic élite of the eighteenth century to the merito/aristocratic Oxbridge élite of the 1970s — only gradual changes in the identity of the families which composed it and in the tastes and attitudes and manners and self-perceptions which made up its culture. That culture the élite public school and Oxbridge served to perpetuate and to transmit from generation to generation.

In Japan, by contrast, the Meiji Restoration (a) radically altered the identity of the power-holders — now a group of rank-and-file samurai bureaucrats, not the upper-samurai fief-holding aristocrats, (b) altered the economic basis of their wealth — from feudal revenues from the land to cash salaries from the State Treasury, and (c) in addition to the effects of this economic change on cultural ethos (think how much of British aristocratic culture was *landed* aristocratic culture) other factors radically altered the nature of upper-class life-styles. The ideals of the old régime were discredited; associated with decadence, defeat and national humiliation at the hands of foreigners. The new cultural symbols were the admired manners and ideas of the West — brought back by the lucky students who had gone abroad to study, or taught by the foreign teachers hired at great expense for Japan's *new* schools. And it was only new schools which could propagate that culture; not old schools of the old régime.

[1]The document is quoted in Passin (1965). This is the best general source for the development of education in the modern period, but see also Nagai (1971); Japan: UNESCO (1966); Japan: Education (1965); and Dore (1964).

To be sure there was a good deal of ambiguity and ambivalence in all this — the same sort of ambiguity as gives rise to the nationalist cries of cultural imperialism and cultural dependency today. The 'Westernisers' did not have everything their own way. As they moved rapidly from the position that Japan needed the West's material techniques for her own defence to the position that these techniques needed backing by the West's *social* institutions, and thence to the automatic reflex assumption that West is best in everything, so the opposition they aroused increased. The traditionalists struck back; primary education was later infused with a heavy dose of Confucian ethics and Shinto nationalism designed to instil in every Japanese a proper patriotism, a proper confidence in the intrinsic worth of Japanese cultural traditions — eventually, in the thirties, a belief in the inherent racial superiority of the Japanese.

But the Westernising enthusiasm of the first years of the new régime had brought many changes that were irreversible. The old feudal system could never be put back together again. Official court dress remained the frock coat. The continuity with the past had been broken — both the continuity of cultural and educational traditions, and the continuity of the class structure. Thus the construction of an integrated educational system was made possible.

Growth of the system

The growth in elementary school attendance proceeded steadily with a final spurt after fees were abolished in 1900. (The private elementary schools — mostly Christian missionary foundations — never accommodated more than 1 per cent of the school population.) The rate of increase paralleled that of Britain — but note, in Table 1, the enormous disparity between the two countries in the degree of industrialisation which provided the background.

Still in 1910 the vast majority of elementary school pupils were in

Table 1

Year	Percentage of labour force in non-agricultural occupations		Enrolment ratios; percentage of the age groups of relevant ages					
			Primary		Secondary		Tertiary	
	Japan	Britain	Japan	Britain	Japan	Britain	Japan	Britain
1870	17	85	28	40	1	2	—	?
1900	29	91	81	83	4	2	1	1
1910	41	92	98	100	12	4	2	2

Sources: Dean (1962); Allen (1962); Japan: Education (1965); Britain: Education (1950).

rural schools; they were there because by this time literacy, the ability to deal with government officials, the ability to 'speak properly' and to use in village meetings the sort of words one learned only in school, were becoming part of the normal village definition of a self-respecting citizen. The majority looked forward to a future as farmers: school was to make them better farmers. Younger sons who were not in line to inherit their family farm might expect to be adopted into another farming family, or to join the steady migration to the towns. If they were bright and poor — and from the sort of honest hard-working family that establishment interviewers would judge to be 'of good stock' — they might be encouraged by their teacher to take the entrance examinations for one of the two cheapest routes into the middle class: the normal schools training teachers and the officers' academies for the army and navy. If they were reasonably bright and members of the upper stratum of village families — the 30 per cent or so who owned all their own land and perhaps had a few acres of woodland to fell and sell off to finance a younger son's education — they might apply for entrance to the middle schools which charged higher fees but which would lead to a university or a professional training.

But (worth noting for reference when we discuss the later late-developers) until the early years of this century — until primary school attendance was practically universal and taken for granted — the number of secondary schools and the proportion of primary school graduates hoping to enter them was still very small. Except in a few middle-class residential areas of the cities, preparation for secondary education and coaching for secondary school entrance examinations played a rather small part in the life of the primary school. Teachers did not see their primary rôle as preparing their charges for the competition to enter the middle class. If they believed what their Minister of Education told them in 1890 (and there is evidence that a good many of them did) their job was 'in the first instance to nurture virtuous characters in their charges and to teach them to observe the Way of Man; in particular it is necessary to develop a spirit of patriotism and reverence of the Emperor, to prepare pupils to become loyal and good citizens who will work hard at their trades and be of exemplary behaviour'.

The proportion of the school week directly devoted to such endeavours — not only the history and Japanese language classes but also special ethics classes — was large. But there was also a good deal of severely practical arithmetic, and some not insignificant general science. And the ethics classes, too, the equivalent of Britain's religious instruction, went a good deal beyond the simple morality of family life, filial piety and neighbourly kindness, or the civic duty of patriotism and loyalty to the emperor. They dwelt, too, on the virtues of enterprise and scientific curiosity and public-spirited community improvement. And the hero models included Benjamin Franklin and William Jenner and obscure bridge-builders otherwise celebrated only in the pages of Samuel Smiles, as well as Japanese historical figures, paragons of loyalty to the throne.

The rise of the qualification

By the 1920s, however, the significance of primary education had changed for a much larger proportion of the population. There were more secondary schools; a higher proportion of each age group went to them; and preparation for them became a more important pre-occupation of primary school children and their teachers.

This reflected a change in the structure of Japanese society: in particular a change in the way jobs were attained. Japan has become a 'qualification society' much more rapidly than England.

The first and most obvious reason why this happened was because the Japanese had to modernise Japanese society by *importing* knowledge. And by and large the most obvious thing to do was to import packages of knowledge as they had been systematised in Western universities. Engineering is a good example. A few young Japanese learned some of the elementary principles of engineering from the French technicians employed at the Yokosuka shipyards and the British engineers who constructed the first railway lines. But a mere handful of apprentices, their learning hampered by communication difficulties, was hardly an effective nucleus of a modern engineering profession. Some students were sent to the engineering departments of foreign universities, but the decisive act was the establishment of the Imperial College of Engineering in 1873. Japanese talent scouts in Britain discovered a 25-year-old Scot who was scornful of the engineering education he had received in Glasgow and was full of ideas about new methods of training derived from Zurich and elsewhere. He was allowed to pick a team of eight compatriots and together they founded the Tokyo College, producing their first ten graduates in 1878. (The Scot in question wrote a book about Japan which quotes several glowing tributes to his own achievements; Dyer, 1904.)

Thus, from the very beginning of Japan's industrialisation process, from the very emergence of a recognisable engineering profession, the pre-career qualification pattern of recruitment was already established. (An incidental consequence is that, unlike the British institutions which are still dominated by practising engineers, the equivalent Japanese engineering societies — the first of which was founded in 1879 by the very first crop of graduates from the Tokyo College — are generally presided over by professors and have their secretariats in universities.)

Other professions similarly had their origin in a government school — the merchant marine, veterinary surgery, pharmacy, music. In medicine, it was a long time before the graduates of the Tokyo University medical school and of the similar schools established later were providing the bulk of the medical services actually rendered. Traditional practitioners continued to practise and continued to train successors by informal training methods, but from the very first the medical schools set licensing standards and their products formed the only professional body.

In other professions, above all in administration and management, routes of entry were not formalised so quickly. For the first twenty years of the new régime the situation was fluid. Government was still the most honoured profession. Recruitment into the civil service was still a rather haphazard affair, partly of patronage, partly of the recognition of ability. But ability tended to mean the possession of genuine (Western) knowledge. Numerous private academies sprang up in the 1870s and 1880s to provide it. Most specialised in law — British, French or German; some in foreign languages; some in accounting or commerce; some in philosophy or art. There were at first no controlled standards; no formal marketable qualifications. One justified one's application for a post by what one could claim to have learned; one might, for a government job, be given an *ad hoc* test to see how well one had learned it.

Gradually, however, the system became routinised and formalised. The decisive event was the reform of the state university — the Imperial University in Tokyo — and the systematisation of its entrance standards, followed a year later by the beginning of a regular system of examinations for the recruitment of civil servants — from which, however, law school graduates of the Imperial University were exempt. (Another example of the compressed time scale of the late developer: civil service entrance tests came to England only after a century of industrialisation; to Japan a mere decade later — at a time when there were hardly more than 1,200 establishments worth the name of factory in the whole country.) Not only for anyone seeking to enter the technical professions, but also for administrative posts, a university qualification became essential. By the end of the first decade of this century many of the business corporations were restricting their recruitment to graduates; so were the major newspapers — a trend in which Japan was far ahead of Britain. In a sample of leading businessmen drawn from a Japanese *Who's Who* of 1955 — men who began their careers between 1900 and 1920 — 70 per cent were found to be graduates of universities or higher technical schools (Asô, 1968, p. 219). A sample study of British managers in 1958 found that 21 per cent were university graduates. Among a sub-sample of 200 top managers in top firms, the proportion was 24 per cent (Clements, 1958, p. 184).

The late development explanation
Why this difference? One can think of several reasons. It will be useful, to bring out the main argument, to divide them into cultural factors (C) and late development (LD) factors.

C1. First, the Japan of the immediate pre-industrial period was a Confucian Japan in which learning and scholarship in themselves carried high prestige. In the largely agnostic society of the samurai upper class, the school and the Confucian scholar combined in one institution the functions which in Britain were divided between schools on the one hand and the church on the other. The school was the only institution outside the family which had charge of morality and the building of character; the Confucian scholars had no effective rivals as the source of philosophical and moral wisdom. The very idea of education, therefore, was given higher value than in Britain's more philistine society.

C2. Secondly the two professions of the samurai, fighting and governing, remained the most honoured professions — despite the efforts of Japanese disciples of the utilitarians (see Fukuzawa (1969), Blacker (1964)) to disparage the importance of the state as against society, of the official as against the entrepreneur. They were the chief goal of youthful ambition; the examination course which led into the First High School and thence into the Law Department of Tokyo University and thence into the civil service was the hurdle race that schoolboys were most likely to be coached for. It was because the civil service had such high prestige, perhaps, that the larger business corporations were more inclined to imitate its methods and criteria of recruitment.

LD1. But, of course, it was because Japan was a late developer, importing institutions from the more advanced countries, that the system of recruitment by examination for the civil service was institutionalised at such an early stage of development — while the enterprises which were to spearhead industrialisation were still in an embryo stage of organisation.

LD2. And it is equally a characteristic of late developers that the big enterprise — more likely by virtue of its very bigness to be bureaucratically organised — plays a much more dominant role in the process of industrialisation than in the earlier developing societies of Europe.

LD3. Equally characteristically for a late developer, Japan continued for a long time to be a wholesale importer of foreign techniques and institutions — importing to *change* society. For all that the pace of change in nineteenth-century Britain was fast as compared with the

eighteenth century, it was still probably slow enough for most businessmen and manufacturers, when they came to recruit a young trainee
manager, to see themselves as looking for someone who would 'carry
on' the business — not as looking for someone who would *transform* it.
But Japanese in responsible positions *did* have a sense that the whole of
their society had to be transformed — most acutely in the 1870s; still to
a very important degree in the 1900s. And transformation meant the
application of Western knowledge — the knowledge to propagate
which Japan's colleges and universities had been founded. Hence it was
natural that they should attach importance to formal pre-career
qualifications.

LD4. The discontinuity of ruling-class traditions — and in the
composition of the ruling class — meant that Japan did not have
available one obvious alternative to the use of educational qualifications: that of filling its managerial positions with men whose education
had bred in them 'the power to command', that certainty of one's divine
right to guide and direct the lower orders, that sense of the responsibilities of leadership, which the public schools bred in upper-class
Englishmen. Japan *had* families — the former samurai families — with
those traditions, and those traditions continued to help members of
that 6—7 per cent of the nation's families to get into top positions.
(They made up 59 per cent of the entries in a 1903 *Who's Who;* 37 per
cent in 1915 and, in 1928, the last year that it was respectable publicly
to record such origins, some 26 per cent; Asō, 1968, p. 211.) But there
were no élite schools, kept as the exclusive preserve of those families, to
specialise in the transmission and reinforcement of that élite culture.
Because of (a) the historical discontinuity in the status system, in the
composition of the élite and in the school system, (b) the simultaneous
importation of Western principles of organisation and (c) the strong
'mobilise all the talents for the defence of the nation' motive for putting
emphasis, *among* those imported organising principles, on the
principle of merit selection — for this combination of reasons, Japan
had schools which could guarantee the cognitive skills of their products,
but not their 'breeding'.

LD5. The unbending use of the examination merit principle within
the school system — for entry into middle schools, high schools and
universities in the state system — meant that the school system
functioned as a general intelligence testing device in a way that the
British system could not. The fact that a man graduated from Oxford
or Cambridge in itself told one nothing about how bright he was (even
if, in a few cases, the fact that he got a first-class degree might). In
Japan, however, by 1896, 25,000 pupils were competing for the 18,000
places in middle schools, and 2,159 sat the examinations for the 1,210
places in upper secondary schools which led directly and almost

automatically to Tokyo University. (There may have been some double counting of students taking more than one examination; for a fuller discussion see Dore, 1967, p. 132.) Several thousands more, probably, were attending private cram schools trying to get themselves sufficiently within striking distance of success to make it worth paying the examination fee. By 1909 the applicant/successful ratio was nearly 2:1 for middle schools and over 4:1 for upper secondary. The net was fairly widely drawn, too. Clearly middle-class children had very great advantages; but there was a far from negligible chance that a village schoolboy of exceptional ability would find some patron to see him through the system, however poor the family. In the only pre-war count available — for 1939 — 16 per cent of Tokyo University students were peasants' sons — doubtless the majority from the more well-to-do strata of villagers (Shimizu, 1959, p. 110).

There was a reasonable assurance, therefore, that anyone who even got *into* Tokyo University had a high level of scholastic ability. And those qualities of intelligence and capacity for persevering effort which go to scoring high marks in examinations are also highly relevant to successful performance as a civil servant or industrial manager too (though not, of course, the only factor determining success).

Totally irrespective, therefore, of *what* a man studied, or of its relevance in preparing him for his future career, there was every reason to favour the graduate of the élite universities if you were looking for a newspaper reporter or a trainee manager. His capacity to learn had been demonstrated. And, of course, the fact that university graduates *were* given preference for these reasons enhanced the value of university degrees *in general* — with the spill-over effect of making more valuable even the degrees of second-rate universities which were *not* so selective in their admissions.

Growth of the system

The number of such universities grew steadily in the twentieth century. As degrees became more important for getting jobs, naturally the demand for the opportunity to get degrees intensified. The state system expanded: a second (Kyoto) university was added in 1897, a third ten years' later. But the demand grew faster. The private academies, in particular the law schools, which had been founded in the 1870s and the 1880s expanded to fill the gap. Some of them still operated, at their lower levels, as second-chance cram schools preparing candidates for the entrance examinations of the state system. Some were given, by the state, other licensing functions — for middle school teachers, for doctors. Others developed their own specialisms, recognised in the non-official world — Waseda for journalism, Keio for business training. But all gradually acquired the general function of giving — at a much higher price than the state universities for there was no subsidy — degrees in law and other arts and social science subjects to those who lacked the necessary ability to get into the state universities. This function became even more important after the major private colleges were granted the use of the title 'university' in 1918. By 1940 there were twenty-six such universities, in addition to nineteen state universities (including a number of single-faculty medical schools, schools of commerce, etc.) and two municipal universities.

The process of expansion was a familiar one. The rush to get degrees resulted — in the depression periods of the twenties and thirties for instance — in enough overproduction of graduates for the social problem of graduate unemployment to receive widespread comment. 'I've got my degree but now what?' was the title of one noted book. The disaffected were eventually absorbed, of course — into small banks and minor trading enterprises which until then had not aspired to recruiting graduates but thereafter took their right to insist on a degree for granted. And so it became even more necessary, for anyone who wanted a respectable middle-class job, to get one.

The post-war period and certain institutional changes introduced under American pressure, or simply as a voluntary adoption of American practices, accelerated the process slightly after the war — the requirement of full university degrees for primary teachers, for example, and the establishment of graduate library schools. But by and large the post-war expansion of higher education was simply the same process as that taking place before the war, vastly accelerated by the spread of affluence. A steadily increasing proportion of the population were able to contemplate the expense of sending a child to a private university — or at least of supporting him till the age of 18 or 19 to give him a crack at the (much cheaper) universities of the state system. And because of the middle-class homogeneity of Japanese culture — itself partly a product of the universality and uniformity of the elementary school system — there were fewer 'not for the likes of us' status considerations to damp down aspirations. By 1969 there were 379 universities in Japan, 270 of them private universities charging quite high fees. There were an additional 473 junior colleges giving two-year post-secondary courses. About 20 per cent of each age group was receiving university education: nearly 30 per cent of each male age group.

The system today
The university system grew from the top downwards. Tokyo Imperial University was there first. It set the paradigm of what a good university should be — the more so since Japan is a tightly knit monocentric society, certainly as compared with such polycentric societies as the US and even as compared with Britain. The other state universities which

followed it did not quite acquire the prestige of Tokyo University. Few people with an open choice would have failed to choose Tokyo. One therefore needed higher marks to get into Tokyo. This confirmed the general impression that Tokyo students were brighter. And this confirmed the superior prestige of Tokyo University — which confirmed the preferences which made everyone converge on Tokyo, redoubled cramming efforts, raised standards, made the examination more selective, further confirmed the superiority of Tokyo graduates, further raised the prestige of Tokyo . . . And so on and on in a never-ending process. The result is a steeply-graded hierarchy with Tokyo University at the top, a second rank of other state universities, then some of the most selective private universities and, in different segments of the bottom of the pyramid, the mass-production private universities with teacher/student ratios of 1:120, and the more gentlemanly (or more often, more ladylike) smaller and more expensive institutions for the not-so-bright children of the upper-middle class.

The system works well enough. It may, of course, actually *teach* something useful; it almost certainly does in the technological and professional fields which occupy a minority of the student body. Even the majority who are studying humanities and social science subjects may actually develop intellectually from the experience of being at the university. But that is not what one means, primarily, when one says that the system 'works' well. One means that it provides a method, relatively satisfactory to employers and accepted as legitimate by the employed, of distributing each generation among the available middle-class jobs. The position in the hierarchy of any man's university, indicating the level of entrance examination he was able to get through, is a useful indicator of his 'general ability'. The top companies offering the most desirable jobs recruit from the top universities. In the labour-shortage years since 1960 there has been such competition for Tokyo University graduates that they have been able to get their job arranged in the second or third of their four years at the university. Employers are not much interested in how well a student performs there: that he got through the entrance exams is proof that he is in the top 2 per cent, say, of his age group on a combined rating of his intelligence and capacity for sustained persevering effort. And that is what they want to know. Lesser companies recruit from lesser universities — right down to those which would admit an intelligent chimpanzee provided his guardian made a large enough contribution to the university building fund. Their graduates are absorbed for the most part into family businesses, or else into some struggling firm whose middle-school-educated boss feels that employing a graduate will give him something to boast about in the bath house.

It works; provided one thinks of it as an enormously elaborated, very expensive intelligence testing system with some educational spin-off, rather than the other way round.

But the cost is high, as Japanese critics of their society are constantly pointing out (for a summary, see OECD, 1971, pp. 87—90):

— the cost to the universities of the devaluation of university education which results from the fact that employers are more concerned about the university a man gets into than about what he does there;

— the cost in the anxiety and stress in late adolescence as the years of entrance examinations approach. Since such importance attaches to getting into university as high as possible up the hierarchy, many students try for two or three successive years, spending the intervening period in special cram schools. Entrance examination time is one of the annual journalistic festivals. The photographers can always count on finding one old lady kneeling outside the examination hall with her rosary to pray for her grandson's success. In the 1950s Japan had one of the world's highest rates of adolescent suicide; affluence and labour shortage giving everybody some place in society to look forward to has presumably been a major factor in relieving Japan of this distinction;

— the sheer economic cost of all the cram schools, the numerous special magazines for exam-competing youth, the numerous publishing houses producing guides to last year's entrance exams; the agencies producing mock tests for youths in high schools and, of course, the conduct of the entrance examinations themselves. One estimate put these costs at 50 million dollars in 1962, plus another 80 million in earnings foregone by the crammers.

— the increasing inequality of opportunity as more wealthy parents resort to private middle and (to a lesser extent) primary education in order to maximise their chances of getting their children into the top (state) universities.

— the devastating effects on the curricula of high schools which results from their preoccupation with preparing for the entrance examinations; the backwash into the middle schools, preoccupied with preparing students for the entrance examinations for the 'best' high schools — those which have the best record for getting students into the top universities; the backwash into the primary schools arising from the entrance examinations to the private middle schools — and so back to the pre-pre-kindergarten which was reported in 1970 to have failed to devise adequate tests for 2 year olds and decided to test their mothers instead.

There are mitigating factors — notably that still, despite all, Japanese continue to believe in *education* and frequently get it in spite of the system. Recently new methods of allocating students between public schools (partly by lottery) have reduced the backwash into the middle schools. The increasing deliberate use by top universities of tests which emphasise reasoning power rather than memory, and the incredible sophistication of high school teachers in diagnosing the exact spot on the university hierarchy which their charges are capable of entering, have reduced the number of child years spent in extra cramming (and at the same time made the system more and more overtly like an intelligence testing system). But 'the examination hell' remains a priority social problem for journalists and liberal commentators.

One suspects that Japan's more conservative leaders, though they are prepared to shake their heads over the system with those who deplore it, are secretly well satisfied. The examination hell sorts the sheep from the goats; a man who can't take the psychological strain would be no use anyway. If you need convincing of the virtues of meritocracy — of getting top brains in top places — look, they would say, at our economic growth record. And as long as you can keep adolescents, in those crucial years when they might otherwise be learning to enjoy themselves, glued to their textbooks from 7 in the morning to 11 at night, the society should manage to stave off for quite a long while yet that hedonism which, as everybody knows, destroyed the Roman empire, knocked the stuffing out of Britain, and is currently spreading venereal disease through the body politic of the United States.

At least one rather suspects that must be what they are thinking.

Chapter 4

Sri Lanka

The pattern of educational development in Sri Lanka is a good deal more complex than that of either Britain or Japan. The complicating factor is the linguistic one intertwined, as it is, with the shape given to the country's social structure by over four centuries of colonial rule. Japan, too, *began* its absorption of Western knowledge largely through Western languages. English, German and French were essential tools. But gradually the translators caught up with the backlog. Foreign teachers were replaced. Medicine, at first a German-language study, became a Japanese-language study. With the replacement of the former (British) professor of naval architecture by his Japanese successor in the first decade of this century, the last course of English-language lectures disappeared from the Tokyo University calendar. Knowledge had been indigenised.

When Sri Lanka tentatively began the same process some seventy years later she faced infinitely greater difficulties. There was much *more* knowledge to be indigenised. There were two native languages, Sinhalese and that of the minority Tamils, not one. The total potential market for translated books was smaller in a population a quarter the size of Japan's in 1870. And, worst of all, knowledge of English was no mere possession of an instrumental cognitive tool; it was symbolic of a position in the social structure, of a relation to past colonial masters.

Yet, despite this enormous complication, and despite the fact that her educational system was so clearly modelled on Britain's, one can discern ways in which Sri Lanka differs from Britain in the same direction as Japan only more so. Starting later than Japan on a deliberate state-led drive to industrialised modernity, she shows the 'late-development effect' in an even more acute form. The reliance on educational qualifications in selecting for jobs starts earlier and is more complete; the tertiary and secondary levels grow faster, relative to the primary levels, from an earlier stage.

Colonial education
Pre-contact, non-Western forms of education were less well developed in Sri Lanka than in Japan (though a good deal more significant than

51

in, say, Africa). It was not a *secular* educational tradition as it had been in the Confucian societies; for the villager who learned to read at the temple school there was not much else *to* read besides the scriptures. Even in the Kandyan Kingdom, at the time of its conquest in 1815 there was only the most sparing use of writing outside of the religious life — for a limited range of land titles and official chronicles.

Hence when colonial Ceylon began to build schools it was, as in Japan, a *discontinuous* beginning. Ceylon did gradually develop élite upper-class schools on the British model; but the culture of that upper class was in itself something largely *created by* the schools, not, as in the case of the British public schools, something already existing in society which the school simply transmitted (with only marginal modification, by zealous Dr Arnolds) from generation to generation.

When the British succeeded the Dutch in 1796 they found some Dutch schools already in existence — as indeed had the Dutch when they took over from the Portuguese 140 years earlier. They catered for the settlers — the Burgher families — and also for a limited stratum of low country Sinhalese who had retained their Catholicism since Portuguese days, or had been converted to the Dutch Reformed Church.

The British colonial government restarted some of these schools but in the English, not the Dutch language (and the Burgher population itself switched to English as its family language in a few generations). Government efforts were reinforced by the various missionary societies which arrived in the first two decades of the century and were especially important in the northern Tamil area. The content of the education given in these schools was uncompromisingly Western. Religious conversion was, indeed, ostensibly as important a goal as education in the mission schools — and really so in the lower-level schools which taught in the vernacular, but less so in the English language secondary-level élite schools which the missions developed for the Ceylonese middle class. Like their Trollopeian counterparts back home, the clergymen teachers of these middle-class schools had a sensitive appreciation of the needs of Mammon as well as of God; of the bourgeois as well as of the Christian virtues. There was, in fact, little difference either in style or function between these and the élite government school (later Royal College) founded in imitation of the new wave of British public schools in 1836.

The Burghers and Eurasians (even in 1911 their number was only 27,000) formed the original core clientele of the upper tier of these schools; they were joined by increasing numbers of families from the upper stratum of the traditional society — chiefly landowners, merchants, practitioners of ayurvedic medicine, perhaps teachers in the vernacular schools. The demand expanded because opportunities expanded. The steady growth of the colony with the development of export agriculture — coffee and coconuts, later tea and rubber — created ever more jobs in the middle and lower ranks of the government bureaucracy and the trading firms. The growth of this Ceylonese middle class required the services of increasing numbers of doctors and lawyers and divines. And educational qualifications determined who would get these opportunities. Local recruitment into the colonial government service was rationalised by selection tests earlier than in Britain (The East India Company had, after all, set the pattern for Britain itself. In a colony the anxiety of the power-holders not to lose their rights to patronage did not hinder a reform as much as at home, for the colonial officials did not have nephews and clients among the natives who were to be sorted out by the local recruitment procedures.) Hence, from the very beginning, the first of the nineteenth-century wave of schools were schools the majority of whose pupils were there to *qualify* rather than to get educated. They were not children being prepared for a future which their birth had marked out for them and guaranteed them; they were pupils being prepared to earn a qualification which would give them a future they could otherwise not expect, pupils seeking escape from 'manual toil, from work they regard as degrading, in an education which [could] lead to posts in offices in the towns', posts which would entitle their 'holders to the respect of the class from which they believed they [had] emancipated themselves' (Jayawardena, 1972, p. 13, quoting a report on the 1911 census). Not all of them found such posts. One colonial ruler spoke contemptuously in 1852 of a 'class of shallow, conceited half-educated youths who have learned nothing but to look back with contempt on the condition in which they were born — and who desert the ranks of the industrious classes to become idle, discontented hangers on of the courts and public offices' (W. J. Sendall, quoted in Pieris, 1964, pp. 438—9). However, despite this early appearance of educated unemployment, the opportunities for mobility steadily increased. In the first half of the nineteenth century Burghers and Eurasians had practically monopolised the government jobs. By 1901, although government service remained the preferred Burgher occupation, and Burghers were still disproportionately represented in the higher posts, 93 per cent of government jobs were held by non-Burghers. There was a total of 12,600 clerks in government and the trading houses at the time of the 1911 census, and a good number of managers, administrators and professionals (Jayawardena, 1972, pp. 13—14).

There was a ratchet effect at work. Mobility was mostly up; less often down. When a man had acquired English literacy, Christianity and a government job, he was able to confer such advantages on his son (linguistic help at home; fees to get him into the better schools) that the dice were enormously loaded in his favour. The son of a prosperous cultivator who had gone to a bilingual school, starting in Sinhalese and learning English in the upper forms, might get a clerkship. His son, started at the kindergarten stage in an all-English school, could well hope to do better than his father — and *his* family, when he married, would be likely to be English-speaking at home. His children could aspire to the top schools which coached for the British matriculation examinations and opened the road to Oxbridge or the Inns of Court. At this point the family would have reached the very top stratum of Ceylonese society — what the civil servant commentator on the 1911 census called the 'vernacular illiterates — practically de-nationalised in the sense that they can neither read their own native papers nor write in their mother tongue to their relations, friends and servants . . . yet [they] have received a . . . liberal education in English . . . and have been educated to meet a demand' (quoted in ibid., p. 72).

And 'liberal' *was* by then becoming a fairly accurate description of the education they received. Because of the ratchet effect, because upward mobility required such a difficult process of acculturation which was heritable once a family had achieved it, the upper-strata children who attended the top schools did have a fairly secure future. Many of their families had acquired landed property and the backing of a private income. The life-style which went with landed property — the 'season' in the hills at Nuwara Eliya; the race weeks at the Colombo track; the garden parties at Queens House — reinforced by the experience of schools run by British schoolmasters as if they were British public schools which happened by chance to be in Ceylon, bred men whose manners, 'breeding' and connections were themselves valuable marketable commodities quite irrespective of any academic attainment. They did not have to cram; they were not at school primarily to engage in a qualifying rat-race. That could be left to the lower-middle-class swots of the lesser secondary schools who needed their marks and their certificates to climb a little farther up the ladder.

To be sure, the children of the very secure élite never so completely predominated, even at the very top schools such as Royal and St Thomas, that the origins of Ceylon's schools as sifting, acculturating, certifying devices for recruiting a new colonial sub-élite were entirely pushed into the background. But some patterns were established which have persisted to the present day. For example, plantations and private industrial firms recruiting managers — especially plantations — are still, like the British managers who signed the army's advertisement in *The Times* (p. 30), likely to prefer the 'good all-rounder' straight from one of the élite secondary schools rather than a university graduate. Perhaps, indeed, the character and self-confidence of the man who can stand on his verandah and quell a seething mob of Tamil labourers with a steely glint in his eye *is* more important than the brains needed to work out a production schedule, but these are considerations which have never prevailed in other late-developing societies, such as Japan, which have not had élite schools whose primary function was the transmission of an established upper-class culture. In this way, the direct importation into Sri Lanka of British educational traditions and British managerial styles established patterns which have proved resistant to the rising flood of certificationism, and created an exception to the generalisations which can be fairly safely made about late-developing societies.

The eve of independence

The system gradually expanded. The proportion of the population which could claim at the census to be literate in English reached 2.3 per cent in 1911 and over 7 per cent in the 1960s. The number of vernacular schools increased too. The only major structural change before the Second World War was the beginning, in the 1880s and 1890s, of Buddhist, Hindu and Moslem schools, expressions of the embryo nationalist movement. These were not in any direct sense heirs of the religious schools which had existed, teaching in the vernacular languages, since before the colonial period. The founders of the new wave of schools were just as much members of the new colonial middle class as the patrons of the English-language establishment schools. But they were dissident elements, no longer content, as one of them said, 'to follow blindly the white man', cultivating a taste for Pears soap and Huntley and Palmers biscuits, and buying Lancashire cloth while Ceylon's weavers starved (ibid., p. 75). Their nationalism, indeed (a last ironic twist of the phenomenon of cultural domination) derived its decisive stimulus from visits to Ceylon of Annie Besant and other theosophists; when Anglo-Saxons started to say that Buddhism was superior to Christianity, people began to listen. The schools thus founded were, consequently, Buddhist or Hindu counterparts of the Christian mission schools; teaching secularly useful knowledge by modern methods, but with a different kind of religious instruction; not by any means eschewing the English language, but emphasising national traditions rather than seeking simply to extol the glories of the British Raj (Ames, 1967).

The other major change, a gradual one, was the increase in government support of education (an Education Department had been set up as early as 1865). Subsidies were given to the denominational schools — at first only to the Christian schools but later to Buddhist and Hindu schools too. Government control increased. *Pari passu,* so did the interference of central teacher training schools and examination boards. By 1939 one could accurately speak of a school 'system' — a two-tiered system, with the 10 per cent of students in the English-medium schools which prepared their pupils for the London or Cambridge certificates getting almost twice the per capita subsidy of the vernacular schools, only a small proportion of whose pupils survived to take the locally-set Sinhalese or Tamil senior certificate (Jayasuriya, 1969, pp. 4—5).

The creation of a unified system

In 1939 there was no certainty that Ceylon was on the 'eve of independence'; five years later it was a foregone conclusion. The work of transforming the educational system was begun — prompted not only by the approach of independence, but also by the new wind blowing in Britain as the 1944 Education Act put the finishing touches to the process of fusing the different strata of British state schools into a single hierarchy.

The first step in Sri Lanka was to democratise access. Although the 'free education' ordinance of 1945 was not finally enforced until 1951, it did eventually oblige the élite schools either to renounce subsidies, or to renounce the right to levy fees. All but fifteen chose to enter the state system — after bargaining for changes in the subsidisation system which especially favoured schools with a high proportion of senior pupils.

The second major change was in the direction of greater centralisation and increased state control. The management rights of the religious denominations was one major issue, not settled until 1960. The other was the standardisation of the examination system. British examinations for the Grade 10 leaving certificate were finally abandoned in 1948. Thereafter there was a single school certificate (later known as the Ordinary level General Certificate of Education or O level), granted on examinations of identical content in English, Tamil or Sinhala. In 1964 the next grade of examination, the university entrance Advanced level General Certificate of Education (known as 'the A level' and taken in Grade 12) was similarly consolidated and henceforth locally set and supervised.

But the most difficult issue of all was the language issue. Was English to continue to be the medium of instruction in the older-established schools? It was no simple matter; many considerations came into play.

1. Education in the English language gave access — important at the university level — to a vast range of literature in all subjects unavailable in the meagre stock of translations into Sinhalese and/or Tamil.

2. A common knowledge of English language and culture provided a

unifying bond between the Tamil and the Sinhalese members of the governmental and intellectual élite.

3. But the continuing use of English in administration, in the newspapers read by the educated, in the learned journals in which the country's academics discussed the problems of the nation's development, sharpened and widened the gap between the élite and the mass of the people.

4. It represented, too, a derogation of the nation's cultural integrity which became the more glaringly indefensible as nationalist feeling was intensified after independence.

5. And as long as English-medium and Sinhalese/Tamil-medium schools co-existed, the terms of the competition — for entry into the élite schools, for entry into the most desirable jobs — were bound to favour those from the English-medium streams, and hence give advantage to that 7—8 per cent upper crust of the nation's children who had parents literate in English. The change to free education was a mockery as long as the selective entry tests to the élite schools favoured children from English-speaking homes; it meant little change in the composition of the pupil body at such schools; merely that well-to-do parents received even larger subsidies from public funds.

The debate on these issues started in the 1940s. Some continued to argue passionately for freedom of choice of medium. Their opponents charged that this was merely a cover for the perpetuation of privilege. They demanded that teaching in vernacular languages should be made universally compulsory and English relegated to the status of a merely optional second language. The first measures were a compromise: all teaching was to be in local languages up to grade 8 by 1955, except in science and maths which were to be indigenised the following year, but English was to be a compulsory second language thus keeping open the possibility of retaining English-medium universities.

The popular pressure against the privileges implicit in the retention of English proved too strong, however, particularly after the 1956 elections revealed the strength of popular Sinhalese nationalist feeling. By 1959, teaching in the vernacular was made compulsory right up to Grade 12 for all subjects except science, mathematics and Western languages, and in 1967 for science and mathematics too. The universities followed suit: by 1970 only in a few departments, chiefly medicine and English literature, were any courses given only in English.

The pyramid consolidated

Thus were the class-linked barriers of the inherited system at least eroded. A neatly pyramidical structure of free education was created which made it possible for children from poor rural homes where only

Sinhalese was spoken to win their way by examination success into that small select band, that 1.5 per cent of each age group, which earned a university degree. Of course children from middle-class homes were strongly over-represented in the upper reaches of the school system for a variety of reasons, but the overt institutional barriers were removed and there were enough examples of children reaching the top from humble backgrounds for there to be a widespread assumption that the competition was genuinely open.

And an increasing proportion of the population saw their children as actively engaged in it. Though Ceylon was a caste-stratified society, the vast majority of the population belonged to the 'middling' castes of farmers or fishermen. Only a relatively small proportion of the population was predisposed by a traditional low self-image to believe that higher education was not for the likes of their children. By the mid-1960s more than 90 per cent of the nation's children were reaching Grade 1 primary, and all the evidence suggests that a high proportion of them had their sights set on the university which only one in a hundred would ever reach.

Many were discouraged early. Promotion from grade to grade depended on performance in an attainment test. In 1971 28 per cent of the children in the first grade of primary school were repeating their first year, having failed the promotion test (Ceylon: Education, 1973, p. 59). The proportion of repeaters diminished gradually grade by grade — from 20 per cent in the second grade down to 14 per cent in the fifth. But that was largely because the experience of repeated failure was sufficiently discouraging to deter the less able children from going to school at all. If the proportion of the age group starting school was around 90 per cent, the proportion still in the system at the end of Grade 5 would be only about 57 per cent. (These figures are arrived at by calculating what would happen to a cohort which went through the school system experiencing the drop-out, repetition and promotion rates current in 1971/2.)

Those who survived that far were likely to be children who hoped to get at least a secondary education. The 57 per cent at the end of Grade 5 only reduced to about 52 per cent on entry to Grade 8 two years later. That was a crucial grade, since the test at the end of Grade 8 determined the track on which the child's future would be set.

Those who did very well in these tests — about 8 per cent of the age group — were admitted to the science streams of secondary schools — if they were lucky, at one of the better-equipped central schools or at one of the former middle-class élite schools; and if they were very bright, with some scholarship assistance to cover the costs of their boarding at such a school away from home. The day has long since gone when the 'humanistic bias' of traditional education prompted the ablest children to prefer those arts streams which led to the most honoured, power-wielding professions of law and administration. In modern Sri Lanka it is the engineer and the doctor who can be sure of high-salary employment — *and* the chance to brain-drain away to the rich countries, should creeping egalitarianism keep salaries too low or otherwise make life too difficult at home.

Those who did not do quite as well in the Grade 8 tests, or who did not live close enough to one of the schools which had adequate facilities for teaching science, could be admitted to the arts or the commerce streams of secondary schools — if they were lucky, in one of the old-established schools, or one of the well-endowed new central schools; if they were unlucky, in a low-morale country secondary school whose managers and local MP had so far failed in the competition to get it a prestige-conferring science stream. The least lucky might find themselves in what was little more than an overflow extension of a junior school. In 1970 about a quarter of the age group entered these arts and commerce courses, making a total of about one-third of the age group entering Grade 9 in all subjects.

Most of them stayed at least the full two years to take the Ordinary level certificate examination at the end of Grade 10. Few had much success, however. At one quite highly regarded central school, over three-quarters of the students taking the examination for the first time gained passes in not more than three subjects — generally including Sinhalese language and Buddhist civilisation, the subjects which had overall pass-rates over 65 per cent. Only 6 per cent — all of them from the science stream — gained the six passes (including the subjects like English and arithmetic with pass-rates around 20 per cent) necessary to go straight on to the A level course (Ceylon: Commission, 1971, p. 90). Two-thirds of those who were disappointed tried again. The success rate is slightly higher the second time round, but not very much higher — just over 20 per cent of the repeaters earned the right to continue their education in the school just quoted. After a second failure children must leave school, but many move on to further coaching in a private tutorial establishment (most of them run by university graduates who have failed to get a satisfactory job). In the late sixties about a third, by 1973 43 per cent of the children sitting for the whole or part of the Ordinary level examination were taking it for the third or fourth year running.

Thus, of the 33 per cent or so of the age group in the O level course, only between 5 and 6 per cent survived to enter Grade 11 and embark on their preparation for the Advanced level examination two years later. This was quite explicitly the university entrance examination. The rank order of marks determined who was admitted and to what faculty (or, rather, the rank order of marks 'standardised' as between the language media and further adjusted by district quotas in a very controversial manner designed to prevent over-representation of Tamil and urban students, apt to occur especially in science subjects). The best performers in maths and physics entered the engineering department, the next best going to the technical institutes for a diploma course. The students who offered biology and zoology were distributed, according to their rank order, between the medical, the veterinary, the agricultural and dentistry departments — and so on. Three-quarters of those who took the examination failed, even after two or three tries, to get a place. They had perhaps the acutest sense of disappointment of all, having got so close to 'success' but instead gained nothing except one or two certificated A level passes which did little to improve their job chances.

Employment, aspirations and the pressures on the school
'Job chances', of course, are what it is all about. In the days when the modern school system was beginning to take shape, just after independence, the small élite (0.3 per cent, say, of the age group) who got university degrees could confidently expect to receive — largely in the public service — interesting and well paid jobs. Those who had O level certificates (3 per cent, say, of the age group) could be reasonably certain of jobs as clerks, teachers, technicians. But it is, alas, far easier to expand the school system than it is to expand the modern sector economy and increase the number of job opportunities. Now, the much larger numbers leaving senior secondary schools and universities can no longer look so confidently to the future. The arithmetic of the labour market is stark and simple. There are about a million jobs in the 'modern' wage and salary sector of the economy, covering about a quarter of the work force (the other three-quarters being in farming and fishing, plantation labour or casual — chiefly agricultural — employment). Death and retirement at around 2 per cent creates perhaps 20,000 job opportunities a year; expansion of the modern sector might add another 50,000 (though given the labour-saving nature of most new capital investment, it may well be that this 5 per cent increase in employment requires something like an 8 per cent increase in output, which is a good deal higher than the Ceylonese economy has recently achieved). At the most, then, there are some 70,000 job opportunities a year, of which perhaps a half may be desirable white-collar professional and administrative jobs. By contrast, the number of young men and women reaching working age annually is in the region of 300,000, and of those, by 1971 nearly 100,000 had had the ten years or more of schooling which they thought (because that *was* the case not so very long ago) ought to entitle them to a decent job.

Some of those who are not going to get 'decent jobs' are not entirely without future prospects — the eldest sons of farmers or small shop keepers, for example, can look forward eventually to inheriting a family livelihood. But that prospect does not necessarily diminish their desire for a job, for the independence of having their *own* job, for the superior prestige and status, as well as probably the superior income, of a job in the modern sector.

Half a million people openly unemployed (over 15 per cent of the labour force); four-fifths of that unemployment concentrated in the under-25 age group; among the 20—24 year olds with at least three O level passes, unemployment rates of 55 per cent for men and 74 per cent for women — these, in 1971 were the facts of the schools' social context which were overwhelmingly important in determining what went on within them. If there are no jobs for O level leavers anyway, what is to be lost by taking the examination for a third or even a fourth year running in order to improve the attractiveness of the piece of paper which is all one has to impress possible employers? Why not try desperately hard to press on to the next higher level — for although unemployment rates rose with educational level up to the O level point (only 8 per cent of the 20—24 year olds with no schooling at all were counted as 'unemployed', presumably because they have never seen themselves as having pretentions to a secure wage job), and were still high for those who left at A level, they were negligible for graduates of university science streams, and although higher again for general arts graduates, especially girls, there was always the hope that, as it did in 1971, the government might start a special scheme to create jobs for unemployed graduates on the grounds that the loss of their manpower is a *serious* under-utilisation of resources.

And, at all levels, if one knows that only one in three or one in four of one's contemporaries will get the few jobs available, what could be more reasonable than to concentrate every effort on trying to ensure that one gets into the top quarter of any achievement test ranking that might influence employers' choices?

The consequences for the quality of education
It is not surprising that examinations *dominate* the curriculum, that all learning is ritualised, that curiosity is devalued, that no one is allowed to stray from the syllabus, that no one inquires about the usefulness, the relevance, or the interestingness of what is learned. The story of the Ceylonese teacher of civics to 16 year olds who just could not conceive of discussing her teaching except in terms of the examination syllabus was recorded in Chapter 1 (p. 10).

With the devaluation of any kind of learning activity which does not contribute to passing examinations goes, also, the devaluation of those subjects which are less crucial to examination success. No one takes

Buddhist civilisation or Sinhalese literature, which have pass-rates of 65
—70 per cent at O level, quite as seriously as arithmetic or English,
with pass-rates of around 20 per cent. And as for woodwork or
agriculture or needlework, they are the subjects to be sacrificed if extra
periods are required for dry-run mock exams — the very subjects,
which unlike the mastery of quadratic equations or memorising the
length of the world's largest rivers, *could* conceivably contribute
something to the future lives of those children (the majority even in
Grade 8) who will, from sheer economic necessity, have to find their
future livelihoods in farming or forestry or petty commerce.

Here is what the Minister of Education said of his school system in
May 1971.

> From the time the child enters school the target is set on the university.
> Each year only 1% of the school population enters universities. So all
> the effort, expenditure and preparations are for the benefit of this
> 1% . . . The school should not worry about them. The school instead
> should concentrate on the vast majority . . . They should be made to
> feel that the society wants them and they are doing something useful to
> the betterment of the country. They should not be made to feel that
> they are rejects who could not enter the university. (*The Nation,*
> 30 May 1971.)

'They *should* be made to feel . . .' The prescription is easy: the
fulfilment difficult. The path of Ceylon's educational development is
strewn with the wrecks of earlier schemes to make school education
relevant to the needs, not just of the minority destined for the modern
sector, but of the majority who are not. The 'central schools' founded
in 1941 had, as one of their three chief aims:

> To correlate the education imparted to the needs of the locality: to
> prepare pupils for life and according to their ability and natural
> equipment; by creating a love for their village environment and by
> concentrating on occupations, traditional or otherwise, which could
> be developed nearer the pupil's home to counter as far as possible the
> tendency of village lads to migrate to towns and semi-urban areas in
> search of employment and thereby to swell the ranks of the un-
> employed and to become useless to themselves and to the com-
> munity. (Quoted in Jayasuriya, 1969, p. 98.)

Within two years, as the historian of the period records, the aim was
as good as abandoned. The schools were 'unable to make children,
most of all the good ones, interested in agriculture and handicrafts'.

These subjects became 'the Cinderellas of the Central Schools . . . over-shadowed . . . by the superior prestige of the pure Arts and Sciences' (ibid.).

One possible solution, of course, is to divide children into different streams. If the race is a race to get to the top, and if only 1½ per cent will get there, is it necessary for 30—35 per cent of the nation's children *still* to be competing in *that* particular race at the age of 15 or even, in many cases, 17 or 18? Surely it must be obvious that the majority of children in that group are not going to 'make it'. Should they not be switched to some channel other than the 'academic' university-preparatory one?

At least twice in the last two decades, Ceylon's educational administrators have tried to create a British-style system of differential secondary education geared to children's diagnosed 'aptitudes and abilities'. Twice they have failed.

The 1951 scheme was the compromise outcome of an original proposal to divide pupils after the fifth primary grade. The administrators settled for a division after Grade 8 — a 13-plus rather than a 10-plus. There were to be, in addition to the regular secondary schools leading on to universities, senior schools (which *could* lead to polytechnics) and practical schools (which could lead on to trade and agricultural schools).

The regulations remained a dead letter. The opposition was too widespread and too intense — particularly from teachers who objected strenuously to being expected to take the responsibility of eliminating *any* child from the only race that anyone seemed to consider important. The ministry came back to try to take that fence again sixteen years later. There was to be a similar array of selective secondary alternatives, but the selection was not to be any casual affair depending on Grade 8 examinations. It would emerge from subjecting 'the pupils in Standards 6, 7 and 8 . . . to a very close scrutiny . . . guided by trained teacher-counsellors who will also conduct regular conferences with parents'. There would be 'every possible safeguard . . . to protect the interests of the late-developer' (Ceylon, 1966, p. 12). This proposal got as far as being embodied in a parliamentary Bill. But it was never officially pressed. The opposition was too great.

Why was it impossible to introduce in Sri Lanka a system of selective secondary education which proved acceptable in Britain between 1945 and the late 1960s? The answer is, presumably, that the unwillingness of parents to see their child eliminated from the central competition, the ideal of equality of opportunity, the demand that doors should be kept open for a 'second chance', the pressure to postpone to as late an age as possible the point of definitive selection and rejection — all the pressures which have made it increasingly difficult to operate 11-plus selection in Britain and forced recourse to comprehensive alternatives, albeit only as a camouflage for very much the same selection process as took place before — all these pressures were in fact stronger in Sri Lanka than in Britain. Sri Lanka's school system, essentially the creation of the post-independence period, was from the first seen as above all a channel of social mobility, a single-peaked pyramid which everybody could climb. Britain's more slowly, more haphazardly growing system was still only gradually emerging from its stratified past. The secondary moderns of the Butler Education Act still had a couple of decades to go before their acceptability declined to vanishing point. And they were acceptable because the principle of division had historical roots, because the secondary modern was familiar as a reincarnation of (indeed some improvement on) the old upper elementary schools designed for a working class which gave little thought to, saw little prospects of, their children's ascent up the educational ladder to higher class status. Ceylon's more homogeneously 'middle-class' population did not have the same long tradition of resigned subordination to an educationally distinct upper class. *Its* subordination — to a colonial upper class — was supposed to have ended with independence.

Thus the pattern of the single-peaked pyramid whose purpose is defined in terms of its peak proved resistant to amendment. It became even more deeply entrenched as unemployment grew, increasing the importance of getting to the top. Several other consequences follow besides the dominant importance of examinations leading on the one hand to a ritualisation of learning and on the other to devaluation of all but the difficult academic subjects.

First, the sense of failure of the 'drop-out' is reinforced. The only way to resist the intense pressure for expansion of upper secondary schools and universities is to 'fail' large numbers of children. Those who leave the school system at O level after Grade 10 are more likely to see themselves as having failed to get into the A level course than as having successfully completed ten years of useful education.

Secondly, it is an important cause of the high level of primary drop-out. The fact that over 40 per cent of the nation's children fail to finish five years of schooling is partly because primary education is not seen as an end in itself, but only as the first qualifying step to higher things.

Thirdly, one should consider the likely effects, already discussed in Chapter 1 (pp. 11—12) on the successful ones who get jobs, especially on the graduates who become the future controllers of Sri Lanka's destiny. If they have, for sixteen long years, been trained to docile acceptance of the authority of teachers and examiners, warned that success depends on producing the answers which we expect those in authority to expect, are they likely suddenly to become imaginative managers and administrators noted for their independence and integrity? If their intellectual curiosity has never been encouraged to develop whenever it has strayed beyond the bounds of an examination syllabus, if they have never learned for the sheer pleasure of mastery, are they likely to be capable of adding to their motives for work the craftsman's pride in seeing a job well done, the pleasure of solving difficult problems?

The answer is that some do. The human intellect has surprising resilience. But the odds are that these are, and will remain, rather exceptional people.

The tragedy is that all these features of the education system seem bound to get worse — as a result of that paradoxical mechanism of the labour market qualification spiral which ensures that the more the job-getting value of educational certificates declines, the more important it becomes for the individual to press on to higher and higher levels of schooling leading to higher and higher levels of certification. Thus, the future seems to hold out no prospect for Ceylon's schools and their pupils except continuous pressure for expansion of facilities, increasing intense competition at every entry port and selection post, increasingly anxious dominance of the curriculum by examinations, and an increasing experience of individual failure within the school system, and of the frustrations of unemployment on leaving it.

That the prospect was a grim one many people in Sri Lanka were prepared at one time to believe. But situations which deteriorate by imperceptible degrees do not usually galvanise people into action. An insurrection, however, is a different matter. The revolt of Ceylon's youth in April 1971 (Obeyesekere, 1974) failed to overturn the government, though it did destroy many police stations and control large areas of the country for several days. The young men and women who joined the movement — 14,000 of them ended up in detention camps and many others were killed — had a variety of different motives, different sources of alienation. Some were educated and unemployed. Some, were idealistically contemptuous of the ineffectiveness and posturings of their politicians. Others among those who had got jobs were among the first generations of the Sinhalese educated who still felt themselves slighted and disadvantaged as they entered the subordinate ranks of a still predominantly English-using élite. And for the large numbers of university and secondary school students who joined the movement, the hopeless frustrations of a meaningless education leading to no prospect of a useful life must have been a dominant motive. The very occurrence of the insurrection highlighted the great gap between what society needed from its educational system and what it was getting. The aims and declarations of the insurrectionists, reflecting the naivety of schoolchildren nurtured on a narrow curriculum and discouraged from any real inquiry into the society about them, emphasised that disjunction. It would be wrong to say that the government was galvanised into action, but at least the urgency of educational reforms was seen to have a new dimension. There is good reason to believe that the response is hardly adequate to the challenge, but that is a topic to be taken up in a later chapter.

Chapter 5

Kenya

In comparison with Sri Lanka's, Kenya's educational system is both newer and less complex. It is less complex partly *because* it is newer — most existing schools were created *after* the establishment of an integrated national pyramid and did not have to be awkwardly slotted in afterwards — and partly because the diversity of local languages leaves English unchallenged as the language of secondary and higher education.

Kenya's earliest schools were, of course, mission schools, and Kenyan education was still in the mission-dominated phase at the time of independence. As a British government statement of educational policy put the matter in 1925, their major function was to 'make the conscience sensitive to moral and intellectual truth' and to 'impart some power of discrimination between good and evil, between reality and superstition' (Britain: Advisory Committee, 1925). For most of the children who went to them, however, probably a more important function lay in providing the chance of jobs in the colonial modern sector — but, still, almost until independence, only subordinate jobs. Whereas Sri Lanka had distinguished native jurists and intellectual leaders already in the mid-nineteenth century, and at independence had families which had been educated at Oxbridge for four generations, Kenya did not produce its first graduate until the late 1930s, and there were estimated to be less than 1,500 African graduates in the country at the time of independence (not all of them Kenyans). At its University College established three years before, only 17 out of over 100 posts were manned by Kenyans.

As soon as the independence issue was settled, as soon as it was made clear that the white settlers had lost the battle for control, and more especially after independence itself, expansion of the educational system had top priority. Primary school enrolments increased from 780,000 in 1960 to over a million in 1965 and 1.4 million in 1970; secondary and university enrolments at an even faster growth rate. Predictably, the growth in school outputs has outstripped the growth in desirable modern-sector jobs.

In 1960, probably about 13 per cent of each age group was getting to the end of Standard 7 in primary school and over half of them were staying the extra year for Standard 8. They had good prospects of a job in a factory, office or government department. But soon, as their numbers increased without much increase in the number of job openings, the school-leaver employment problem became a major concern. By the end of the decade, however, Standard 7 leavers, now making up nearly 60 per cent of each age group, had adjusted their expectations to reality. They had, in the words of one writer, been 'cooled out [as they competed] to grasp in the 1970s the sort of openings that preceding cohorts despised in the late fifties: shoe shiner, *shamba* boy, spanner boy, day labourer on the building sites, tea and coffee picker' (King, 1973, p. 7).

Now, the only worthwhile focus of ambition was on getting to secondary school. Hence, not unnaturally, all parental political pressures were concentrated on the expansion of secondary school opportunities. If the government would not build a secondary school in the district, the parents built one themselves, hoping that their *fait accompli* would eventually force the government to incorporate it into the subsidised system. The Harambee self-help secondary school movement spread throughout the country (aided, sometimes, by external missionary donors impressed by the movement's zeal in the cause of education).

For Kenya we can follow the course of the education explosion with some accuracy, thanks to excellent tracer studies. The year which first saw the onset of secondary leaver unemployment was 1968. Until 1967, less than 1 per cent of those who left school after the Form 4 certificate exam were still unemployed a year later. In 1968 that proportion rose to 15 per cent — 35 per cent among those whose certificate grades put them in the bottom fifth of the class (Kinyanjui, 1973, pp. 18 and 83). By the early seventies the problem of secondary leaver employment was recognised to be acute. The new self-help movement started at the next level: politicians from each major area of the country launched subscription lists for polytechnics to absorb the secondary school graduates who could neither get jobs nor get into the single state university. The government had no politically feasible alternative but to announce its support. The onset of unemployment for those with degrees and diplomas is still some years ahead.

Still, among the 200,000 or so young Kenyans who reach working age every year, a certain proportion, at the most 16 per cent,[1] get some kind

[1]This assumes (a) that there is a 3 per cent replacement rate in the wage and salary labour force, (b) that the net increase in that labour force registered for 1969—70 in the Labour Force Survey was both accurate and typical (see Kenya Min. of Finance and Planning, *Stat. Abstract*, 1971) and (c) that school leavers took *all* the 33,000 net vacancies thus created. (Even 3 per cent greatly exaggerates — perhaps even doubles — the replacement rate, so that 16 per cent is certainly an over-estimate.)

of wage employment. Perhaps not more than a half of those jobs offer a fair security and the sort of income that makes one of, and not just in, 'the modern sector'. And 8 per cent is precisely the proportion of the age group which in 1970 was getting a Form 4 secondary certificate. Hence the role of the secondary school entrance test as the major filter determining life chances. (The test still bears the name 'certificate of primary education', as if its function remained that of confirming and applauding what primary school children have accomplished — a certificate designed especially for those whose education is coming to an end!)

The examination is nationally standardised. The last two or three years of primary school are devoted to preparing for it. In those years . . . the interest and relevance of a particular piece of information will increasingly be determined entirely by whether or not it is likely to be asked in the examination. During the last year extra study periods will probably be arranged; before or after school, in the farm holidays, or even at night. A good deal of attention will be given to the specialised technique of answering multiple-choice questions. The class will be told of the careers of former pupils who passed the examination well (Somerset, 1973, p. 65).

Children who can afford it will buy the crammer's guide — a comprehensive compendium covering all aspects of CPE cramming techniques.

The top performers in this exam (the one outstanding pupil out of seventy to eighty) will get the chance (and only in the rarest cases refuse it) of taking a place on the region's quota at one of the four national élite schools. These schools, originally built by missions, three for boys and one for girls, have the highest reputation because of their selectivity, and by the same token can attract able teachers. Attendance at such a school itself confers high prestige. Old boys who have 'made it' to such schools are a legend in their primary schools back home.

There is another group of national élite schools (two for boys, five for girls) which also recruit from all over the country, but charge higher fees (they were formerly schools for Europeans only). Their entry standards are correspondingly less high; they are privileged, but less 'élite'.

The next level of students, still those of well above average performance, get places at the local maintained secondary schools. Their careers are less assured; their chances of a university place are a good deal slimmer than for the children at the national schools, but still they are the objects of envy — they can expect to be among the 13 per cent of their age group who can leave school with an O level certificate.

And for those who are left, those who have missed either of these chances, there remains — unless they are prepared to change their name and place of residence, smuggle themselves into the top form of another primary school and try (illegally) a second time — the chance of going to a Harambee self-financed school.

Of the efficiency of the sorting system — efficiency in its own terms, i.e. its ability to predict *later* academic achievement (which, of course, it in part determines) — there can be little doubt, at least if subsequent examination performance is any guide. In 1969, in the East African Certificate Examination which came at the end of the fourth secondary year, the average mark at the national schools (both high and low cost) was close to the mark of the 20th percentile in the overall national distribution. At the local maintained schools it was a little over the 50th percentile, i.e. close to the median for all examinees. The average for the Harambee schools equalled the mark of the 80th percentile (Somerset, 1973, p. 66).

The differentials are widely understood, and that makes it worse. The fact that he knows everybody knows that he has been relegated to a lower-grade school is what is apt to sap the self-respect of a once-ambitious Harambee pupil and what prompts his younger brother to redouble his efforts to avoid such a fate.

And in the secondary school the pressure to get good marks does not diminish. One has to get a good Form 4 certificate to enter Form 5 and stay on the royal road to the university. Even if one does not aim so high, even if one hopes only to be one of the lucky ones who gets a job, marks still count; employers *do* take them as an indication of 'general ability'. The tracer study showed that in 1968, the first year of secondary school unemployment, the grade average of the 15 per cent who were still without a job a year after graduating was 45 compared with 35 for the whole sample (the lower the mark, the better the score). Among the 9 per cent who were still without a job a year later, the average mark had dropped (i.e. increased) even further — to 47 (Kinyanjui, 1973, p. 96).

Kenya, in terms of the total *volume* of unemployment, is still some way behind Sri Lanka. Yet it is catching up fast as Table 2 indicates. this is not just a statistical illusion due to the fact that Kenya started from a smaller base. There are three plausible reasons for thinking that the pressures — for growth of the system and for competition within it — are greater in Kenya than in Sri Lanka. The first is because, lacking anything like Sri Lanka's hereditary upper crust, differentiated by language, culture and 'breeding' from the rest of the population, Kenya has no *alternative* criteria of excellence to challenge school achievement as the legitimator of high position. There are no families, no élite schools with a century-old tradition, which are thought to give their children specially potent doses of confidence and judgement and character. Patronage and particularistic 'connections' can, indeed, make up for poor marks on occasion — but hardly for the public service (which employs 70 per cent of the secondary leavers who get jobs and a higher proportion of university graduates), nor for the large-scale private firm, still, probably, dominated by European managers.

Table 2 *Enrolment growth rates 1965—70, proportions of cohort enrolled 1970 and selection ratios, 1970*

Level	Enrolment growth	% of age cohort enrolled	Ratio (university = 1)
		Kenya	
Standard 7	6% p.a.	57%	197
Form 4	23% p.a.	8%	23
University 1st year	31% p.a.	0·5%	1
		Sri Lanka	
Grade 6	5% p.a.	72%	70
Grade 10	2% p.a.	39%	36
University 1st year	0% p.a.	1·2%	1

Secondly, few Kenyan families — a good deal fewer than in Sri Lanka — have family businesses which are thriving enough for their children to see taking over the family business as a *preferable* alternative to getting an employee job. Only 10 of the 1,200 children in the tracer study who left Form 4 between 1965 and 1968 went into self-employment (including one musician and five who got their own farms). All the rest had become, or were trying to become, or training to become, employees, and therefore needed their marks.

Thirdly, the absence of hereditary class or status group divisions makes the competition even more open in Kenya than in Sri Lanka (just as I argued in the last chapter that it was more open in Sri Lanka than in Britain). A generation ago everybody in Kenya was a village boy. The first graduates, the present leaders of the country, were village boys. Why should not every other village boy follow in their footsteps? Except for certain groups such as the Masai who are marginal to the polity, everybody can consider himself in the race.

Chapter 6

The Late-Development Effect

It is time for some general propositions. I will offer three. Other things being equal (we'll consider what things later), the later development starts (i.e. the later the point in world history that a country starts on a modernisation drive):

the more widely education certificates are used for occupational selection;
the faster the rate of qualification inflation; and
the more examination-oriented schooling becomes at the expense of genuine education.

Let us look at each of these in turn.

. . . the more jobs depend on qualifications

Chapter 3 has already tried to show how and why educational qualifications counted for more in Japan than in Britain. To be sure, 'late development' is not the only factor. Britain's non-reliance on formal qualifications was extreme, even among early developers, partly, presumably, because Britain has never since Cromwell experienced the sort of modernising spurt which in Napoleonic France created the Grandes Ecoles, or at least established them in such a position that they soon acquired very important qualifying functions for government and industry. But the 'late development effect' is clear. Certificates undoubtedly counted for more in Sri Lanka in the 1950s than for, say, Japan in the 1910s; more for Kenya in the 1960s than for Sri Lanka in the 1950s. It is easy enough to explain why. Part of it is the later developer's need to catch up fast — by importing knowledge and skills in formal educational packages. The most important part is the general tendency of the late developer to import the *latest* technology from the metropolitan models — social as well as machine technology. And, as a piece of social technology, the device of making even more refined and universal use of educational certificates for job allocation is becoming — as we saw *à propos* of Britain in Chapter 3 — more and more 'perfected' every year. Thus, Sri Lanka, earlier in the century, followed then current British practice in providing apprenticeship/ mid-career-training routes into accountancy and engineering. Kenya, starting later, did not, but instead adopted the degree-entry practices which were just becoming formalised in Britain.

But it is time to look at that 'other things being equal' clause. Some other factors do over-ride the tendencies just described.

There are a few odd corners, even in what is conventionally thought of as the developing world, where a man's ability to make his way in the world does depend a good deal less than in most on the educational qualifications he carries. Hong Kong is such — though decreasingly so. It is one of the few places where industrialisation has been the product of the same sort of small-scale entrepreneurship as laid the basis for Europe's (especially Britain's) industrialisation. Most men's income and status have depended on what they actually know and can do — on their skills and their push and intelligence more than on the pieces of paper they have been able to show potential employers. Hong Kong does not have the same sharp dualistic division between a highly desirable modern sector and an impoverished, despised, traditional sector typical of most developing countries. There is, rather, a steady graduation in enterprise size and modernity and considerable movement along the gradient.

The reasons for this are complex. It is partly because Hong Kong *does* have an unusually high quotient of clever, innovating businessmen who were capable of expanding tiny family workshops into larger, wage-employing viable firms. Another reason is because, as a colony, with a government which was solely concerned to hold the ring, state employment — given the small range of government services and the absence of state enterprises — has played a small part in total employment and so been less influential than in most developing countries in setting the general patterns.

Even Hong Kong is changing now, however. Government employment is expanding. The big multi-national corporations which always did tend to recruit by certificate are more firmly entrenched and have expanded their recruiting needs; more and more of the home-bred Chinese enterprises have grown big enough to have specialised personnel managers and to adopt the 'rational', 'modern' methods of recruitment by qualification.

In countries where big organisations — the state or large corporations — have dominated the industrialisation/modernisation process from the beginning, and where thrusting small-scale entrepreneurs have been lacking, or even positively discouraged by harassing licensing restrictions, the division between the traditional and the modern sector is sharper and the importance of educational qualifications correspondingly greater. Of the total working-age (15 to 59) population of

Senegal, about 6 per cent are in jobs secured by social security provisions — modern sector jobs within the purview of the labour inspector. Of these nearly a half are government or public sector enterprise jobs, and of the rest a large proportion in big rationalised French-owned firms which set minimum educational standards for nearly all jobs. In Tanzania the corresponding figures are about 6 per cent in modern sector jobs (in establishments employing more than ten workers) of whom (1970) 58 per cent are in government or in parastatal corporations. A glance at Tanzanian newspaper job advertisements will show how finely graduated the correspondence between jobs and educational levels has become. A parastatal printing corporation wants a proof reader: 'Form 6 leaver with good passes in Swahili and English'; a Security Officer: 'at least Standard Seven'; a Costing Clerk Grade II: 'at least Form 2 leavers'. It is not a bad generalisation that the almightiness of the certificate varies in direct proportion to the predominance of the state in the development process. Weber made insistence on qualifications part of his classical definition of bureaucracy as an ideal type — and for very good reasons; certificates are objective; governments need, among other things, standards of impersonal judgement which protect them against charges of corrupt favouritism.

The other feature of countries like Senegal or Tanzania is the cliff-like nature of the separation of the modern sector from the traditional one. The twilight zone of what it is now fashionable to call the 'informal sector' — the roadside and empty-lot mechanics who will weld on a Bournville cocoa tin to mend the exhaust pipe of the civil servant's Mercedes, the leather workers making hand-made bags for the tourist trade, the furniture-makers, the men who collect empty Essolube cans from the garages twice a day and have them processed into serviceable oil lamps by sunset — this twilight zone is small in total size, and its tiny enterprises, which are mostly family affairs offering little wage employment, rarely show much prospect of expanding into modern enterprises, particularly in those African countries where the people who have in the past shown entrepreneurial skills (the Asians in East Africa, the Lebanese in Senegal) are coming under increasingly nationalist restrictions of their activities.

Hence the 'informal sector', the 'transitional zone', is *not* in fact a transitional zone for individuals. It is not a means by which one moves from rural traditionalism into the modern sector by easy stages. Its entrepreneurs have little hope of achieving the life-style or the prestige of the modern-sector managers: its workers are not likely to graduate to more secure, better paid jobs in big firms. They are working in the twilight sector precisely *because* they have failed to get jobs in the modern-sector firm — and their chances of doing so are likely to diminish rather than increase as the new jobs which do become available are snapped up by their educationally better qualified juniors. Where the informal sector is that small and insignificant, then, it does not offer a route up the cliff-face from the traditional to the modern sector. The only way to make that transition is by the cable cars of the educational system.

But, of course, the tendency for government to play a leading rôle in the development process is *also* something which tends to increase the later development starts — because of the greater weight of the élite's 'sense of backwardness' among the motive forces for development, as Gerschenkron argued *à propos* of the successive generations of European development (Gerschenkron, 1965).

Likewise the tendency for dualism to be more exacerbated the later development starts is another part of the 'late-development effect'. (First, there is a greater technological gap between the traditional economy and the current generation of techniques available for import; secondly, in so far as the living standards of the modern sector are pulled up by the influences of rich country standards, the higher the latter go the greater the gap is likely to be. The Japanese Emperor in the 1890s required only imported horses and a locally made carriage. President Kenyatta needs a Benz or a Lincoln.)

So both these factors can be assumed to be subsumed in the proposition that later developers are more bemused by qualifications. That leaves three things as independent sources of variation:

(i) the presence or absence of people with thrusting entrepreneurial talents *à la* Hong Kong;

(ii) the presence or absence of the political will deliberately to counter the forces leading to dualism and qualificationism — *à la* China;

(iii) the economic and strategic circumstances which may limit the scope of these last two factors. It may be, for instance, that even if Senegal were peopled by Chinese, its poverty of resources, geographical position, and the entrenched nature of French influence would leave so little room for manoeuvre that things would still not be too different.

. . . the faster the rate of qualification inflation
Qualification inflation results from a faster growth of the school system than of the number of modern-sector job opportunities. Our proposition can therefore be translated either: the later development starts, the slower the rate of creation of modern-sector job opportunities; or, the later development starts, the faster the growth of school enrolments.

The first proposition is unlikely to be true, though there are *some* forces pushing in that direction; the later the timing of industrialisation, the more capital-intensive and less labour-intensive it is likely to be, hence the fewer jobs created for any given volume of investment. Two countervailing forces, however, are a probable faster growth in service-sector jobs, particularly government services (because of the greater role of government, see above), and faster overall growth rates. The Japanese economy grew faster in the early stages of industrialisation than the British, the Ceylonese than the Japanese, and the Kenyan than the Ceylonese.

It is the second proposition which is the crucial one: school enrolments grow faster — so much faster as to counteract any tendency there *might* be for job opportunities to grow faster too: hence an imbalance which grows at a faster rate in later starters. Compare the figures for our four countries:

Growth in secondary enrolments (% p.a.)

Britain	1864—1893	3%
Japan	1900—1910	8%
Sri Lanka	1950—1960	14%
Kenya	1960—1970	20%

Taunton Commission (1868), Vol. 1, Appx. VI; Bryce Commission (1895), Vol. 1, para. 52 and Vol. IX; Japan: Education (1964); UNESCO (1963, 1971). British figures are for seven sample counties only; endowed and proprietary schools only.

The first reason why this should be so is fairly obvious. It follows from the first of our three propositions. The greater the degree of credentialism, the more the schools are the *only* channel of social mobility; the more complete the absence of any route up the cliff to the modern sector except the educational cable car. Studies of educational aspirations in Malaysia show that there is a smaller proportion of children hoping to press on to the university among the Chinese, who are supposed to be ambitious, persistent and energetic, than among the Malays who are supposed to have rather smaller doses of these qualities. The reason, clearly, is that, for the Malays who dominate the bureaucratised government (and, through government, expatriate big business) sectors of the economy, certificates really count; for the Chinese Malaysians whose opportunities lie in the small business sector, they have less value (Malaysia, 1972).

A second part of the explanation is that the later development starts, the more firmly implanted in the international consensus is the idea (still highly controversial in Britain as late as 1870) that it is a proper, indeed essential function of the state to provide for its citizens' education — and, one might add, to provide schooling and the hope, however fallacious, of escape into the modern sector, is often easier than, say, carrying out a land reform or otherwise redistributing resources in ways that might make life in rural areas more productive and more tolerable.

Thirdly, the later development starts, the worse the dualism is likely to be — the greater the modern-sector/traditional-sector differential in income, power and prestige; the greater the attractions of trying to scale the cliff. Indeed, where population growth, or the initial disequalising effects of economic growth, have actually worsened living standards in rural areas, there may genuinely be no way out but to try to scale the cliff — push factors not just pull factors, as the students of rural-urban migration say.

Also, fourthly, later developers have better means of communication available; hence the late developer's villages are more integrated into the polity and more subjected to demonstration effect. Tokyo, where all the university graduates were, was a pretty remote place for the vast majority of Japanese villagers in the 1890s; a place on the end of a telegraph line, described in the newspapers which came three days late. A good proportion of Kenya's contemporary villagers have seen Nairobi on a television screen, hear its broadcasts instantaneously on the radio; can join their cousins there for the relatively inexpensive price of a bus ride. More people, in other words, know something about life up on the modern-sector plateau and are likely to be susceptible to its attractions.

And they are more likely to see access to that modern sector as feasible as well as desirable because, fifthly, the later development starts, the more the meritocratic ideal of equality of opportunity is entrenched in the international consensus; the more likely, therefore, an integrated school system providing subsidies, scholarships, etc., for poor children to reach the top — given, sixthly, the additional factor that the 'sense of backwardness' is likely to be greater, greater also the urge to catch up, greater the premium placed on efficiency; greater therefore the arguments for meritocracy as a mean of mobilising all the talents. What these last four factors all combined to produce, therefore, is a *greater intensity* of *popular demand* for education, particularly for schooling at the sort of levels at which valid job certificates are thought to be produced.

One could argue, finally, that the later the timing of development, the less a government is likely to be able to resist that demand — because the more deeply the democratic notion that governments should be responsive to popular will is likely to be built into the system.

However, *some* governments, for some time at least, can resist — which brings us to the first variable one has in mind when one puts the 'other things being equal' qualification to the proposition that qualification inflation is worse in later developers. Tanzania, for example, can still make some claim to be the manpower planners' dream land. In the planner's ideal world, qualification-escalation just is not allowed to exist. He will allow expansion up to 100 per cent enrolment in a basic primary open-access span of education which is not presumed by anyone to confer any job rights in the modern sector. Beyond that he seeks to fix for all time what he has assumed to be the 'correct' equations between qualification levels and job requirements, and to regulate numbers allowed into each secondary and tertiary education stream according to the numbers of jobs predicted to be available; so many entrants to the medical faculty, so many for general arts degrees, so many to be admitted to general secondary education.

Tanzania still operates such a system. The budget for Form 2 leavers, Form 4 leavers, Form 6 leavers and university graduates is set for some years ahead, and the government declares its firm intention of allowing just that many and no more into the secondary schools — however strong the mounting pressure for more secondary places as the number of children reaching the end of primary increases annually and each individual child's chance of getting to a public secondary school correspondingly diminishes. Even in Tanzania, however the state has not been able to present the growth of a 'spill-over' private secondary sector, a growth which was accelerating in the more prosperous areas in the mid-seventies.

In Kenya next door, as the last chapter described, the government has all but given up attempts, even within the public sector, to dam the flood at the secondary entrance stage, and is in fact abandoning any attempt to do so at the tertiary stage. The most obvious explanation of the difference lies in the contrast between the collectivity-oriented philosophy of Tanzania's leaders and the individualistic philosophy of Kenya's, but other features of the political structure also play a part — the degree of federalism, for instance, and the dependence of governments on popular election.

India, the authentic home of the BA bus conductor, famous for its 60,000 unemployed graduate engineers — many of them already with master's degrees — is a good example of the importance of those latter features. Every responsible Indian who writes on problems of his country's education deplores the unbridled expansion of higher education of unemployables when 60 per cent of the population still either never reach or fail to finish primary school. But in India control over education is decentralised to the state level, to decision-makers for whom the manpower planning concerns of the central government have little relevance and less force. The device — a British legacy — of founding satellite colleges, which establish themselves by taking externally the degrees of already established universities, makes it possible to begin a plausible tertiary institution with much more exiguous resources. The existence of real democratic party competition makes the political pressures infinitely more irresistible than in a one-party state like Kenya. Schools and colleges are one of the most tangible ways of winning the electorate's favour; the yield in votes gained per rupee of public money expended is likely to be higher than for bridges or agricultural credit schemes — particularly in states like UP where, such is the level of sophistication in the factional use of education, that (over and above the general goodwill created by providing educational opportunities) schools and colleges act as electoral bridge-heads for the politician who creates or captures them, their staff and students mobilised into active workers in his vote-getting machine (Rudolph and Rudolph, 1972).

One other important variable affecting the rôle of qualification has already been discussed in the preceding chapters: the degree and type of social stratification. In some 'older' societies with long-established status systems, the 'lower orders' have been conditioned for generations to see themselves as 'naturally' condemned to underdog status. If the only primary school available is one which peters out after the third grade, they are not much upset; they do not bewail the foreclosing of chances of mobility they have hardly conceived of. By contrast, in African societies which had little stratification before they were colonised (even in the kingdom of Buganda or the emirates of northern Nigeria there was little elaborated hereditary *cultural* differentiation between the upper and lower strata) the 'modern sector' is equally new to everyone. No particular group is seen as having a preternatural right and everyone is free to compete. One can hardly imagine a Ministry of Education *anywhere* in the modern world setting out, as the Taunton Commission did in Britain in the 1860s (Taunton Commission, 1868, Vol. 1, Appx. 2), to calculate the number of 'upper and middle class school-children' as a means of estimating the requirements for secondary education (though it may be, of course, that the enormous educational advantages which accrue to the children of university-educated parents will lead to sharply entrenched class divisions very rapidly (O'Connell and Beckett, 1975).

The problem is not new in India. Indeed, already at the beginning of the century, the headlong expansion of higher education was sufficiently widely recognised to be a problem that legislative controls were introduced. Nothing better illustrates the marvellous Canute-like hubris of the British Raj than Lord Curzon's confidence that he had settled the problem once and for all. It is worth recalling his words before the legislative council. If he had not acted, he said,

. . . the rush of immature striplings to our India universities, not to learn but to earn, would have continued till it became an avalanche ultimately bringing the entire educational fabric to the ground —

Colleges might have been left to multiply without regard to any criterion either of necessity or merit; the examination curse would have tightened its grip on the rising generation; standards would have sunk lower and lower; the output would have steadily swollen in volume, at the cost of all that education ought to mean; and one day India would have awakened to the fact that she had, for years, been bartering her intellectual heritage for the proverbial mess of pottage. (Quoted in Mazumdar, 1972, p. 6.)

All that, he claimed, he had stopped. Once and for all. In 1904.

Finally there may well be cultural differences, also, which over-ride the 'late-development effect'. Cultural differences can affect the vigour of the competitive impulse; the extent to which peoples easily 'take to' the new pursuit of qualifications of status and of 'place' in the modern world. Quite apart from between-country comparisons, compare the reputations, for example, of the Masai and Kikuyu within Kenya, or of the Hausa and the Ibo within Nigeria. Another dimension of cultural difference is in the importance attached to education as such — the intrinsic prestige traditionally accorded to 'learning' and the 'scholar' — a point made in Chapter 3 when comparing Japan and Britain.

Not that *that* factor cuts much ice these days as it becomes harder and harder to imagine that 'schooling' has anything much to do with 'learning' and 'scholarship' rather than the pursuit of certificates. As for the other factors, how strong they are in 'washing out' the late-development tendencies is a matter for debate — and observation. We shall see whether Tanzania has managed to hold to its disciplined policy in ten years time, and whether the Hausa and the Masai have remained so relatively unimpressed by the attractions of qualified employment in the modern sector.

. . . the more schooling equals exam-taking

The mechanisms of this third proposition are obvious. They follow from the last point. If it is to get certificates that people go to school, if it is the need for and desire for certificates rather than knowledge which explains the popular demand for schooling, then the more the schooling process itself is likely to revolve around certification.

Once that process begins it has inbuilt mechanisms that make it self-reinforcing. The more consciously children are sent to school to get certificates and the greater the demand for schooling for that purpose, the greater the number of primary schools geared up to prepare children for secondary entry, the tougher the competition, the more primary schools' and teachers' performance is measured by their proportion of secondary entrance 'successes'. The greater, therefore, the teachers' emphasis on teaching for the examination, sticking to the syllabus, concentrating on learning to remember rather than to understand, showing extra attention to the bright boys who have a chance of making it; in short, demonstrating in all they do, *their* concept of exam results as the be-all and end-all of schooling — and consequently the more the qualification-orientation of the *children* and their parents is reinforced, which in turn reinforces those tendencies in teachers, and so on.

There are three other factors which make the situation worse in later developers. The first is another facet of dualism. Schools themselves belong to the 'modern sector'. Their buildings and furniture are patterned after imported designs if not actually imported. The contracts and modes of payment of teachers follow the conventions of the civil service and the factories, not of traditional rural areas. The rhythms of the school conform to the imported seven-day week, not to the moon phases of local calendars. And, most important of all, the knowledge and attitude content of what they purvey is remote from the context of village experience. In other words, the gap between the culture of the school and the culture of the home is likely to be greater, the more pronounced the dualism of the country's development pattern — which is itself a function of late development. Japanese schoolchildren in the 1890s learned about steam engines which perhaps only one person in their family had ever seen; they learned about Benjamin Franklin, and public libraries. But at least more effort was made to relate them to village life than was done for the children in, say, Jamaica's schools in the 1930s (see V. S. Naipaul's hilarious account of the writing of formal compositions on family holidays at the seaside; Naipaul, 1961, p. 322). The point is, at any rate, that the more remote school work is from daily experience, the more easily it becomes a mere ritual, a merely instrumentalised means of getting marks.

Because of the tremendous pressure to expand school enrolments on exiguous budgets, schools are poorly equipped. Qualification-orientation obviously gets worse if there *are* no laboratories and libraries even to provide the opportunity of developing discovery methods of learning, if there *are* no alternatives to chalk and talk, memorisation and testing.

Finally, in the later developers the birth of a school system and the development of a qualification-based occupational system are likely to be simultaneous. The very concept of 'school' and of formal education entered the society in recent times as part of the package of 'modernity' brought by the imperialist powers. By contrast, most of the older industrial countries have formal pedagogical traditions (and some educational institutes) dating back to pre-industrial times *before* educational certificates acquired bread-and-butter value — dating back, in other words, to the time when learning was thought to be about getting *knowledge* or wisdom, to make a man respected or holy or righteous or rich. These older traditions still persist in the older countries. They serve to maintain the fiction that education is about moral and intellectual uplift and enrichment. And such fictions *are* important. What men define as real is real in its consequences. The fictions *do* serve as a countervailing force to weaken tendencies towards qualification-orientation, particularly when they are boldly reasserted by rebellious students demanding the end of examinations, and urging that universities should stop prostituting themselves by subserviently acting as graders of human material for the capitalist system (even if they do falter and fall into confusion when any university teacher offers to take them at their word and abolish all degree *certificates* as well as examinations). In later-developing societies, where all except the very first generation of purely soul-saving mission schools (and even some of those) had selection/credentialling functions, these useful countervailing fictions, having no roots in any local past, are harder to establish and sustain. The pursuit of certificates can be even more naked and unashamed.

This aspect of the late-development effect is perhaps even more subject to 'other things being equal' qualifications. There are other things besides cultural gaps which lead to bookish ritualism in schooling. When Britain was being modernised by the importation of Renaissance culture, it may have been partly the cultural gap which made the classical learning of the Elizabethan grammar schools such a ritualised product, but it was sheer inertia which kept it in such a desiccated state for another three centuries. Similarly, the possibility and strength of countervailing tendencies depends very much on idiosyncratic national and cultural traditions. It is striking how much genuine intellectual concern survives in Japan, despite the fact that, as the late-development thesis would predict, Japanese high schools are a good deal more certificate-oriented than Britain's. Consider, for instance, the title of one of the typical products of Japan's multi-billion-yen cramming industry, a monthly magazine produced for those students in high schools or (second and third-chance) private tutories who are preparing for the university entrance examinations. It is called *Keisetsu-jidai, Snow and Firefly Days,* after the legendary Chinese peasant whose love of learning (of *learning*) was so great that he studied under the most unpromising conditions — by the glow of caged fireflies in summer and in the moonlight reflected off the snow in winter. And if one looks through the 350 pages of a typical issue one will indeed find older educational traditions shining through the anxiety-ridden discussions of examination techniques, reports of impending changes in certain universities' entrance examinations, assessment of the relative job values of the degrees of Japan's 600 universities and so on — one will find articles on 'Savouring the Beauties of the Tsurezure-gusa' (the diary of a thirteenth-century monk), for instance; articles on Laos and biochemical warfare and women's lib. (These examples are taken from the April 1971 issue, published — yet another indication of Japanese anxiety to get ahead of themselves — in March 1971.)

But setting aside all questions of the truth of *general* propositions of the kind 'the later development starts, the more . . . ', one thing we can assert with confidence. In the Third World today the importance of qualifications is greater than in the advanced industrial countries. Educational systems are more likely to be geared to qualification-getting, and the consequences for the society and its pattern of development are likely to be even more deplorable than in our society.

Here ends the diagnosis. The next five chapters look at possible solutions.

Chapter 7

Education and Development: the Academic Debate

Not many people whose opinions history records have expressed the view that schooling of the young is anything but a good thing — at least until the deschoolers burst upon the scene in the last few years. But for most of history it has generally been left to philosophers and divines and educators to explain why; to argue about the relative importance of spiritual or cognitive or physical or moral development, and about the true purposes of such development — whether education should develop the humanity of human beings, or fulfil God's purposes, or conduce to an orderly and harmonious society. Even Adam Smith was speaking as a distinctly political student of political economy when he claimed that:

> an instructed and intelligent people are always more decent and orderly than an ignorant and stupid one . . . they are more disposed to examine, and more capable of seeing through, the interested complaints of faction and sedition, and they are, upon this account, less apt to be misled into any wanton or unnecessary opposition to the measures of the government. (Smith, 1937, p. 941.)

But eventually economists got involved. As I shall argue later in this chapter, the problem is that they have not merely been involved but have tended to *dominate* thinking about the relationship between education and development. And the education profession, by and large, has just stood by and let them do it. Whether this *trahison des clercs* was due to the fact that it was the economists who commanded the money, or whether the educators were mesmerised by the economists' use of funny numbers, or whether they were just over-awed by the superior professional status of the economics profession (in that academic pecking order determined by consensual perceptions of the 'toughness' of different courses and the marks required to get into them) is a matter for speculation. But the results have been deplorable.

That economists were right to get involved, that education also has consequences for the economy, and that improving its provision might improve the nation's level of material welfare, became increasingly taken for granted in European countries as it came to be seen as a major function of government to create the conditions for economic progress — in the mid-eighteenth century in Russia (see Kahan, 1965, p. 4); a century later in Britain. The connection between British politicians' awareness of Britain's lagging economic growth and Forster's 1870 Education Act was mentioned earlier, and so was the faith of Japan's reformers in the 1870s that education could transform the society and the economy.

But apart from an unusual group of Russian economists working just before and after the revolution, it is not until the last twenty years that economists — chiefly in the United States — have begun seriously to tackle the problem of measuring the precise ways in which, and the precise degree to which, education contributes to economic growth.

Several approaches have been tried. One of the most aggregative is cross-country comparison. If, the argument runs, education contributes to economic growth, then countries which have had more education should have more economic growth. This is a fascinating game to play for anyone with a taste for regression analysis. The range of variations is infinite. For education, does one choose a measure of primary, or secondary, or tertiary enrolments, or a weighted measure of all three? And should it be enrolments in relation to total population which is easier to measure, or in relation to the relevant age groups which is more difficult? And should it be enrolments, anyway, at a particular time, or school outputs, or the stock of schooled people in the labour force, or should one use some quite different indicator such as the volume of educational expenditure, or an estimate of literacy levels? Economic growth levels, too, can be measured in any number of ways: GNP *per capita*, the number of kilowatt-hours generated, the percentage of the working population in agriculture, etc. And having settled on the indicators, should one compare enrolments, say, at a given time with *per capita* income at the same time, or a decade or two decades later, or should one compare enrolments with the *rate of increase* in income twenty years later — or even the rate of increase in enrolments with subsequent rates of increase in income? And can one usefully refine the analysis by adding some other variable which might be thought to mediate the relation between educational investment and economic payoff, such as, for instance, the degree of egalitarian openness of the educational system, or the level of 'political mobilisation' or 'political modernity'?

All of these have been tried in some form or other, and with a lot more other variations too, depending upon the imagination or the *hubris* or the naivety of the researcher. The results have not been spectacularly informative. (They, or the pre-1970 ones at least, are conveniently summarised in Blaug, 1972, Ch. 3.) Perhaps one of the best-known findings is that of Bowman and Anderson (Bowman, 1963) which has the merit of simplicity and consequently of results which are more clear-cut than most. They used straightforward measures of 'literacy' (though with wildly varying definitions between countries, of course) and of dollars *per capita* GNP. The overall correlation is of less interest than the details. All the countries with less than 40 per cent literacy were in the poorest (less than $300 *per capita* bracket), all those with over 90 per cent in the richest ($500+) bracket. But for the countries in between there was precious little correlation between the two variables. One of the authors showed later that the notion of a '40 per cent threshold' — the idea that sustained economic growth does not begin until 40 per cent of a population are literate — did seem to be roughly borne out by our historical knowledge of European countries (Anderson, 1965).

Other studies using measures of secondary and tertiary enrolments have found only small and ambiguous relations to economic growth. When time-lags have been introduced income levels at one time seem to provide as good, or better, predictions of enrolments twenty years later, as earlier enrolments dc of later income levels.

There may be some indication that the later the time period treated, the poorer the correlation. One of the latest studies uses 1965 income data and 1950 enrolments (Meyer, 1973). One consistent finding, however the data are analysed, is that among the less-developed countries, the higher a country ranked in tertiary enrolment levels in 1950, the more it was likely to have sunk in the economic performance rankings by 1965. The relationship is not a very strong one but about as strong as the more expected positive relationship between secondary and primary enrolments and subsequent income levels.

The evidence from these studies is confused, but at least not inconsistent with the hypothesis that follows naturally from the arguments of previous chapters, *viz.*, that schooling for the purposes of education may well contribute to economic growth, but schooling in pursuit of certification less probably so, that the world is having more and more of the latter kind of schooling than the former, and that this is particularly the case for the developing countries. Thus one might well expect a *declining* positive correlation between those countries' enrolments and growth rates — and even the appearance of negative correlations.

These gross correlational exercises, have been as much the work of sociologists and psychologists as of economists, but the technique has also been used by accredited members of the economics profession as a tool of educational planning. With the discovery by the development profession in the 1950s that the deployment of 'human resources' was as important as the accumulation of physical resources, 'manpower planners' became essential members of the various planning teams which rich countries and international organisations sent to the developing world to prescribe their confident recipes for economic development. Estimating the needs for engineers or architects or accountants — specific skills requiring specific vocational courses — was easy enough. It could be done, especially in small countries, with surveys of present and predictable vacancies, plus a little guesswork. But the needs for general education, for products of academic secondary schools and the humanities and social sciences courses of the universities, to man a wide range of clerical and commercial and administrative posts, was much harder to estimate. (Even though manpower planners did, by and large, simplify their problem by operating with 'fixed coefficient' assumptions, i.e. that there was an ideal 'schedule of correspondences' between educational level and type of job: a costing clerk should have ten years of schooling: a personnel manager should have a university degree, etc, which was valid in an absolute sense. In practice, of course, they generally assumed that the 'schedule of correspondences' actually current in their own country was precisely that ideal one, rather than being the contingent outcome of, the current state of play in, a long process of qualification inflation in their own country.)

Regression analysis offered a possible solution to the estimation problem. If you take a hundred countries and chart the relationship between level of GNP and primary and secondary and tertiary enrolments, you can arrive at a formula which offers the best possible means of guessing a country's level of GNP if all you know about it is its school enrolments. If you stand this formula on its head and make the whopping assumption that *grosso modo* all countries (even if they do locate themselves very untidily around the assumed trend line) are *essentially* following the same growth pattern, with some just having got a little bit further along than others, then you can say by how many per cent primary, say, or secondary enrolments are likely to increase for a given percentage increase in income level (*provided that* the various forces which hitherto have operated to produce the historical trend line discovered by the analysis continue to exercise their determining influence). If, then, your economic plan tells you how fast GNP will grow (and it needed more than experience to weaken the faith of planners that that was precisely what their plans *did* tell them), then you know how fast to expect *enrolments* to grow too. Well, not actually *expect,* since there were supposed to be planners in charge of the matter — how fast to *make* enrolments grow — on the curious, and rather Taoist, assumption that the aim of good planning should be to achieve a consonance with the underlying forces of History — a daring *non sequitur* of enormous subsequent influence, as one writer remarks (Blaug, 1972a, p. 73).

Others not only stood the formula on its head but also turned it inside out, seeming to argue that if you increased your primary, secondary and tertiary level enrolments in the right proportions as the model prescribed, then economic growth would follow (ibid., p. 69 on Harbison and Myers, 1964), an argument which, as one critic remarked, in view of the lag studies mentioned above was rather like saying: rich men have Cadillacs; therefore we should get some Cadillacs in order to be rich (Sato, 1972, p. 3).

It is not surprising that such exercises were thought to give economics a bad name. What is surprising, though, is that the alternative developed in the sixties, rate-of-return analysis, should ever have been thought likely to give it a better one. Attention shifted from the macro to the micro level. The assumption was that one demonstrates the connection between education and development, not by seeing how *societies* with more of the one get more of the other, but by seeing to what extent, within particular societies, *individuals* with more education contribute more to development.

The first assumption one makes is that the income a man receives is a fair measure of his contribution to development — not unreasonable if one has already swallowed the (enormous but more common) prior assumption that growth in GNP is a reasonable measure of development (particularly since, in the service industry, for example, incomes are anyway translated directly into contributions to GNP). Next one discovers, by censuses or other data, the average income after tax, of people at different ages, who left school at 15. Then, assuming that all the people leaving school *now* at the age of 15 will follow that income curve as they grow older (that their income at age 50 will be the same as present 50 year olds who left school at 15) one can work out the future lifetime pattern of earnings of those now leaving school at 15.

One does the same for those leaving school at 18. One subtracts for each age the earnings of age-15-leavers from those of age-18-leavers and the difference represents the lifetime flow of cash benefits from staying on for an extra three years at school. One can also calculate the costs of staying on at school to the pupil and his family — not only fees and books, but the income foregone by studying instead of working between 15 and 18. After that all you need is a modest computer which can then tell you what discount rate will equalise the present value at the age of 15, on the one hand of those additional lifetime earnings beginning after leaving school at 18, and on the other the costs incurred between the ages of 15 and 18. That rate would represent the return which a 15 year old would eventually get from his investment in another three years' schooling if he decides to stay on. This is called his 'private rate of return'. If you add into the calculations on the cost side everything that the state and other public authorities spend on his education and, on the benefit side, all the amounts that he will pay in taxes in the course of his lifetime, then you can arrive at the 'social rate of return' — you can say that if society (the state, local authorities, the man himself and his family) spends this much on those extra three years of education for that man, it will get an economic contribution to society out of him equal to x per cent a year return on the investment. Each step in the educational ladder can be treated in the same way: one can work out the returns on completing primary education (as compared with staying out of school) or on completing a PhD (as compared with being content with an MA).

There are broadly three uses to which this sort of analysis can be put. The first is to use the calculation of private rates of return in the search for reasons why people should seek to get more education; the assumption being that the higher the rates of return, the more eagerly people seek educational opportunity — and that if you can alter those rates you will be able to alter educational aspirations.

Some devotees of the technique sometimes talk as if peasant parents who have never been to the city or read a newspaper can somehow intuitively make, and base their decisions about keeping their children in school on, calculations involving highly complex juggling with obscure, little-known, aggregate data, the results of which sometimes surprise the economists who juggled them. Even if they do not go quite that far, a major point of such exercises does seem to have been to try to demonstrate that 'people' are rational just like economists. Thus Blaug and his colleagues, in their study of graduate employment in India, were clearly glad to be able to discover that the people flocking to the universities to face certain unemployment afterwards need not be assumed to be irrationally motivated by status concerns rather than hard-headed economic advantage. Even if they did face a lengthening 'waiting period' in the queue for jobs after they graduated, their investment was still 'worth it'; they could, in fact, make a respectable 9 per cent rate of return, given the high salaries graduate occupations still commanded and the low cost in income foregone if, as a secondary school leaver, you were most likely to be unemployed anyway (Blaug, 1969).

Things did not appear quite so reassuring to the rationalist cause, however, when in the Philippines calculations were made of the costs and benefits of going to *particular* universities. The 9 per cent or so rate of return to the *average* graduate was shown to aggregate the very high rate of return of the boy who passes the stiff entrance tests to the élite state universities (where he pays a little and the state pays a lot) and the low — or in many cases *negative* — rate of return of those who had to make do with low-prestige private universities, pay the whole cost of their education themselves — and end up in jobs with much lower salaries than the products of the élite schools (ILO, 1974, Special Paper No. 17). All this adds up to a salutary reminder of the danger of making inferences about individual micro-economic decisions from highly-aggregated macro-economic relationships. (For other problems in the use of private rates of return for the analysis of motives — different subjective time preferences, different real costs for different income strata see ECAFE, 1974, p. 77.)

It is hard to believe that the Philippine results would not be duplicated in India or many other countries. Certainly the modest 9 per cent rate of return calculated for university education in Japan in 1961 (Psacharopoulos, 1973, p. 62) does not — especially when compared with, say 26 per cent in Turkey or 35 per cent in Nigeria — seem an adequate explanation of the enormous appetite for higher education shown by Japanese high school students and those who spend one or two extra cramming years after high school preparing for university entrance examinations. It becomes a little more explicable if one accepts that what people are hoping and competing for is entrance to one of the élite state universities which (for £20 a year in fees) open the royal road to success. But, having set off on the university track, they may well, if they are unsuccessful in the entrance examinations, set off for a private university and pay twenty times the fee for a much less saleable certificate, perhaps get a negative rate of return, but still feel that they have, at any rate partially, lived up to their expectations of themselves and acquired something which gives them prestige.

All of this must be taken into account if one seeks to move from 'understanding' to 'policy' and use these calculations of private rates of return to affect outcomes. An obvious market-economist recipe for graduate unemployment is to reduce the demand for education either by raising the costs of going to university or by paying lower salaries to graduates. It is possible to calculate *how much* of a fee charge, or *how much* of a compression of the salary differentials inherited from the colonial period would be necessary to reduce the rate of return to university education which in, say, Ghana, in 1967 was calculated to be 37 per cent p.a. to, say, an Israeli level of 8 per cent (*loc. cit.*). It would only be a rough guide, perhaps, but particularly if the calculations were publicised so that they affected as well as predicted outcomes, a possibly useful one. Not that it helps with the real problem, of course — the political one of getting such measures accepted. A so-called authoritarian military government in Ghana was forced, by vocal opposition, to withdraw a scheme which would have modestly reduced rates of return by turning the university students' scholarships into loans (Williams, 1973).

That particular cautionary tale brings us to the second use of private rates of return — to clarify the equity effects of educational expenditure. If there are very high private rates of return to individuals from university study — 30 per cent rates are common in African countries and in some Latin-American countries — it raises questions about the equity of either the salary system or the volume of state subsidy for higher education; it deals a body blow, for example, to the argument that people *deserve* high salaries because of their 'sacrifices' and 'investment' in getting educated. If the Ghanaian government had publicised the rate of return university students were calculated to be getting, it might have had a little more success in stirring up support outside the university for its measures.

Social rates of return
With the third use of rate-of-return analysis, however — the use of *social* rates of return as a guide to public educational investment policy — we move into, if not exactly cloud cuckoo land, at least its border areas. The exercise seems harmless enough when it is used only to say: look how important education is in bringing economic growth — as Denison used it, for instance, in a famous study which concluded through a calculation of the contribution changing educational levels should have made to increase in wages, that education was responsible for 23 per cent of the economic growth which took place in the US between 1929 and 1957 (Denison, 1962; see also the analysis in Blaug, 1972, pp. 89-97). It becomes altogether more alarming if anyone argues that since the social rate of return to secondary schooling is 15 per cent and to a proposed hydroelectric scheme only 13 per cent, a wise economist ought to go on putting money into secondary schools rather than generating stations until the rates of return to secondary schooling fall. Few economists have argued quite that crudely — it is obvious, for one thing, that it takes too long for a surplus of secondary school leavers to affect their wages enough to bring the rate down to 13 per cent — but they have argued the reverse case — returns to education are too low to warrant diverting funds from physical investment projects to further expansion (Blaug *et al.,* 1969 and ILO, 1974, p. 317) — and even more frequently argued that if the returns to one level or type of education prove higher than to other types, it is that level which should be expanded. This, for example, has been seriously suggested as a reason why investment funds in developing countries should be diverted from secondary and higher to primary education (Blaug, 1973, p. 19).

Many other people these days similarly urge the diversion of funds to primary education, for all kinds of good reasons — because they have a strong intuitive sense of the uselessness of universities, because they are afraid unemployed secondary and university graduates will revolt, or because, like Mr McNamara and the World Bank, they have 'discovered' the plight of the 'poorest 40 per cent' and the need for special 'from the bottom up' development policies to help them. Perhaps one should pragmatically welcome the economists who join the chorus with the argument that their calculations of rates of return show them generally to be higher for primary than for secondary and higher education.

Unfortunately the argument itself scarcely bears examination. The returns to primary education in most of the developing countries where they have been calculated (Thailand, Kenya, Ghana, Nigeria, for example) are based on the earnings of those lucky earlier generations who *could* get modern sector jobs with their primary certificates. Further expansion of primary education now means bringing into the schools those who are almost certain to spend their lives as farmers or self-employed craftsmen rather than as wage-earners. No rate-of-return analyst has ever tried to calculate how much schooling raises *their* productivity and earnings, though such indirect evidence as there is (see Harker, 1973; Colclough and Hallak, 1975) is not very encouraging. Economists, in neglecting such calculations, have accepted and helped to confirm the popular assumption that getting a modern-sector wage job was what schooling was all about. Until they take self-employed earnings into account, their calculations will not have much relevance to policy — even though they may provide *otherwise* well-meaning bureaucrats with a few spuriously impressive figures to dazzle politicians with.

Social rates of return: objections

The particular case of primary rates of return apart, there are several other, rather devastating, objections to the use of social rates of return either as an explanation of education's relation to economic growth or as a guide to policy.

First, they assume that the future earnings of people leaving school with ten years of education now will be the same as those who came out of Grade 10 between five and forty years ago. We have said enough about the rate of qualification escalation to know how unrealistic is *that* assumption for most developing nations. Even in the developed countries, to infer from returns to education in the 1920s anything about the return to education today is, as one critic put it, 'like identifying a crystal radio set with Telstar' (Balogh and Streeten, 1964, p. 387).

Secondly, social rates of return make the assumption that somehow or other market forces ensure that everybody is paid what he is worth: that a man's wage equals his marginal product. We all know, however, that Providence doesn't quite work that way. It is hard to believe that because the social rates of return to higher education work out at 23 per cent in Mexico (1963) and only 6 per cent in the Netherlands (1965) an extra Dutch graduate would be likely to make a lesser *real* contribution to the welfare of his fellow men than an additional Mexican graduate. A much more likely explanation is that the political structure in Mexico and its class base perpetuates an inequality of income distribution in Mexico many times greater than that in the Netherlands. To be sure, no one who has ever used overall GNP as a measure of economic welfare (which implies all kinds of similar assumptions about the justice of the market) can throw stones at the economists of education for this assumption. Fortunately, the usefulness of GNP measures of welfare is increasingly doubted; so, too, should be that of social rates of return as a guide to educational policy.

It is the final objection to a social rate of return argument that is most germane to the theme of this book, however. We observe people who have had certain kinds of education subsequently (on average) getting higher levels of income than other people with less education. But how do we know that this enhanced earning power is *because* of their education (implying, on a broader scale, that more education in a society would make that society more productive)? Is the 'investment' metaphor genuinely justified? Is it true that the education *changes* a man, *enhances* his capacity to work and in this way alters the price at which he can sell his labours?

Economists, to give them their due, have not generally claimed that it was wholly a matter of changing people. Conventionally they have tended to assume that only about 60 per cent of the additional earnings that a graduate, say, gets above a high school leaver's income can be attributed to the effects of his education; the rest to other factors.

When one starts to consider the other possible factors, though, it begins to seem unlikely that 40 per cent is an adequate weighting of their importance. The range of possible explanations for the observed fact that people with more education have higher incomes — over and above the obvious one, 'because their education has made them better at their job' — is very wide. (For an extended discussion, see Dore, 1976.) Let us list some of them.

1. Because of other characteristics which correlate both with having a lot of education, and with earning a lot of money, e.g.
    (a) having rich parents who can set you up in life (especially important in societies where only rich parents can buy their children higher education);
    (b) being 'naturally' more intelligent, diligent, etc. (especially important where secondary schools and universities have selective entrance examinations and low fees).
2. Because of various institutional mechanisms which *automatically*

give good jobs in bureaucratic organisations to those with certificates, institutions which owe their origin:

(a) to the fact that entry into secondary and higher education is by competitive achievement tests, so that educational level — and grade records — can be taken as proxy measures of general ability;

(b) to beliefs about the virtues of, or the correlates of, education which may once have been true and are no longer ('all graduates are highly intelligent' was reasonably true in Japan when the only universities were highly selective state universities, not, later, when expensive free-for-all private universities started), or may have been true elsewhere, but not in the country in question ('secondary schools teach one to think' may be true in Europe, less true — see Chapter 7 — in developing countries);

(c) to the pressures of self-interested professional groups (including educators; the sellers of certificates);

(d) to the need of employers to sort out floods of job applicants in some way which is both convenient and legitimate (see p. 5).

3. Because of the halo effect. A degree bolsters a man's prestige, and hence his morale, raises people's expectations, and increases the chances that they will selectively perceive his good points and give him encouragement. The certificate itself, in other words, not the schooling, helps people to 'grow to their job'.

There is at present a lively debate between proponents of the 'screening hypothesis', who urge the importance of these latter mechanisms (and so throw doubt on the extent to which education actually improves people or their society) and the traditional 'human capital theorists' who persist in believing that people earn more because their education has *changed* them and that the 'investment' assumptions of their rate-of-return analysis are correct.[1] There is another debate among those who accept the importance of schooling in changing people but cannot agree whether the most significant way it does so is:

(i) by pumping cognitive knowledge into them,

(ii) by giving them all kinds of mental abilities and attitudes — powers of reasoning, the urge to get problems neatly sorted out, curiosity, the ability to categorise and classify, to handle abstractions, to generalise and check generalisations against evidence, to foresee consequences, to sort out an argument persuasively, to 'interligate', to think laterally, etc.,

(iii) by changing their social attitudes and self-perceptions; giving

---

[1]Arrow (1974); Berg (1970); Blaug (1972, 1973); Taubman and Wales (1973); Wiles (1974), Baghwati (1973); Layard and Psacharopoulos (1974); Miller (1967).

them leadership powers, or alternatively brainwashing them
into the materialist values of the capitalist system, accustoming
them to mindless work rituals, obedience to authority, etc.[1]

The trouble with these debates is that everyone seems to be talking
about *the* rôle of *the* school system in *the* economy — as if the whole
world were the same.

This is, of course, absurd. Different institutional practices, different
social structures, different educational traditions and degrees of equality
of opportunity make the intervening mechanisms between schooling
and earnings levels very different in different countries. What I hope
Chapter 6 has made clear is that, because of their different circumstances, there are some *general* differences between the rich countries
and the developing world which are of crucial significance for the
debate, namely:

1. The institutional mechanisms referred to above have far more
consequence in the highly bureaucratised modern sectors of the
developing countries than in the more fluid economies of the advanced
countries which still have more chances for people to 'find their level'
by mid-career mobility. In many developing countries far more people
get on their 'appropriate' seniority-promotion escalator when they leave
school and stay on it for life.

2. The most plausible argument of the 'human capital' theorists is
that the rationality of the system in rich countries lies in the second of
the three forms of the 'investment affect' listed above: schooling
improves people by developing their mental attitudes and abilities. For
all the reasons outlined in the last chapter, schooling in developing
countries seems less effective in this regard — less effective at
developing any mental muscle except the memory muscle, and *much*
less effective at developing those attitudes which make people find
intrinsic satisfaction in creative mental activity.

Quality in education
How far the schools *do* develop desirable mental attitudes and abilities
emerges, thus, as the central underlying question of the education/
development debate. It is, essentially, the question of the *quality* of
education. Unfortunately, the discussions of the 'quality' of education
in the recent literature on development fail to come near the heart of
the matter, dominated as it is by economists who confine their
discussion solely to that which is measurable. (For a summary of this

[1]Blaug (1972, 1973); Bowles (1971b, 1973); Carnoy (1974); Carter and Carnoy (1974);
Collins (1971); Edwards (forthcoming); Gintis (1971).

literature see Alexander and Simmons, 1975.) Hence their usual measure of 'output' is achievement grading — as if the pumping in of cognitive knowledge *were* the crucial rôle of schooling. Most of the literature on quality consists of attempts to correlate these grades with equally measurable inputs such as size of class, or expenditure on libraries, or on school buildings or on teacher training — usually with the conclusion that none of these factors seems to have much effect — to the great comfort of the rate-of-return analyst who can stick to his homogeneity-of-inputs assumption that a year of schooling is a year of schooling.

All this is very sad because, as everyone knows, a year of schooling is not just a year of schooling; it can be anything from a delight to a torment, anything from an experience of growth and mastery to a stunting and a confining; anything from the continuous exercise of powers of reasoning and imagination to the exclusive exercise of the powers of memory. And which it is makes an enormous difference to the outcome — a difference which footling measures of 'internal efficiency' do not even begin to capture.

And which it is depends largely, as we saw in the last chapter, on the constraining circumstances which make the late developer's situation so different from the rich countries'. Even within those constraints, however, there is some variation depending on the dynamism and imagination and devotion and warmth and responsiveness — as well as the cognitive skills — of the teacher. And that brings us to another reason why economists are allowed to get away with the discussion of the 'quality' of education in such myopic terms. It is because the educational establishment itself has self-interested reasons for accepting the improbable notion that it is the *cognitive* outcomes of education which are important. Educational administrators and planners have their own reasons for perpetuating the assumption that 'educational quality' is a matter of how much a teacher knows, rather than of his dynamism or imagination or how much he 'cares'. Cognitive skills one can do something about. Give us the money and we will put on an extra course.

But who would take seriously a proposal to extend teacher training from three years to four in order to give teachers an extra year's training in dynamism and responsiveness? It would take an unusually accomplished mastery of gobbledygook for a Dean of Education to sell *that* idea.

And it is too much to expect educational administrators to contemplate the alternative — that one might *select* teachers in the first place primarily by the appropriateness of their personalities and mental attitudes rather than admitting anyone who has achieved certain general educational qualifications. It is on the bread-and-butter importance of general educational certificates — on their universal use in job allocation — that the survival of the whole educational industry depends. One could hardly expect that industry itself to devalue their importance.

Chapter 8

Education and Development: The Swings of Policy

It would be wrong to say that the academic debate whose twists and turns were described in the last chapter has had *no* impact on the practical men in educational administration as they have gone about their business of building schools, changing curricula, altering grading systems, getting and spending budgets which are always smaller than they would wish for. Practical men nowadays are less inclined than they were in Keynes' time 'to claim exemption from any intellectual influence' while in fact being 'usually the slaves of some defunct economist' (Keynes, 1936, p. 383). The planning mystique has cast its spell; it is a rare Ministry of Education in the developing world which does not have a planning office or send its officials to international conferences on educational planning and policy at which they rub shoulders with far from defunct economists. The actual impact of academic ideas has, perhaps, been limited, even on first-draft bureaucrats' plans — even more limited as these plans are filtered through the pressure valves of various interest groups in the process of being translated into budgets and policies. (Curle has given a nice blow-by-blow account of the translation process of one such plan; Curle, 1966.)

Nevertheless, there has been some impact. For example, the importance given to expansion of secondary and higher education in many poor countries' development plans in the mid-1960s owed something to the manpower planners' doctrines about the strategic importance of middle and higher level manpower, doctrines which were incorporated into such documents as UNESCO's Asian Manpower Plan, debated and endorsed by meetings of Asian Ministers of Education (though the acceptability of these declarations and their bold targets probably depended on the fact that already strong private demand pressures were building up for an expansion of the upper reaches of the system). The more recent agreement between economists and practical men that the time has come for a reversal — for more emphasis on primary education — was noted in the last chapter; though who has influenced whom is a moot point.

There is, at any rate, a fairly wide measure of agreement in both worlds, the academic and the practical, about what are the major problems of the educational system in developing countries today.

The perceived major problems: primary education
1. First, perhaps, comes the slow progress in the drive to secure a basic primary education for all. Countries have varied widely in the importance they have in fact attached to this objective relative to the development of modern-sector middle and higher level manpower, but every government has at least paid lip-service to 'schools for all', and on the international scene the grand conferences in Addis Ababa and in Karachi at which governments pledged themselves to attain universal basic education by 1980 came early, before the manpower planning emphasis on the higher levels took hold.

Many countries are only just managing to increase provision to keep up with population growth, without any increase in the *proportions* of children getting schooled. India, for instance, which already has as much as 3 per cent of the population getting to a university, probably gets not more than 70 per cent of its children into primary school, and only about 25 per cent to the end of the fifth primary grade. In Pakistan the first grade figure is not much more than 45 per cent. Even in the Philippines, where nearly all children get to school, only about a half of them survive to the end of the sixth grade (ECAFE, 1974, p. 117). These Asian figures could be matched on other continents.

Some countries are showing increasing drop-out rates in primary schools. There are economists who applaud this as yet one more justification of their faith in man's rationality. Unemployment for the certificated means that education doesn't pay. Parents are therefore sensible to refuse to invest in it. The growing drop-out rates probably are, indeed, an indication that the primary school is *not* seen as a means of personal development and enrichment, a means of becoming a self-respecting first-class member of one's society, but rather as the first step on the ladder to a modern-sector job. As the ladder lengthens, as it becomes no longer a primary certificate but a secondary one, no longer a junior but a senior secondary certificate, that is necessary to secure any chance of a job, parents may understandably be easily discouraged — particularly if they discover in their child's first few years at school that he is not showing the kind of academic promise that offers real hope of his getting far up the examination ladder.

2. And there is concern that the idea of primary education as a 'basic right', a 'basic preparation for citizenship and a productive life' should be overshadowed by the first-step-on-the-ladder conception of its purpose. There was a time, in the early days of the new independent states, when the manpower plans seemed to be drawn up on the assumption that somehow or other the rate of development would be so

fast that all, or nearly all, the children who complete primary school could get modern-sector jobs; that somehow Say's Law would operate to make sure that the supply of educated people would produce an appropriate demand. There was, therefore, no particular need to think about the relevance the primary curriculum might have to village life. Many of the administrators in the new states probably had memories of such attempts to introduce 'relevant village-oriented curricula' during the recent colonial past; they recalled how vigorously those attempts had been denounced as a means of keeping a subjugated colonial people in their subordinate rôle as hewers of wood and drawers of water. Now all that would be changed. The school could and should be an agent of modernity; it was very *properly* to be designed as a preparation for a truly 'modern' modern-sector life.

Now, slowly, the sheer demographic arithmetic of the situation is beginning to sink in. It is beginning to be realised that in most countries under no conceivable circumstances can the sort of 'employee' slot in the economy that primary schools ideally prepare their children for be actually provided for the majority of the children completing primary school — not for more than a quarter in either Sri Lanka or Kenya, as we saw in previous chapters. Can or should the primary schools go on giving an induction course into modern-sector occupations? If the majority of their products are going to be self-employed, to continue their parents' occupations as joiners and craftsmen and fishermen and traders, can they not be given something more appropriate to their future possible occupations?

That realisation comes together with a *general* revaluation of the dominant strategy of development which has taken place in the last five years. The criticism of growth in GNP as an indicator of development or as an objective of policy has become commonplace, repeatedly endorsed by the President of the World Bank who speaks of 'institutional reforms to redistribute economic power' (McNamara, 1973, p. 115), of 'prime attention to agriculture' as a means of getting development programmes which will really relieve poverty, eliminate malnutrition and create jobs — and within agriculture, programmes to benefit share croppers and small farmers, not the 'already more advantaged large farmer' with one foot in the modern sector (ibid, p. 66). In the health field, it is no longer a novelty to observe that genuinely 'modern-sector' glass-and-steel hospitals in the capital, manned by expensive consultants, have had far too large a share of budgets, while modest rural health centres manned by inexpensively trained staff capable of dealing with *most* of the commonest complaints of the mass of the population have received far too little (though actually *changing* that situation in the teeth of determined opposition from the medical profession is a different matter).

Hence the realisation that the primary schools, particularly rural primary schools which contain the bulk of the school population in most developing countries, were not doing much for the real futures of the majority of their children, coincided with the revaluation of rural development as a crucial focus of development policies in general and the discovery that the schools were making very little contribution to it. Hence a new demand for relevance.

The perceived major problems: secondary and higher education
3. The third focus of concern, the growth in educated unemployment, needs no elaboration in view of the discussions in earlier chapters.

4. Nor does the fourth, the relentless pressure for more secondary schools and universities in spite of this unemployment — a pressure which is practically irresistible, even in countries with only tiny private education sectors if they are countries where electoral competition is important; and quite unstoppable where higher education is a thriving private industry.

5. And for the fifth focus of concern, the pressure of educational budgets on government revenues (compounded by population growth and attempts to upgrade quality standards as well as to expand educational opportunities), it will be enough to recall the figures for national expenditures on education quoted on p. 4.

6. The final concern is worth a little elaboration; it is disillusionment with the vocational school solution which became the favourite recommended cure when the educated unemployment problem first began to penetrate the educational consciousness in the mid-1960s. The trouble, it was then thought, was the 'academic bias' of traditional education. 'It has been frequently asserted that the problem of educated unemployment has its source in the reluctance of literate individuals and graduates of the schools to accept manual occupations and their persistence in an unrealistic search for white collar employment that they believe to be commensurate with their status as "educated men",' wrote Foster in a much-reprinted article in 1963 (Foster, 1963, p. 148). Somehow, it was thought, if people could be given *useful* skills, Say's Law would make sure that they would find jobs.

One finds the same popular belief among sixth-form children in Sri Lanka today, especially those who have missed by a few marks the opportunity to get into a science stream. Engineers seem to have little difficulty in getting jobs; therefore if everyone were an engineer everyone would have a job! What is surprising is that the educational establishment should have fallen for a similar logic, and not done either the simple sums which would have shown the underlying fallacy, or even undertaken surveys to discover whether there *were* large numbers of unfilled vacancies for technicians.

It was, at any rate, to the expansion of technical education that special efforts were directed in many countries in the last few years. The bulk of the lending operations of the World Bank which moved into the education field in a big way in 1963, was for technical education. Technical institutes for secondary school leavers and vocational secondary schools were to provide viable alternatives to the sterile pursuit of academic education.

Failure was predictable. Vocational secondary education to produce technicians for industry has problems everywhere, notably the problem of striking a balance between teaching specific skills, which may not be the ones in demand, or more general skills which may be *relevant to* a lot of occupations but not so advance competence in any one as to be worthwhile. Also vocational schools have a hard time getting good teachers; if they *do* have good technical skills they may be tempted by higher salaries in industry — particularly in developing countries where such skills are scarce.

But the chief naivety of the vocational school programme, the fallacy on which it foundered, was to ignore the significance that vocational schools would acquire in school systems which are dominated by their selection function, and revolve entirely around the primary-secondary-university axis. At least in those countries where education at all levels is largely paid for from public funds, it can be safely assumed that no one voluntarily *chooses* to get certified as a technician if he has the chance to press on to the top and earn, as a university graduate, several times a technician's salary. The updraft built into the system is too strong. It is a fairly safe assumption, then, that the student in a 'dead-end' vocational stream will have been 'relegated' to that stream, having failed to get a place in the academic secondary schools which lead on to the university. Many children in these academic secondary schools, of course, have little hope of getting to university. Nevertheless, as the vestibule to the university they have more prestige. (No amount of earnest rhetoric by the British Ministry of Education could ever persuade the British public to talk about 'the allocation of children to different streams of secondary education — all enjoying equal parity of esteem — in accordance with their aptitudes and abilities', rather than about 'passing' or 'failing' the 11-plus.) This has three consequences.

First the sense of being 'relegated' breeds a sense of second-class citizenship among both teachers and taught, which militates against effective learning.

Secondly, students are reluctant to give up. They seek a second chance, hoping against hope that at the next level, at, say, high school entry, they can 'make it' back into the main stream — particularly in countries like the Philippines where there is a large private sector of higher education. Schools respond by giving them large doses of general academic education so that they can keep in the race (also because that is what gives prestige, of course). Consequently even vocational schools sometimes have only 15—20 per cent of class time dedicated to genuinely vocational subjects — with their brightest pupils concentrating on the academic subjects, and in fact going on to college.

And thirdly, the final horror, it turns out that employers show little interest in hiring the graduates of vocational schools and frequently prefer to take the products of academic secondary schools and train them from scratch. This seems to be partly because of the poor reputation of the actual vocational training in vocational schools, partly because, if they are going to train a man, what employers are most interested to know about him is his general learning ability. And if X 'passed' into the academic stream and Y 'failed' and was relegated to the vocational, they know what conclusions to draw.

Undeterred, the assembled officials at the 1971 Conference of Ministers of Education and Those Responsible for Economic Planning in Asia included in their composite resolution on vocational education the pious hope that there should be more 'public understanding and support for technical education . . . in order to raise the prestige of technical education' (UNESCO, 1971b).

Solutions

1. Improved channelling of ambitions. If perceptions of the problems are widely shared (what I would add to this list — the problem of what the schools do to maim the minds and spirits of their *successful* products — hardly finds a place in a list of 'generally perceived problems', except under the rubric 'the need to improve quality'), the recipes vary. Perhaps three fairly distinct positions can be observed. The first, the worldly wise or that's-the-way-the-cookie-crumbles view, finds its classic expression in the writings of Philip Foster. Basically the view is: that which is the way it is, is the way it is for a very good reason. It's perfectly natural and healthy that people should want to better themselves. What's wrong with going to school to get meaningless academic certificates, as you call them? If a certificate gets you five times the income of a peasant, is that not 'meaning' enough? What could be more pre-eminently *vocational* than an 'education which provides access to the occupations with the highest prestige and, more importantly, the highest pay in the economy?' (Foster, 1963, p. 145). Material aspirations are the source and life-blood of development. It is all very well for idealists in ivory towers to snipe at materialism and meaninglessness, but it is precisely the efforts which such a system evokes that can develop a country. And (doubtless he would now add, for his chief articles were written before dualism became a fashionable concern) if the people who get to the top because they deserve to be there and because the system has sorted them out as the people best able to do the top jobs, of course they have moved into a different world from the villages into which they were born. Why shouldn't they, if they are doing a modern job as fully qualified engineers and doctors, get the salary that properly qualified engineers and doctors are entitled to in the international community? After all, there *is* a divide between the modern and the traditional sectors. To recognise it is to recognise a reality. Why *should* a Ghanaian doctor identify with a Ghanaian peasant rather than with the international community of doctors? Is there any moral or practical reason to require nationalism — nationalism if you please! — as a matter of conscience?

And as for the problem of educated unemployment, the laws of supply and demand should cure that in the end; people's expectations do adjust to reality. What one has to do — in the name of equity too — is to accelerate the adjustment process by making people pay the real cost of the education they are getting, by raising fees and reducing the element of public subsidy, or at least converting it into *loan* assistance to poor students. If one genuinely makes the investment in a college education less profitable, fewer people will bother getting it (Blaug, 1972, pp. 43-6).

2. Bypass the formal system. The second view is that which is emerging as the new orthodoxy of the international educational establishment as represented by UNESCO, UNICEF and the Educational Division of the World Bank. This concentrates on translating into educational terms the newly favoured 'from-the-bottom-up' development strategy based on overwhelming priority for rural development. Here the key word is *non-formal education,* meaning all the deliberate, conscious, and organised teaching and learning (not including unorganised learning in families and factories which is known in the jargon as *in*formal) which goes on outside of schools — agriculture extension programmes, community development, health education, adult literacy classes, and so on.

The essence of the new strategy is to put as much resources as possible into the strengthening of these non-formal programmes. As a report for the World Bank prepared by the International Council for Educational Development puts it, there must be a 'radically new approach to formal and informal education in rural areas . . . flexible, coherent and comprehensive *rural learning systems* . . . facilitating the transformation and advancement of rural societies and economies . . . diversified and continued learning experiences for all subgroups in the rural population, irrespective of age or sex or previous educational attainment. . . . The system . . . should include a diversity of means for spreading basic education to meet the minimum essential learning needs of all rural young people . . . should culminate in a new type of open-ended rural university . . . a knowledge-generating centre for rural development.' And for 'integration of planning and of operations in specific rural areas . . . multipurpose *rural development centres* connected to networks of modest local development and learning centres (Coombes and Ahmed, 1974, p. 229).

Do not be put off by the heavy weight of Unospeak, the high adjective/noun ratio, the liberal spattering with 'comprehensive', 'integrated', 'coherent', 'well-conceived'; the penchant for the word 'system' (though still, luckily, only 'learning systems', not yet 'learning experience delivery systems'). Underneath it all there are good intentions, generous impulses and a lot of sense. Clearly there is much to be said for the idea of putting less money into the formal school system with its disappointing record as a promoter of rural develop-ment, and more into responding to the needs of people who actually want to learn something useful — though one should not minimise the dangers of formalising the non-formal, of blanketing the countryside with learning systems engineers jeeping out daily from the provincial towns to ascertain and programme the learning needs of farmers — or rather of 'target sub-groups'.

What is not clear, however, is where the formal system fits into all this. For many of the advocates of non-formal education, it seems, it just has to be accepted as an irrelevance or an unavoidable evil. Too much is invested already in the system for it to be abolished; and the possibilities of radically *changing* it are limited by the power of all those who have a stake in the present system — quite apart from the fact that the job of filtering and preparing some of the young for the modern sector has got to be done somehow. Meanwhile, they would say, build a non-formal system in parallel and channel as much resources into it as possible.

Others, while giving up the secondary and tertiary schools and above as beyond redemption, would hope to incorporate at least the rural primary school directly into new rural development centres; places where both children and adults could learn, together or separately, in the mornings or in the evenings; from ordinary 'academic' teachers or from the local health worker or farm extension officer. It is rare, though, that much thought is given to the way in which these transformed primary schools should relate to the secondary schools; who will be prepared for them and how, and what effect such arrangements will have on what goes on in schools (one exception is Bennett, 1973).

3. Reorient the formal system. The third body of opinion (which shades over into the last) is the view that reform should take place *within* the formal system; that with judicious changes the primary and secondary schools *can* be made to contribute genuinely to a healthy pattern of development which tries to carry the nation forward together, not simply to expand a modern-sector bridge-head.

Those, indeed, have been the assumptions of most of the radical attempts to reform school systems in developing countries over the last fifteen years. At least we now know *something* of how such reform attempts work. In chronological order then, a brief review in the next three chapters of events in Cuba, Tanzania and Sri Lanka.

Chapter 9

Reform in Cuba

When the revolutionary government took over in 1959, Cuba was not a 'typical developing country' of the kind we have been considering in this book, at least in one crucial sense. It did not have an educational system expanding at an explosive rate. Primary enrolments were lower than they once had been; they had fallen from well above the Latin American average in the 1920s to 51 per cent, well below that average, in the mid-fifties (Jolly, 1971, p. 212; Bowles, 1971, p. 479).

Expansion was one of the first aims of a revolutionary government which believed firmly in education as a birthright and as the foundation for a new society — expansion pre-eminently for the egalitarian purpose of incorporating those who had been left out of the pre-revolutionary society into the body civic and politic. Mass education was the watchword: in the dramatic 'year of education' campaign of 1961 nearly all the nation's schools closed down so that teachers and students could spread throughout the countryside to run literacy classes. The figures for adult illiteracy are said to have fallen from 24 to 4 per cent in the course of a single year, and the momentum was sustained by offering further courses for the new literates which over the next seven years brought a third of a million adults to a level equivalent to primary school graduation (Gillette, 1972, p. 15). At the same time, regular primary school provision increased rapidly until coverage was close to universal at the end of the decade (ibid., p. 11) and Fidel Castro was already talking of secondary education as a universal basic right — and basic minimum obligation.

This expansion, particularly in the early years, was carried through with great *élan*. Teachers' courses were improvised and a great self-improvement movement was started. Many new teacher training institutes were founded and the first-year course, usually in an austere mountain-top school where the atmosphere was redolent of guerrilla life in the Sierra Maestra, was designed primarily to breed camaraderie, dedication and enthusiasm (Jolly, 1971, p. 224). There was an experimental attitude toward new techniques of learning, especially the use of student monitors (new for Cuba that is), sometimes in conjunction with educational television.

107

The expansion of mass education was very specially expansion of rural education. One of the basic egalitarian aims of the government, at the core of its development strategy, was to destroy the dualism of pre-revolutionary Cuban society. The 'commitment' which the teacher training schools sought to induce, for example, was very much a commitment to work in rural areas.

Education for development

The second major axis of reform was to gear the educational system to the country's development needs. To this end the new régime experimented a great deal with programmes for upgrading workers' skills by part-time study, but the main thrust in this regard was the expansion — and the redirection — of secondary and higher education. The fact that pre-revolutionary Cuba had 20 per cent graduate lawyers for every agronomic engineer is an indication of the bias that had to be corrected. At the secondary level there was a strong drive to increase the facilities for training middle-level technicians: the numbers enrolled in technical and professional schools rose from around 15,000 to around 50,000 by 1963 (though not much thereafter). Expansion of general secondary education was, however, equally rapid, steady and of greater consequence. Enrolments tripled from 1958 to 1968 to reach about 170,000 (Gillette, 1972, p. 5; Bowles, 1971, p. 485). Just how much effort was put into educational expansion can be guessed from the estimate that Cuba devoted some 7 per cent of GDP to education in 1966 (5 per cent is quite a high figure for a developing country; Jolly, 1971, p. 225) or from the estimate that in 1968—9 formal education involved, as teachers and students, something like one-fifth of the working-age population over 14 (Bowles, 1971, p. 483).

It was, of course, a constant concern in all this expansion to *equalise* opportunities, and the concentration of investment funds on building schools in rural areas was part of that policy. The government did not however go farther, as many socialist countries have done, and establish university entrance quotas for underprivileged groups or compensatory educational programmes. The new general spirit of equality was relied on as a guarantee that equality of opportunity would be met with a uniformity of aspiration.

The transformation of attitudes

From 1965 onwards, with the reorganisation of the Communist Party and the more definitive formulation of the doctrines of Cuban Communism, the schools were given a new rôle elaborated especially in the speeches of Che Guevara — to create the new, unalienated, man. In Castro's own speeches about education, this objective has had fluctuating importance and has not had the constancy and priority accorded to mass education and the need for technical skills (Gillette, 1972, p. 9). In large measure, too, the well-springs of idealism have run into the sands of ritualism; the new man, it seems, is largely to be formed by the purely cerebral process of learning doctrine from textbooks.

Something *is* done, however, to develop, through experience in school, the new attitudes towards work which are at the heart of the notion of a new unalienated man, who works because he freely chooses to work and finds some intrinsic satisfaction in doing so. Attitudes to, perceptions of, motivations for, work are the key to these changes. One device in the regular secondary schools has been the creation of 'interest clubs'. Work in the new society is not to be chosen for its extrinsic characteristics — the salary or the prestige attaching it: choice should spring from the intrinsic interest of the work itself. So pupils are encouraged to join biochemistry clubs, photography, citriculture, meteorology, petroleum, food chemistry, geology and construction clubs so that their interests can be developed on the basis of substantive knowledge (Bowles, 1971, p. 489).

Secondly, of increasing importance in the last ten years, is the involvement of schools in actual production — chiefly agricultural production. At first schools moved into simple harvest camps to work — sometimes for up to twelve weeks at a time — with the peasants in the fields, continuing a certain amount of study at the same time. Since 1971, however, the new policy has been to make the secondary schools themselves productive enterprises, situated in the country, usually providing boarding facilities, and owning their own land which students farm on a half-day study, half-day work basis, covering as far as possible the expenses of the school by their earnings. It was planned to have 300 such schools by 1975 — and to be able to make this kind of junior secondary education available for all children by about 1980 (Gillette, 1972, p. 32).

The selection function
How have all these changes altered the quality of children's educational experience, altered the way the schools function to mould mental and social attitudes and abilities? It is hard to tell. In the new Cuba, nothing has been done to alter the selection function of the schools, the link between schools and jobs. One still gets into the more highly prized occupations by getting pre-career qualifications; the opportunity to get such qualifications depends on marks in general school achievement tests; the higher the prestige of the occupation, by and large the more lengthy the pre-career qualifying training and the more marks one has to score in the selection exams to get into it.

It seems a recipe for the creation of a competitive atmosphere, not

for a co-operative learning atmosphere 'totally devoid of selfish senti-
ment' as Castro once described the education of the new man (Bowles,
1971, p. 482). On the other hand, there *are* reasons for expecting that
the competitive pressures for self-interested ambitious advancement
might be weaker in Cuba than elsewhere. Income differentials, at least,
are narrower; the 'successful' boy who gets to the university will not
earn *that* much more in his superior profession. There is, moreover, no
great danger of unemployment and insecurity for those who do not
move up the ladder. Secondly, income differentials apart, the *prestige*
attaching to non-manual work must surely have been eroded both by
the school learn-and-work programmes in which manual labour is
invested with the aura of enthusiasm and dignity, and by the extension
of this to adult life — the scheme for white-collar volunteers to join the
peasants for cane-cutting in egalitarian work camps. The fact, too, that
it is the best workers, not the best students, who get the leadership
posts in the harvest camp also weakens the association between prestige
and scholastic performance (Bowles, 1971, p. 494). Thirdly, the notion
that differences in occupation should be simply an expression of
differences of interest, the notion embodied in the 'interest clubs',
might well, if still a fiction, be a useful fiction which does something to
counter alternative conceptions — built into the very structure of the
school system — of a job hierarchy in which everyone naturally wants to
get as high up as possible.

These changes must surely have done a lot to mitigate the competitive
pressure. Are yet there must still be — and children must surely see
there to be — a difference between being able to cut cane occasionally
for a change of pace and with a great sense of one's own noble public-
spiritedness, and *having* to do it for a living? At any rate sympathetic
observers still find considerable preoccupation with the achievement
tests which determine career chances. 'Exams and grades still seem to
be a central element in the motivation of students, thus maintaining a
structure of rewards external to the process of learning and analogous
to wages in the capitalist labour market' (ibid., p. 497). 'The test and
mark system is still omnipotent' (Gillette, 1972, p. 31). With this go
instruction methods which 'could best be described as a catechistic,
authoritarian, teacher-centred approach characterised by a single
teacher talking at a class of passive students', in which 'little genuine
motivation or interest was evinced by the students' (Bowles, 1971, p.
497).

Structures of competition or the inertia of tradition?
It is hard to tell how far it really is the examination-selection structure
of opportunities which is responsible (compliance in an educationally
arid ritual being assured by the strength of ambitions for future career

advantage) and how far, alternatively, it is a matter of cultural inertia, of authoritarian teachers successfully imposing on students their preferred pedagogical mode in which the test, the exam, the distribution of praise and blame, are chiefly a means for ensuring docility, a means whose effectiveness is guaranteed by its firm institutionalisation — by the fact that nobody expects the school to be any different? Or is it a little of both? It is hard to tell in the absence of any good research on learning motives in Cuba, and it seems not the kind of thing anyone is much prompted to do research on; perhaps *because* there is an uncomfortable awareness of the gap between the selfless ideology of the system and the self-interested competitiveness which keeps it going? *Prima facie* the evidence from Cuba seems to lend support for the view that it is hard to give schools an entirely new educational rôle, if the selection functions which those schools retain continue to reinforce old patterns.

Chapter 10

Reform in Tanzania

Tanzania in the early 1960s was one of those countries where the dualism of the dualistic pattern of development was most clearly apparent. The modern sector was so small; the subsistence farming life of the villages was so economically undiversified and so clearly visible on the edges of the small cities. There was no declension, only contrast between the city streets built for the Mercedes Benzes of the senior civil servants and the villages where there was little animal power, even, to take the burdens off human backs; between the sparkling modern buildings of the university and the huts in which the majority of the people lived.

But similar circumstances elsewhere have not provoked, as they did in Tanzania, wholesale attempts to reform the system of education — chiefly, perhaps, because other countries have not had presidents with the conscience and quality of mind of Nyerere, nor, perhaps, had an élite so small that one man of high prestige could dominate it and successfully require it to sacrifice at least *some* of its material interests and established conceptions.

Diagnosis: the need for reform

The educational reform came as part of the general package of reforms which followed the Arusha declaration. The latter were designed (like the Cuban reforms) to break the dependence of Tanzania's development on foreign assistance and control, and to alter radically the expand-the-modern-sector-bridge-head-outwards policy which was intimately linked with it. It had, though, been in the educational system itself that one of the first instances of overt conflict over the privileges of the favoured modern-sector enclave occurred. The government had ruled that university students, on whom the government was annually spending, *per capita,* several times the income of the average Tanzanian family and who were assured, when they graduated, of jobs at a *starting* salary over five times the minimum wage, should spend the first twenty-one months of their working life in government-directed employment. The students objected at this infringement of their liberties by an oppressive government; the university was closed for a while and several hundred students were sent home, expelled from the lost paradise of modern-sector living (Cameron and Dodd, 1970, p. 220).

Another source of concern, specifically with educational problems, was the appearance of the first signs of educated unemployment and the qualification inflation; in this case the first-stage manifestation of the phenomenon as 'the problem of unemployed primary school leavers'. With this, and the pressures for secondary school expansion which accompany it, went, inevitably, the pressure on government revenues of rising school budgets.

The key document of the reform, Nyerere's *Education for Self-reliance* (Nyerere, 1967), clearly reflects these concerns. It begins with diagnosis, acknowledging, first, the efforts that had been made to develop the educational system and take it out of the colonial past in the six years since independence. All racial and religious segregation had been removed in all government-aided schools: numbers had been rapidly increased (though there were still only 830 pupils reaching the sixth class of the secondary school, compared with 176 in 1961) and a great deal had been done to introduce 'Tanzanian content', at least in history, music and dancing lessons, and in civics courses for secondary school pupils.

But these were still only modifications of a colonial system of education which, 'based on the assumptions of a colonialist and capitalist society', 'emphasised and encouraged the individualistic instincts of mankind instead of his cooperative instincts' and so was unsuited for the socialist society of post-Arusha Tanzania which was to be based on the three principles: 'equality and respect for human dignity; sharing of the resources which are produced by our efforts; work by everyone and exploitation by none'.

The schools, he suggests, have got to face up to the poverty of Tanzania, to the fact that the vast majority of Tanzanians are, and for some time will be, farmers, and that equality demands that their needs should dominate — but in a national endeavour to use all the nation's resources for steady progressive development. And it is a remarkable feature of this document that it is primarily in terms of mental and social *attitudes,* rather than of knowledge and skills, that the purposes of education are defined. A man should leave school with 'an enquiring mind; the ability to learn from what others do, and reject or adapt it to his own needs; and a basic confidence in his own position as a free and equal member of the society, who values others and is valued by them for what he does and not for what he obtains'. Instead, Tanzania's schools in 1967 were, he says, liable to breed intellectual arrogance. The 13 per cent of primary school leavers who 'pass' into secondary school have no doubt that they *deserve* the promise of success. The 87 per cent who don't 'pass' are regarded, not as people who have finished primary school, but as people who have 'failed' to get to secondary. Secondly the schools breed, not only feelings of inferiority and superiority, but also of separateness. The (mostly boarding) secondary schools are 'an enclave'; the university is even more separated from the life of the society. Even when the university student goes home in the vacations 'he will often find that his parents and relatives support his own conception of his difference, and regard it as wrong that he should live and work as the ordinary person he really is'. Thirdly, schools purvey a distorted bookish notion of knowledge as something derivable *only* from formal education, to be taken seriously only if it is certified by a degree. 'I recently visited a very good tobacco-producing peasant. But if I tried to take him into Government as a Tobacco Extension Officer, I would run up against the system' — because he wouldn't have the qualifications. And finally the schools take young people out of productive work. Healthy and strong young men and women, the 25,000-odd secondary school children in their middle and late teens, for instance, 'consume the output of the older and often weaker people' and are protected from rough work even during the holidays.

The blueprint for reform
The main lever for an attack on these problems is the primary school. Expansion of secondary schools *cannot* be a solution of the primary school leaver unemployment problem: the country cannot afford to spend more on education than it spends already. Secondary schools and universities are for training those people like teachers and extension officers who need more than seven years education to be prepared for 'life and service in the villages and rural areas of this country'. The only publicly provided 'education for education's sake' must, for a long time to come, be the seven years of primary education.

And that primary education is to be a complete education in itself, a preparation for life 'instead of . . . being geared to the competitive examination which will select the few who go on to secondary school'. Two principles should determine the content of primary education. If there are examinations it is they which should be geared to the curriculum, not vice versa; Tanzanian examinations were 'geared to an international standard of practice which has developed regardless of our particular problems and needs'. Secondly, schools should not be dominated by the intention to provide a preparatory basis for the next cycle of schooling — thus basing the whole educational structure ultimately on what engineers and administrators need to know.

One radical change expected to help shape the curriculum is the suggestion that all schools, but especially secondary schools, should contribute to their own upkeep, should also *be* a farm, or craft workshop — not just have a school field for training purposes.

Self-reliance is something to be taught by doing; pupils should lose their sense of being a pampered élite, learn the connection between work and reward, learn what it is to share in *community* endeavours, learn to learn experimentally, learn to participate in decisions, learn about planning and the sharing of responsibility and, not least, learn about farming. Profitable work activities would also make possible the expansion of primary schools to give everyone a full seven-year primary education without intolerable pressures on educational budgets.

Primary school should start later — at the age of 7 or 8 — so that the children who have finished the seven-year cycle (all the economy can afford to aim at, at the present stage) will be old enough to start a normal working life as soon as they leave school. The faster learning of slightly older children would compensate a little, perhaps, for time spent on working and maintaining the school and its buildings, but even if it did not, even if conventional academic 'standards' were lowered; no great loss.

> For the majority of our people the thing which matters is that they should be able to read and write fluently in Swahili, that they should have an ability to do arithmetic, and that they should know something of the history, values and workings of their country and their government, and that they should acquire the skills necessary to earn their living. . . . Things like health science, geography and the beginning of English are also important, especially so that the people who wish may be able to learn more by themselves in later life.

And for selecting those who are to move on to higher education? 'There is no reason why Tanzania should not combine an examination, which is based on the things we teach, with a teacher and pupil assessment of work done for the school and the community.' That would both be a method of selecting more appropriate people for higher education opportunities, and also an important symbolic assertion of the new values. And that, of course, also needs reinforcing in the society at large.

> . . . examinations should be down-graded in Government and in public esteem. We have to recognise that although they have certain advantages — for example in reducing the dangers of tribalism and nepotism in a selection process — they also have severe disadvantages too. As a general rule they assess a person's ability to learn facts and present them on demand within a time period. They do not always succeed in assessing a power to reason, and they certainly do not assess character or willingness to serve.

The reform in practice

Even seven years later, the ideas of this document have not lost their freshness and directness. Some of its more graphic phrases have become familiar in Tanzania; they are to be seen framed and hung on the wall of headmasters' studies. At least the idea that schools should be integrated into, and designed to serve, their communities is known to and quoted by every member of the education profession. The declaration of policy has certainly made an impact. The Ministry of Education was, however, showing more optimism than accuracy when it said, in its 1967 Report, that as a result of *Education for Self-Reliance* 'the Primary School and its curriculum were completely changed. . . . Primary education ceased to be regarded as a stepping stone for higher education, and became complete in itself, aimed at fitting young people for gainful self-employment in their respective communities' (Tanzania, 1967, p. 13).

Much, indeed, has changed. Whereas the language of instruction at the upper primary forms used to be English, it is now Swahili, with English taught as a second language from an early stage. New curricula have been designed in history, geography, mathematics and science with greater emphasis on local relevance and on solving problems rather than on learning facts. Textbooks for the new syllabuses are gradually being produced, though poverty of resources means that the provision lags woefully behind need. Schools have mostly started their own farms, though few of them contribute a significant fraction of the school's income. There have been some, though fewer, changes in the secondary schools, notably changes in the history and civics courses and an attempt to include vocationally relevant studies, especially for those who go on to professional training or direct employment after their fourth secondary year.

How far the social definitions of school and schooling have been genuinely changed, however, is a moot point. Some impressions from a brief visit in 1972 suggest that the notion of the primary school as providing a complete terminal education, its function as a preparation for secondary school being a minor, if not incidental part of its rôle, is a hard one to implant in a system in which the *structure of opportunities* is not greatly changed.

In the first place one might question the decision to concentrate primary expansion on topping up existing schools, many of which had previously offered only the first four years, so that all primary schools could offer the first seven grades, rather than on building additional schools which might have only the first four grades — particularly since it was estimated that still, at the end of the sixties, less than 50 per cent of children were getting to school at all (Bienefeld, 1972, p. 175). One can see some merit in the justification usually given, namely, that after only four years' schooling the dangers of relapse into illiteracy were great, given that the cultural background of rural areas was not such as readily to sustain literacy, particularly in the areas where schools were fewest. (Regional diversity is very great, particularly in educational matters, with primary enrolment ratios varying from 90 per cent in the Moshi district to 20 per cent in Shinyanga.) But why the jump from four to seven if not because it is from Standard 7 that one enters the secondary school and parents would be less than enthusiastic about continuing their children's education into the fifth or sixth year if the school did not provide such opportunities — particularly given the cost in fees which was 60 shillings a year in Dar es Salaam or about a week's wage of those lucky enough to be employed in the modern sector, at the legal minimum rate.

The idea of learning through working has caught on, but work is still a very subordinate activity. One primary school had a share in raising poultry at a nearby agricultural centre from which it earned 11,000 shillings a year, and it got another 4,000 shillings from the sale of bananas and pineapples, furniture, beadwork and other handicrafts. The upper forms spent most of one day a week at such tasks — but they came to school on Saturday morning in order not to fall behind in the examinations. A headmaster can hardly afford to do otherwise: if children in other schools spend more hours in study and less in work, his children will be disadvantaged in the national competitive examination for secondary entrance. A headmaster explained that it was not his aim to compete with other schools; he sought merely to get a few people into secondary school and to help the others to be self-reliant, to be able to go back to the villages and play a full part in improving the livelihood of everybody, though he admitted that parents did not quite see it in the same way. At the secondary school, the headmaster explained that it was not intended by the President that schools should cover their own expenses, but that they should manage, by their own efforts, to produce things like maize and eggs that they might otherwise have to buy. 'It isn't the intention that schools should be production-centred; they should be educative, teaching people how to do things by themselves. The President did not suggest that classroom work should be reduced. We must not neglect our classroom work.' Clearly, everyone finds what he seeks in *Education for Self-Reliance*.

The selection function
The pattern of selection for secondary schools *has* been changed on the lines suggested in Nyerere's speech. Methods have varied, but in 1972 the unenviable task of selecting the 8,000 secondary entrants from some 2,000 schools was done in each region by a committee chaired by

the regional education officer, with representatives of the Ministry, of the Tanzania Parents' Association, of the National Party, TANU and in industrial areas, of the national trade union. They were to make their judgement on the basis of marks in the national examination, plus teachers' reports on a child's attitudes, initiative and commitment. Some committees doubtless took the easiest line and used almost exclusively the objective criterion of marks. Some sought for subtle variations in teachers' ratings of initiative, etc., and shut their eyes to the problem of varying standards of judgement. Others, it was widely suggested, judged cases by such extraneous criteria as whether the parents were supporters of TANU. (It is hard *not* to see the award of a place as a gift to *the family*. A university professor remarked how anxious *he* was for his son, about to take the examination. 'But we say: well, this is egalitarianism. If I get two or three of my children into secondary and the next one doesn't make it, we say "Oh well, let my friends' children have a chance". Think of the poor man with four children who doesn't get one of them in. They all have to go back to the land — and there is absolutely nothing for them there. No stimulus. No opportunity.') The inevitable assumptions of favouritism were sharpened by the fact that individual examination marks are not known. (Partly because the regional quota system for allocating secondary places, designed to prevent *all* the places going to the educationally rich areas such as Moshi, Bukoba and Mbeya, results in quite disparate 'pass marks' between these and poorer areas and, understandably, the Ministry did not want the size of the gap to be known.) Teachers complained that everyone *assumed* that the relatively high 'success ratio' of teachers' children must be due to favouritism, though it was of course due to the better coaching teachers' children had, but in the absence of any published marks they were unlikely to be believed. As a result of these criticisms it was decided the following year to decide on the basis of marks in the selection examination plus the cumulative record of performance kept by the school — not specially written reports. The cumulative records would, of course, chiefly reflect performance in earlier tests.

The next hurdle, transition from Form 4 after the first secondary certificate to the advanced certificate course in Form 5, was almost entirely a matter for decision within the school. Three things were taken into account; the examination marks in each subject; the record of performance over the year; and a rating on such things as 'curriculum interest and attitude towards nation-building'. According to one headmaster, they took into account willingness to volunteer for the adult literacy classes which the boys conducted in surrounding villages, and the 'attitudes' displayed in political education classes; but it was still, it seemed, older criteria of 'character' and 'leadership' which counted for most: 'Hockey (captain), basketball, badminton, football, attitude is alright' was a typical entry under this head.

No one mentioned or seemed to remember Nyerere's suggestion that pupils might take part in the assessment of pupils. No one actually said it, but one does sometimes sense the unspoken comment: 'Mwalimu, our Teacher, is a great man and we love him and he is an inspiration to us, but, my, some of his ideas!'

Clearly the change in attitudes has been less than complete. In 1972 the front page of the *Daily News* was still reporting, as if it were hot news, that the Minister for National Education had made a speech calling on parents to recognise that the purpose of primary education was mainly 'to prepare the pupils for life in the rural areas and not for white collar jobs' (15 September 1972). Income differentials *have* changed. There were cuts in top salaries after the Arusha declaration, and severe limitations on second incomes, and since then the lowest incomes have been raised while higher levels remain frozen. But the gap is still very wide; the élite is still élite, and secondary school boys are still conscious of the fact that they are on their way to join it. 'Students should have more comfort while travelling home or back on holiday', wrote one student to the newspaper. 'We stand throughout the whole journey from Mwanza to Dar es Salaam because of women who travel in large numbers to the capital. We go without sleep throughout these days, a thing which endangers our health, etc.' (*Daily News,* 21 September 1972). That trains could put on extra coaches for these predictable migrations of large numbers of students is a not unreasonable point, but the implication that students, as opposed to mere women, are rather important people does come through rather clearly.

And that students in primary school should still compete for the chance to join that *élite* is not surprising. Selection methods may change, but examination marks remain the major criterion for success, and in any case the only one that students can more or less predictably influence by their own efforts. And so examination preparation remains the major focus of schooling, particularly in the later years of primary. A dialogue at a teachers' training college:

> You see, the government is trying to wipe out the idea that manual work is only for failures — to give children an appreciation of the usefulness of manual labour. Admittedly the achievements so far have not been great. In fact you could say that there hasn't been much progress. It is the parents that are the trouble. The teachers try to explain and to discourage it, but it does no good; at home the parents still press the child to study for the exams. If he fails they call him a failure. It's the pressure from parents that's the trouble.

Well, yes, but you're probably a parent too. One can understand it. I'm sure if I was a farmer, say, with an income equivalent to 2,000 or 3,000 shs a year — and if my son was coming up to an examination which would give him a chance of 2,000 shs a *month* and absolute certainty of getting 500 shs or alternatively, if he failed, the barest chance of a wage job at 240 shs a month or just staying in the village — I'm sure I'd worry.

Yes, I suppose you're right. But that's why the government is putting such emphasis on rural development. If we can make rural areas attractive that would change people's ideas. They will find more interest in staying.

But that requires enormous investment.

Ah, but you don't realise what a lot of self-help there is. It's not just money. But to go back to cramming for the exams, it *is* partly the primary schools that are to blame. Every term every child comes home with a report — a formal letter from the head. It sets out his character, also his attainment; his test score in each subject and finally his overall standing — forty-eighth out of fifty, for example. At least they don't do as they did in the old middle schools — label children as first, second and third class students and failures. But it's about as bad.

Certainly the problem is not solved. The Ministry would have liked to do without selection exams, but it's just not possible. Teachers are certainly not happy with the present system. I was talking to a headmaster of a primary school in Dar. He said that for two years running he didn't get any children at all into secondary — out of a two-stream standard of ninety pupils. He said he simply couldn't face the parents. The children lost all respect for their teachers. In fact they went berserk and broke all the windows of the school. In the end he had to be transferred.

Two things must be said. Tanzania is still desperately short of people with higher-level professional skills. The supply of students qualified to study science-based subjects at the university was for a long time below the targets (only 217 compared with a planned 296 in 1968 for instance; Tanzania, 1969, p. 9) partly because of 50 per cent failure rates in the examination. Tanzania *does* have a mobilise-the-national-talents need for *efficient* selection of intelligent children who are quick and per-severing learners. Secondly, particularly in a country like Tanzania, where economic life has moved at a leisurely pace, and where practices of husbandry have not been notable for efficiency, care or timeliness, one can see point in the argument that at least the hard slog of examination study, motivated however it might be by the prize of a modern-sector job, does create a capacity for hard work, self-discipline and per-severence, which if economic development is the goal are no mean virtues.

Nevertheless, one thing seems fairly clear. Tanzania's schools are still, in spirit, a long way from the pattern set out in *Education for Self-Reliance;* and one of the reasons for that is to be sought in the way ambitions relate to jobs and jobs relate to certificates, and the effect of these things on motives and modes of learning.

Chapter 11

Reform in Sri Lanka

Chapter 4 left the story of Sri Lanka at the point of crisis. The links of causality between the educational system, the employment problem and the insurrection were much disputed, but that there was a relationship no-one seriously denied. Nor was anyone disposed to believe that the employment aspect of the situation could do anything other than get worse. And indeed it has. In 1969 there were half a million people who counted as officially 'unemployed', i.e. felt they had a claim to a wage or salaried job but could not find one. By 1973, that figure had grown to 800,000; from 14 to 17.4 per cent of the total labour force (Sri Lanka, 1974, p. 3).

That the educational system had to bear some responsibility for the situation was widely accepted. The 'Five Year Plan' published some six months after the insurrection spoke of the need for reform.

The present divorce of education from the world of work has uprooted an entire generation from the type of production which can be readily developed in the country and has pushed the person who would normally have gone into some productive activity into a fruitless search for white-collar employment the expansion of which can no longer be supported by the country's productive sectors. (Sri Lanka, 1971, p. 5.)

There had, said the Plan, to be a change in the 'academic-type curricula . . . framed to cater to the needs of the small minority' who are likely to end up in professional jobs.

Even if the Ministry of Planning did not manage to show what were the types of production which the half-million unemployed could 'readily develop' if only they were not bemused by the prospect of a white-collar job, it remained an undeniable truth that getting white-collar jobs was what the educational system was all about, and that there was something wrong with a system which annually induced 350,000 children to sit an examination socially defined as an entry port to the kind of jobs of which, at the most optimistic estimate, only 30,000 become available each year.

122

The diagnosis

The Ministry of Education's plans for reform emerged gradually. The major defects of the system, as the ministry identified them (Sri Lanka, 1974; see also Wijemanne and Sinclair, 1972), were as follows:

1. Too many resources were focused on the two years of Grades 9 and 10 which preceded the O level examination, the main life-chance selector, to the neglect of attempts to improve either the primary school curriculum (still characterised by 'dull, drab mechanical learning') or the middle school Grades 6 to 8 where, for instance, plans to introduce general science in 1957 had been abandoned 'for want of enthusiasm'.

2. Premature specialisation, dividing pupils into arts and science streams at Grade 9, depriving the majority of any contact at all with science, and limiting students to four subjects at Grade 11.

3. The non-integrated assortment of optional subjects both at O level and A level — which cannot be integrated, either, because they have to be independent optional units.

4. The inequality of opportunity involved in the unequal provision of science teaching facilities between schools and regions — given that it is the science stream which offers much the best career possibilities.

5. The effect of the schools' single-minded concentration on the competition to pass into the A level stream and university in

> under-mining the realisation of most of the aims and objectives of good education. . . . Parents complain that their children . . . have to rush every afternoon from one private tuition class to another. . . . Class teachers complain that their pupils have no time to ponder and study on their own and assimilate what they are taught in class and heads of schools complain that their most promising pupils are being removed from their sports and other extra-curricular activities because they have to concentrate on their studies. . . . Quite a few [pupils] break down unable to stand the pressure and tension that goes with this experience. Private tuition also undermines the operation of examinations as valid instruments of selection.

And at the source of it all, says the Ministry's frank and perceptive diagnosis, was a *misdirection* of egalitarian pressures which sought to change the two-tier system inherited from colonial times.

Right from the beginning and all along, the question that was being asked was 'How can the chances of the child from the poor home to enter the privileged circle be improved?' The question 'How can education be made to contribute its little to the betterment of the mass of the underprivileged?' *was never asked.*

The reform of the system

From this diagnosis were conceived ideas for reform. And those ideas begat proposals, and those proposals begat threats to the comfort and security and the hopes and ambitions of many people, and those threats begat counter-pressures, and from the final shotgun marriage between the proposals and the counter-pressures was born, in late 1971, a plan of reform. Its main points were:

1. In place of the eight years (five plus three) of general education, with two years' O level preparation, the new 'open access span' of the school system would consist of a five-year primary school and a four-year middle school — nine years in all instead of ten, but with the same school-leaving age, since school entry would be postponed from age 5 to age 6.

2. All possible resources for curriculum reform would be focused on the middle school. It would provide a uniform general education (covering languages, religion, maths., science, social studies, aesthetic studies and two units of pre-vocational studies), and the whole thrust of the reform — not only in the introduction of the new pre-vocational studies, but also in designing the content of science, maths and social studies courses and in integrating content across subject boundaries — would be to correct the academic bias of the present curriculum, to relate what is learned to the present and future circumstances of the majority of children who will proceed no farther in the system.

3. Grade 9 would end with an examination in all ten subjects of the curriculum. All pupils would take all ten subjects; they would be graded A to E (not pass/fail) according to a mixture of (national) examination marks and school-based assessment. Only one repeat (following a repeat year in school) would normally be permitted, though a third try would be possible if still under 17. But there would be no 'private candidates', no more private tutories for repeaters.

4. Admission to Grade 10 for two years of further, more specialised, study would depend on results obtained in this National Certificate of General Education. But instead of a fixed standard of attainment (which could mean steadily rising numbers of successful entrants), the entrance standard would be varied to keep the success ratio to about 10 per cent — the proportion currently gaining the A level transfer requirements, and approximately the proportion of the age group which could reasonably hope for a non-manual job.

5. The curriculum of these two senior secondary years would also be reformed, notably by the innovation of a core curriculum (socio-economic and cultural studies, statistics and management, English and first language) taking up 25 per cent of the time, and by the attempt to develop curriculum streams which could *both* lead directly to middle-level technical employment and provide a preparation for professional

training at the university — the universities themselves being already at work on the development of 'development studies' degrees in a range of a dozen or more professional specialisations, ranging from mining to tourism.

The first test of the new system came when the first reformed age group which started in Grade 6 in 1972 took the first National Certificate Examination in 1975. Already, in 1974, the pressure was building up for a relaxation of the rule that there should be only one repeat attempt at the exam, and that there should be no automatic right of promotion if a 'pass' standard were achieved. Both threatened entrenched concepts of fairness, the feeling that *effort* should be rewarded; the former particularly was a dire threat to the livelihood of the many thousands of people who run private O level tutories. Their opposition has been vocal and not without influence, but the ministry has fought back; no one can regret the decline of private tutories, says a recent report, 'when one sees the cramming that goes on in these institutions in the name of education, the manner in which numbers of adolescent boys and girls are led astray by some ruthless people, the extent to which utterly unrealistic job aspirations consequent on obtaining "the certificate" are promoted, and the tragic end of all this in the form of large numbers of frustrated youth'. Even the sacrifice of the chances of a small number of late developers would be a price worth paying for the mitigation of those abuses (Sri Lanka, 1974, p. 18).

Prospects for success
If the ministry succeeds in withstanding the pressure there will certainly be some gains. All the pupils who reach Grade 9 should have some smattering of science. No one will consider the Grade 9 certificate as a job-entitlement and those who get the higher certificate which *will* be so regarded might actually get jobs. The selection for those charmed higher certificate courses will be fairer, since lesser advantages will accrue to those with access to schools with specialist science streams.

But, how far will the reforms succeed in making the curriculum of the middle schools genuinely educational, useful and relevant to the lives of that 90 per cent of the children reaching Grade 9 who are destined not to proceed on to the circles of privilege? Will the certificate ever be seen by the pupils, teachers and parents as a genuine 'school leaving certificate', if few of those who leave school after Grade 9 are ever likely to find a prospective employer to show it to? The examination is much more likely to be seen as an intensely competitive selection exam, with all hopes concentrated on becoming one of the lucky 10 per cent 'successes'. The intensity of cramming concerns can only be enchanced by the more narrow constriction of the upward route, by the percentage rule, and by the now-or-never character of the examination under the only-two-shots rule.

How far can this be overcome by valiant efforts of curriculum designers and teachers to insist, by the sheer force of their inspirational convictions, that this is *not* what it is all about, and that the school is there to teach children to be useful citizens and productive workers — in particular the sort of productive workers who do *not* go whoring after wage jobs in the city, but will go zestfully into traditional sectors of employment to improve the efficiency of the nation's farms and fisheries and artisan production, developing new or under-utilised resources?

Pre-vocational studies

Apart from the new science and social studies curriculum, the main hopes for this transformation are concentrated on the new pre-vocational studies courses. Three out of the forty hours a week are to be devoted to handicrafts as they have traditionally been taught, and another weekly hour alternately to the study of the country's natural resources and to geometric drawing. The chief innovation is the other half of 'pre-vocational studies', the study for three hours a week of locally practised vocations (between one and three over the four years, depending on their complexity) according to syllabuses devised by schools themselves following models provided by the ministry. Some eighty-two vocations had been registered by mid-1974, ranging from meat preservation and joss-stick making to palm-leaf craft and gypsum production. The objectives are not only to give knowledge of the vocations and an awareness of the way 'knowledge gained in other studies such as mathematics and science can be applied in studying about vocations', but also 'a feeling of confidence and pride in [one's] ability to participate in the production of marketable goods and services' (Sri Lanka, 1974, p. 21c). There is no doubt that some teachers and officials have thrown themselves into the task of devising pre-vocational study units with enthusiasm and imagination. Consider, for example, this conversation with a regional education officer who had acquired a considerable reputation for his promotion of pre-vocational studies. On his desk was a product of one of his schools' work; a lampshade made of bamboo and cane, a basic cylinder with circular extended 'eaves', professionally finished off with varnish.

> We look on pre-vocational studies more as a medium not a subject — as a means of introducing the pupil to an integrated variety of aspects. It should be flexible and creative, but not the personal expression of interest of a particular teacher which would collapse if that teacher moved. It must be the product of a group of teachers

who work together, and who can interpret and create something that can survive the removal of any particular teacher.

You mean that it has to be formalised?

Well, let me give you an example of a unit of study built up around basketwork. Take this lampshade for instance. Now to start with, here's bamboo. This gives an opportunity to teach the biology of the bamboo in relation to the plants of the same group. The same with the canes and grasses used.

Now we come to the making of these two rings which form the ends of the cylinder. Children learn how to peel off a strip of bamboo. Here again physics and biology come in. The tissues flow one way, not the other. Why? Then we get the concept of springiness and flexibility. This can be bent, other materials would snap. What makes the difference?

And all the time we come back to making things. With variations on these basic rings, for instance, children can make steamers for string hoppers which have a good sale.

Will you bring in the local craftsmen to teach the children?

No, not actually into the classroom. You see, if you bring in the craftsmen, they will just want to teach the craft. They would inject all kinds of superstitions. No, it will have to be under the control of the teacher, though he would, of course, consult with and learn from the craftsmen. But the aim is not just to transmit traditional crafts but to improve on them, and to train the children to seek ways of improving them, and the teacher has to do that. The teacher has to provide the scientific and intellectual element. For instance, the bamboo is bent into a circular ring. This involves more maths. What defines a perfect circle? Then the cylinder. The maths of the cylinder. The physics of balance — weight, consistency, uniformity, mass, and so on. Then we come to adding this part like an upturned flower basket. First they learn about the geometrical forms involved; then there is opportunity to design their own forms and to combine different forms creatively in new ways.

Then there are opportunities for experimentation and research — what is the maximum candle-power of bulb that could be used in this lampshade without burning it? How do the convectional currents flow? What difference does it make if you cover the cylinder with paper instead of leaving it open, and so on. In the same way there can be experiments with different tools and methods of making the shade. Children can make their own tools.

Again, there are all the economic aspects; the marketing problems, the export opportunities, the economics of growing the cane, the possible uses for the parts of the plant not used in basketwork, and so on.

That seems to me very impressive and imaginative, but I wonder how far one can go starting from a relatively simple craft like basketwork. To fill out a curriculum over several years based on this craft one has to teach a great deal which has not direct relevance to the craft itself. Compare it, say, with teaching children enough about the mechanics of the tractor engine to be able to repair one. That could fill up several years of study without straying too far from the practical purpose in hand. If a school could get hold of an old worn tractor engine . . .

No, no. That's impossible. They are not to be had. In any case we want to concentrate on the sources available in our natural environment . . .

There is no doubt that handled with skill, pre-vocational studies will turn out to be an improved version of old-style project work. They could well, if well taught, be intellectually stimulating, develop powers of observation, arouse curiosity, show the interconnectedness of knowledge. But will the pupils take to their basketwork unit with equal enthusiasm? And will it make them keen to be basketworkers — and *better* basketworkers than their fathers? One possibility might have been to make it special; to emphasise the practical purposefulness of the activity and the need to develop intrinsic interest, by excluding pre-vocational studies from the certificate examinations. But that alternative was very early rejected as hopelessly unrealistic. If we did that, said one official, not 10 per cent of our teachers would take pre-vocational studies seriously. But that is not the end of the matter. Examinable subjects can acquire the reputation of being easy subjects or difficult subjects. In the present O level exam there are subjects like Buddhist civilisation with high pass rates and subjects like maths and English with very low ones. The bright child has no worries about doing well enough in the first type of subjects; he is worried about the difficult subjects and on these he — and his teachers — concentrate attention. Those are the subjects taken really seriously; the Buddhist civilisation periods are hours when one can safely let the attention wander.

There is no reason to suppose that the situation will be any different when the crucial selection barrier is the new general certificate. The difference between the boy with seven As and Bs who gets into the favoured 10 per cent, and the boy with only five who does not, is likely to be their performances in difficult subjects like maths and English.

If pre-vocational studies become an 'easy' subject, then, they may be taken more seriously than if they were not examined at all, but not *much* more seriously. There will be every reason for making them a difficult subject so that they *are* taken seriously.

And how will they be made difficult? It is clear from the official's description that an elaborated pre-vocational unit centred around the craft of basketwork will contain three elements: (a) the knowledge and skills which existing craftsmen use; (b) the knowledge and skills which they *could* use to improve existing techniques, designs, marketing and use of resources; and (c) other knowledge and skills which are unlikely to have such practical relevance (the mathematics of the cylinder, etc.) but which are part of general education which the basketwork theme can be used to lead into. Making the subject difficult then will mean increasing the complexity of the mathematics and general science or economics 'hung on' to the peg of the craft activity, increasing the number of facts to be memorised for reproduction in the examination. And as this happens, pre-vocational studies move farther and farther away from the craft activity which is their supposed focus; they become instrumentalised as another rung on the ladder into the favoured 10 per cent élite; a means of escaping the necessity of ever having to practise the craft in earnest. A further consequence is that the children most likely to have the need to practise the basketwork craft are the most likely to get Es in the subject — a fine emotional preparation for their career!

At present the greater likelihood is that pre-vocational studies will end up as an 'easy' subject. As between the Scylla of not being taken seriously and the Charybdis of being intellectualised and made bookish, it is on the former that the enterprise is more likely to founder. The dilemma is a cruel but inescapable one — inescapable, that is, as long as the life of the school revolves around achievement tests which allocate all-important life-chances.

Social dualism, disjunction, relevance and the selection function
It is a dilemma inherent in the structure of society. Teaching children to write solemn essays on the dignity of manual labour is one thing. For teachers to behave as if they really believed that gaining manual dexterity in basket-making was as intrinsically worthy a pursuit as learning the mathematical properties of cylinders is quite another in a society where it is the brain-workers who give orders to the hand-workers (and have the larger salaries) rather than the other way round.

And, as hand is to brain, so home is to school — at least for the majority of Sri Lanka's children who live in rural areas. The gulf between home and school, the fact that to the child they seem to belong to quite separate spheres, is a potent obstacle to the development of relevant curricula, and that too is partly of the teachers' making. Recall the educational official's rejection of the notion of bringing craftsmen with their superstitions into the schools. Again, this is understandable. The school *is* an agent of change. The rational, scientific intellectual values which it promotes often *are* at variance with the more mystic, intuitive values of the folk society around it. But if the school is to be an agent of real change it must *engage with* that society, not operate in parallel with it, ignoring it, letting the children solve the compartmentalisation problem as best they may. Somehow the school has got to come to terms with the craftsman's superstitions, recognise them as a fact that exists, ask how far they are justified, ask why he believes them.

It is worth citing another example from the new Sri Lanka curriculum. Plans were being made, in Grade 7 and 8, to include an introduction to the stars and the solar system. But there was to be no mention of that essential part which the stars *actually play* in village life as the basis of astrology and horoscopes. One sees and sympathises with the dilemma of curriculum builders. Deliberately to challenge these traditional beliefs, to declare them incompatible with rational science, might be to sharpen the disjunction between home and school (as well as arouse antagonism). Silence might seem preferable. But it is not impossible to find other more subtle approaches — on the one hand to question the accuracy of horoscopes and perhaps to compare the methods of astrology with the methods of making weather forecasts, on the other hand to point out the element of uncertainty and luck in all human affairs, to point out the human need for the security of certainty, and to point out various other forms of anxiety-allayment which that human need produces — including, for example, modern economic planning. The point is to show that improvements in intellectual sophistication and in real technological control over the environment do not alter the basic human constellation of needs and appetites, the basic pattern of capacities for love and hate, for hope and fear. It is at that level of basic humanity that the bridge must be built between home and school.

But the truth is that the disjunction exists. It is a reflection of the disjunction within the society as a whole between the modern and traditional sectors, between the bridge-head of rationality and salaried employment and high incomes and all mod cons, and the hinterland of superstition and precarious self-employment. And as long as it is school performance which largely determines who goes into which sector, and as long as school performance is measured by achievement tests which cover — indeed dominate — the whole curriculum, it is a fairly safe prediction that all the pre-vocational studies in the world, and all the imaginative efforts of the most energetic of Sri Lanka's educators in devising them, will not make Grade 9 school leavers *very* much better prepared for the futures which actually await them than the O level leavers of today — either cognitively or emotionally.

PART III MORE RADICAL ALTERNATIVES

Chapter 12

Deschool?

From the last three chapters would seem to emerge a rather clear, and distinctly gloomy, conclusion. No amount of change in the guiding ideology, no attempt to switch attention from the needs of the high achievers to the needs of low achievers, no search for 'relevance', no change in the overt curriculum, can have any effect on the 'hidden curriculum' — how schools really teach children about their society and shape their values and ambitions and learning patterns — at least as long as school achievement has such overwhelming importance for individual life-chances.

What, then, can be done? Abolish schools altogether is the response of Ivan Illich. Small wonder, perhaps, that such an audaciously simple recipe should have caught the imagination of the editors of Sunday supplements and made Illich and his ideas so widely known that all discussions of fundamental education reform in the mid-seventies must somehow take account of them.

Illich's proposals were, in fact, the product of a decade of joint work by Illich and Everett Reimer, beginning in Puerto Rico in the fifties (whither Illich went to direct a training programme for priests and where Reimer was a manpower adviser) and continued at the educational centre which Illich founded at Cuernavaca, Mexico. Their collaboration did not extend to co-authorship, however, and reading their separate books — Illich's *Deschooling Society* (1971) and Reimer's *School Is Dead: Alternatives in Education: An indictment of the system and a strategy of revolution* (1971) — one can see why. Reimer has the power to develop an elegant and reasoned argument, to think things through, to document. Illich writes like a man who is better at talking — preferably to a large and aroused audience. One can sense the magnetism and guess why it is that so many well-meaning (and well-heeled) American ladies flock to his Cuernavaca centre for the healing experience of a course of deyanquification treatments. Eloquent, fanciful, classically erudite, he writes with supreme confidence, giving graphic illustrations of elusive *nonsequiturs*. As one reads of the Delphic Oracle in the final chapter's re-interpretation of

131

his ideas in terms of Greek myth, one cannot escape the feeling that he too has sat over the navel of the earth, inhaling its sulphurous fumes.

The thesis

Their thesis is a universal one, meant to apply equally to both rich and poor countries, and in elaborating its main outlines Illich and Reimer are in close agreement. The school system is an integral part of the rottenness of modern society, a key mechanism in the perpetuation of that rottenness. Piecemeal change will be difficult, but one has to start somewhere and it is just possible to begin the reformation of society by changing the whole conception and process of education.

That schools fail to give people the right kind of training for their later occupations, or that the selection processes mixed up with the training inculcate the wrong kinds of attitudes to work and society, or that they get in the way of the healthy intellectual and spiritual development of the individual — the burden of the indictment of Third World schools developed in earlier chapters of this book — is only a small part of the Illich-Reimer critique of schools. They are more concerned that:

1. The whole concept of compulsory schooling is an affront to individual liberty. Contemporary schools share one characteristic in common, 'the idea that one person's judgement should determine what and when another person must learn' (Illich, 1971, p. 42). Concerned with the institutional 'processing' of individuals, schools deny their essential humanity.

2. School's compulsoriness, as well as being an intrinsic affront to human dignity, also distorts the learning process. Only that learning is valuable which is freely and autonomously embarked on.

3. In so far as schools do provide 'benefits' they distribute them grossly unequally. In the US, the amount of public money spent on the schooling of the richest tenth of the population is ten times the amount spent on the schooling of the poorest tenth. In Bolivia, one half of the public educational budget is spent on 1 per cent of the age group (Reimer, 1971, p. 46). (This is a point more insisted on by Reimer than by Illich. Illich is more firmly convinced that schooling is degradation and presumably hesitates to argue that the poor are unfairly deprived of it.)

4. Schools perpetuate inequality because they 'define merit in accordance with the structure of the society served by schools. This structure is characterized by the competitive consumption of technological products defined by institutions. Institutions define products in such a way that is consistent with the maintenance of a dominant hierarchy of privilege and insofar as possible, with the opportunities of

the currently privileged class to retain their status in the new "meritocracy"' (ibid., p. 43).

5. Schools not only perpetuate hierarchy, but the whole cancerous pattern of modern living. A major, and pernicious, function of the school is to indoctrinate children in habits of consumption which turn them into obedient, addictive consumers of the products of mass consumption society. School is 'a vast enterprise of equipping man for disciplined consumption' (Illich, 1971, p. 46).

The alternatives

We can all recognize elements of truth in this indictment, even if we cannot share its fervour. But the important question is: what are the alternatives?

First, one learns from work. Illich would give special tax incentives to anyone who would employ children (humanely) for a couple of hours a day between the ages of 8 and 12 (ibid., p. 85). Reimer (more impressed, presumably, by the unemployment figures) would employ teenagers not on routine work, but on ecological and social research projects and artistic projects (Reimer, 1971, p. 51). Secondly, the basic skills of literacy and numeracy do not have to be worried about because the children of literate and numerate parents acquire these skills anyway (ibid., pp. 16-18), though Reimer still leaves open the possibility, under the new dispensation, that parents might hire drill teachers for their children (ibid., p. 146).

But these are minor aspects, dealt with in a few throw-away sentences. The grand design for an alternative is much bolder. It consists of nothing less than abolishing all 'scholastic funnels' and creating instead a 'world made transparent by true communication webs' (Illich, 1971, p. 104). The organised, institutionalised part of education should be entirely facilitative, not directive. It is to provide access — like those other good 'convivial' institutions which will be preserved in the new society: telephone linkages, subway lines, mail routes, public markets and exchanges, sewage systems, drinking water, pubs and sidewalks (ibid., p. 54). There are three prerequisites.

The first is an adequate store of things and people to learn *from* — with computerised directories to lead the learner to them. The existing libraries and museums would be supplemented by thousands of new kinds of 'storefront learning centres' — places where one could go to learn to use or repair office equipment or to try one's hand at printing a community newspaper, factories whose owners are persuaded to provide access to the productive processes now secretively shielded from public view. Junkyards would be opened up *and* consumer demand would lead to the re-emergence of the *repairable* consumer durable instead of the calculated obsolescence of the 'replaceables' which are turning North America into a 'non-inventive society'.

The other kind of resource would be people. Any possessor of a skill willing to share it with others would be encouraged to register with the computer his availability as a skill model. There is a certain ambiguity here: Reimer sticks fairly carefully to the term 'skill model'. Illich oscillates between 'skill model' and 'skill teacher'. Even in Reimer's examples, however, it is not clear whether, say, the would-be typist just watches and occasionally questions the skill-model typist, or whether the latter also explains what he is doing. The native speaker nobbled as a skill model for language learning (another favourite example) clearly has to give his full attention to his modelling, not just get on with his own business as the typist might, but whether he (or anybody else) needs to know about the structure of the language he models is not clear.

The second prerequisite is access to suitably matched peers — someone to share the learning experience; someone with whom to give and take the stimulus to learn. This may take various forms. The computer will equally find one a fellow-beginner who also wants to learn typing, or meet the needs of 'a student who has picked up Greek before her vacation [and] would like to discuss, in Greek, Cretan politics when she returns' (ibid., p. 93).

The third prerequisites are the (three kinds of) educational specialists. These are, first, the administrators who keep the networks of things, the networks of skill models and the peer-matching systems, in good working order. Secondly, there are pedagogical advisers available to advise people on their use of the available facilities. The latter must be extremely versatile. One minute they will be available to help a student who wants to learn spoken Cantonese from a Chinese neighbour — helping 'to judge their proficiency and to . . . select the textbook and methods most suitable to their talents, character and time available for study'. The next they might be counselling the would-be airplane mechanic on finding the best places for apprenticeship (ibid., p. 99).

The third kind of specialist is the educational leader — a mixture of Nobel Prize winner and Socratic guru.

No dogmatic solution is offered to the problem of how to mobilise and allocate all these resources. Mobilisation can be taken care of, it is suggested, by tax incentives or compulsory legislation designed to make the society's potential educational resources fully available. Allocation may be more difficult. First, they recognise that not everyone should be able to claim the attention of, say, a research chemist as skill model. They may need some kind of preliminary knowledge to make use of his example. This may have to be tested. But the tests should be strictly purposeful examinations of capacity, in no way affected by records of schooling, certification, etc.

(And, of course, no one will ever require that this preliminary knowledge should be tested. Or if they do, there will be no pressure to make the tests objective, open and competitive in the interests of fairness. Or if there is, no one will ever have the idea of starting a cram school to prepare aspirants to society's most coveted positions for these tests!)

Illich and Reimer recognise that their scheme of things might still generate a demand on the system greater than the resources available. One way, they suggest, is to price all the services the system offers (or a section of those services, the rest being freely available) in terms of a special educational currency. Each individual would then be given a basic educational credit to be used up over the course of his life. It might also be possible to earn extra credit by teaching others.

This sort of educational system will, they suggest, have liberating ideological effects. Schools will cease to enslave; learning will make people 'educated' in terms of Paulo Freire's definition — 'critically aware of one's reality in a manner that leads to effective action upon it' (Reimer, 1971, p. 162). Freire, who turned adult literacy campaigns in north-east Brazil into a means of developing the peasants' political consciousness, was concerned to direct 'critical awareness' at landlords, property, priests. In North America it is parents and Big Institutions (school, organised medicine, the motor industry) who similarly mystify and conceal in order to warp the burgeoning consciousness of the child and prevent his critical awareness of the way he is being enslaved into his addiction to expensive medicine and six-lane highways (ibid., p. 168).

The plan is as bold as the denunciation is spectacular. Parts of it are as admirable as parts of the denunciation are apt. They are right to insist that most good learning is done by doing, that the school denaturalises knowledge and can emasculate curiosity and the genuine desire to learn. One's heart warms more readily to the man who thinks that a junkyard has more educational potential than a classroom than it does to the older romanticism about single impulses from vernal woods teaching one more of man, of moral evil and of good, than all the sages can. And yet, one cannot help wondering at the naivety. Worse, one cannot help occasionally feeling angry at the evidence, either of the insensitivity to the real sufferings of a large part of mankind, or else of that same capacity for self-deception which enables the questing, protesting youth of North America (for whom, indeed, the book seems to have been chiefly written) to mistake their own self-regarding concerns for social concerns, to conflate their own identity crisis with the crisis of their society.

All the world the same?

The first whopping assumption in the Cuernavaca scheme of things, is that, educationally, there is no difference between the rich and the poor countries (see Illich, 1971, pp. 8, 59, 82; Reimer, 1971, p. 22); their problems and their needs are the same.

But clearly they are not. North America may not need to think hard about the way schools can cure poverty. The poor countries do.

Consider, for example, their facile acceptance of Freire's 'critical awareness' as the highest educational goal; highly appropriate, they suggest, for the mystified United States and obviously appropriate, since Freire's ideas are rooted in Brazil, to the poor countries. But is it? One has nothing but admiration for Freire, working in a situation where any sane prescription for development would require a trans-formation of an iniquitous social system, and where the evocation of political consciousness among peasants can reasonably claim priority *among* educational tasks. But in the first place it is absurd to suggest that that is *all* education is about in poor countries. Freire's peasants, if they ever got the land and water they need, would also need to learn about conserving and fertilising it, about marketing and keeping accounts. In the second place, not all political situations in the poor countries are such as to make critical awareness the first priority. The 'oppressors' of China, even, perhaps, of Cuba or Tanzania, may well be said to do a more efficient job than Brazilian landlords in keeping their people in a state of 'false consciousness'. But it surely makes a difference that they are using their power to make their people richer and to share the wealth of society in a reasonably egalitarian manner. Their programme of rural education is certainly not geared to pro-ducing critical awareness. The only criticism encouraged is self-criticism. The schools teach conformity to the existing order: they are concerned to inculcate the virtues of hard work and the techniques of agriculture and conservation. And the best guess seems to be that this *is* contributing to measurable improvement in the material livelihood of Chinese peasants.

But this sort of disciplined, frankly élite-dominated education aimed at building a productive and cohesive society has no place in the Illich-Reimer scheme of things, and for the very simple reason that they do not recognise the importance of the economic differences between the rich and poor countries. Educational arrangements, say Reimer, again as an apparently universally valid statement, can be 'an outcome of how people, given a wide range of choices, decide to live . . . Technological considerations impose no serious restrictions on these choices. People can have what they want if they can free themselves of habits and preferences, some of which have been frozen into laws and institutions' (Reimer, 1971, p. 36).

Perhaps the United States has reached that happy situation: perhaps if Americans were freed from the brainwashing of Madison Avenue and the AMA and ceased to lust after cars like gleaming battleships and expensive open heart surgery, they would be able to live more happily, as Illich/Reimer suggest, in an economy with a much lower level of productivity. But do they expect nods of agreement from, say, the Indians — from countries where half the population have difficulty in getting enough food to stay alive? (Illich even has the gall to say that poverty in most of the poor countries is only 'modernised poverty', the product of expectations aroused by modern advertising; 'classic poverty' was 'stable and less disabling'. (Illich, 1971, p. 7.) One wonders if he has ever read Lewis' account of how this stable and undisabling classical poverty brutalised life in the villages around Cuernavaca early in this century; Lewis, 1969, pp. 270, 401 *et passim*.)

Given their basic assumptions about what the modern problems of Society — *all* societies — are, it is not surprising that all the practical illustrations they give of how their new system will work concern learning of only two types — acquiring some kind of practical skill (like typing, for instance) or pursuing a personal hobby type of interest — learning Cantonese, or becoming an expert on Greek politics. Theirs, one might summarily say, is a prescription for an individualistic, play-oriented educational system. Admirable, no doubt, for an affluent society that can sink complacently into its affluence and forget about the rest of the world. Hardly what a poor country needs.

But, it might be objected, surely the argument of this whole book is that there should be less instrumental qualification-oriented learning and more 'learning for learning's sake'. It is time, perhaps, to spell out the taxonomy of educational purposes (or educational philosophies if one wants to be more pompous about it) which was briefly sketched on p. 8.

ONE OUGHT TO LEARN

to acquire knowledge or skills as ends in themselves

because the process of mastery gives pleasure (END-IN-ITSELF LEARNING)

because it is a moral duty (to God, to society, oneself) to develop one's full capacities (DUTY LEARNING)

because its acquisition gives one prestige (SNOB LEARNING)

in order to be able to use the knowledge

because the 'open-ended exploratory use of acquired skills' (Illich, 1971, p. 17) is a pleasurable goal in itself (PLEASURABLE USE LEARNING)

instrumentally, in order to win power over others or to gain income from others, or to win respect from others
    by skilful performance in the use of the skills learned (SELF-REGARDING ACHIEVEMENT LEARNING)
    by virtue of qualifications gained through tested learning, and the weight the institutions of society place on those qualifications (SELF-REGARDING QUALIFICATION-SEEKING LEARNING)

instrumentally, in order to make one's community, or one's nation a better place (SOCIETY-REGARDING ACHIEVEMENT LEARNING).

The target of this book is what is labelled above as 'self-regarding qualification-seeking learning' which I see as the chief source of educational iniquity. 'Self-regarding achievement learning' (seeking the knowledge to *do* jobs conscientiously well, not just the certificates to *get* them) is altogether a different and better thing, much more likely (if the 'invisible hand' which channels individual self-regarding efforts to the common good has *any* residual efficacy) to conduce to social and economic development. The Chinese ideal of 'society-regarding achievement learning' may perhaps be a nobler aim, though for me, with my Western prejudices, the nobility depends on whether, in a spirit of beehive conformity, one simply accepts one's rulers' goals as to what one's society is seeking to achieve, or whether one is also educated to criticise and assess the dominant value criteria and so retain the freedom to commit oneself or not according to *one's own* definition of what the society's goals should be. Any wise educationalist, under any of these ruling ideals, would also seek to mobilise the end-in-itself learning motive, the duty-learning motive and the snob-learning motive — if only instrumentally as a concession to the weakness of the flesh. (And, in fact, if he did not also attach some *absolute* value to end-in-itself-learning, he would not, by my lights, be much of an educationalist.)

But Illich and Reimer seem to see the need for nothing else *besides* end-in-itself-learning and pleasurable-use-learning. Their old-fashioned market individualism (see their proposals for educational vouchers to balance the supply and demand) precludes *society-regarding* definitions of goals. Their blithe lack of concern for the problem of poverty explains why they are little interested, either, in *achievement-oriented* definitions of goals.

There is in more ways than one a cavalier lack of discrimination about the Illich/Reimer message. Just as they take little account of the differences between societies, so they take little account of the differences between individuals. All the examples offered of education in the post-school society concern the gifted, inquiring, intelligent youth — the sort of person who can quickly learn Greek in preparation for a summer holiday and has such a high quotient of sociological curiosity that he can spend that holiday probing into local politics. The Illich/Reimer scheme of things is paradoxically élitist. The gifted would indeed do well out of it. It is the not-so-bright who would suffer.

A striking thing about both books is their lack of any sense of the reality of childhood. There is no evidence that either author has experienced at first hand the capacity for wonder, the delight in discovery and eager curiosity of some children, the passivity, the quick recourse to less challenging play of others. Neither seems to have noticed that curiosity and the power to perceive are trained capacities, not, in all children, natural ones. Perhaps Reimer's sons and daughters, with whom, he tells us, he has benefited from 'years of critical conversation about education', were the kind of children who spontaneously noticed that the moon waxes and wanes and asked why, who were aware without prompting of the slight difference in breast colour of a pair of swallows and were puzzled by it. Or perhaps one or two of them did belong to the vast majority of the world's children who don't notice these things until they are pointed out, and it was Mrs Reimer who did the pointing while her husband was away working for the Alliance for Progress.

For the child whose parents are unmoved by moons or swallows and for whom curiosity was what killed the cat, good primary schools in the rich countries often do provide the necessary stimulus to wonder, and develop the appetite autonomously to find out. And for the 'slow learner' in the richest societies, they can do even more. Neither Illich nor Reimer gives any indication he has ever seen or heard about the way in which a gifted and patient teacher can, by careful, conscious, but loving *manipulation,* coax out of the sort of child who scores 65 in an IQ test, the first glimmers of curious interest, the first experience of mastery of an idea or a manual technique, the first glow of self-confidence.

Russell remarks somewhere on the frequency with which philosophers with a passionate concern for the fate of Man show an inconscient indifference to the fate of individual *men*. An awareness of the wide range of difference among men — in capacities as well as in tempera-ments — should be the starting point of any educational theory.[1]

[1]For a more extensive discussion of the Illich/Reimer philosophy, see Dore (1972).

Chapter 13

Some Modest Proposals

Clearly, to deschool is to throw the baby out with the bathwater, for there genuinely *is* an educational baby worth preserving and nurturing in the institution called school. The cure for the problems which beset developing country school systems must be sought in less drastic measures — but measures perhaps only a little less drastic.

One element lies at the heart of nearly all the problems discussed in this book: the diploma disease, the scourge of the certificate, the dependence of individual life-chances on certificates of school achievement.

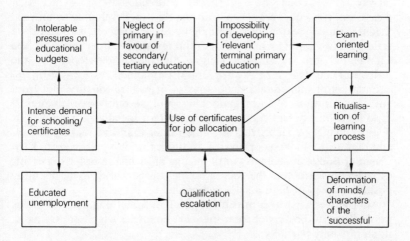

It should, surely, be there that one should look for the possibilities of reform. Somehow, to be sure, society has to find ways of deciding who does what job, and they have to be the ways which (a) are considered by the people of that society just and acceptable ways of awarding the privileges and amenities that go with different jobs, and (b) ensure that the productive efficiency of society is not too much impaired by having too many round pegs in square holes — what may be referred to as the equity requirement and the efficiency requirement. The efficiency requirement, of course, has two parts: choosing pegs from wood of the right grain in the first place, and shaping them to a proper roundness in the second; the selection and the training aspects respectively.

The solution which most societies have adopted throughout most of human history — hereditary succession — is not likely to find acceptance anywhere today; it solves the efficiency problem only in societies with a relatively simple and non-progressive technology where the chief division of labour is between those who always give orders and those who are always on the taking end (family upbringing being the best sort of shaping tool for the attitudes and self-perceptions required for efficient job performance in those respects). And equally, by 1975, hereditary succession was no longer an acceptable answer to the equity problem either, except, perhaps, in a few backwaters of Latin America and North-West Asia which are still very largely unaffected by the flood of egalitarian ideas spreading out from the industrial societies in which they first developed.

And if the alternative which has developed in the industrial 'models of modernity' (both capitalist and socialist) — the alternative of relying largely on selection through the educational system — has such disastrous consequences when transplanted to developing countries, then it is time to search for something better. Even more is this so if we reflect on two points which I hope were established earlier: first (see Chapter 2) the certificate-selection alternative developed in the industrial countries largely *ad hoc* and unplanned, as a result of the cumulation of individual calculations of private rationality, not from any considerations of social rationality; and, secondly (see Chapter 7) in so far as the system does work roughly in a socially rational way, it does so chiefly by identifying the able rather than by creating ability, and that we are fooling ourselves if we think that it is *necessary* to keep a man at Bouleian geometry until the age of 21 just in order to *test* his capacity to learn (on the job, after he starts work) to write pithy position papers or plan a sales campaign.

Alternatives exist. It *is* possible to think of something better. And as we shall see in the next chapter there *are* countries which are trying it, if, so far, only partially.

The essential elements of that alternative are two:

1. Start careers earlier — around the ages of 15—17 — doing as much of the selection as possible within work organisations, and transforming all tertiary education and training into in-career learning, either part-time or full-time, in special educational institutes.

2. At all points where there has to be selection — particularly for the all-important decision as to which work organisation people are to enter initially at the end of their period of basic schooling — avoid using learning achievement tests: whether the alternative be aptitude tests, lotteries, special 'encapsulated' tests (see below), the essential thing is that they be tests which cannot be (or cannot much be) crammed for.

Early recruitment into work

Let us spell out the implications of these suggestions in more detail. First, the patterns of recruitment and training. The civil service, for instance, would no longer recruit graduates. There would, instead, be a single major entry port for all grades at the age of 16 (or whatever were fixed as the school leaving age) and everyone would start as a clerk; some, on the results of internal tests, or on the basis of work performance, would be promoted fairly quickly to the executive grades and given such further training as was necessary, and some of those would similarly be selected — and educated/trained — for administrative posts. The same pattern could apply to other professions. Future engineers could train first as craftsmen; some of the craftsmen could be trained as technicians, and the ablest of those sent off for full training as engineers. Doctors could begin as medical assistants; teachers as pupil-teachers; university teachers as research assistants or secretaries or schoolteachers; architects and accountants and quantity surveyors could begin as clerks and be selected for professional training — a variant of the 'articling' system still practised in England. (Even the quip 'so you would start surgeons off as butchers' boys!' might not be too fantastic; one can learn a lot about anatomy in a butcher's shop, and certainly get used to the sight of blood!)

Such a change would pose very considerable problems, but consider, first, its advantages.

A cure for educated unemployment. It would, in the first place, cure the problem of secondary and tertiary educated unemployment, and the pressure on educational budgets for indefinite expansion of secondary and tertiary education which leads to the neglect of basic schooling for the masses. If there was no graduate recruitment into the professions, there would be no point in a student in India or Sri Lanka slogging relentlessly on taking O levels three times and A levels four times, putting himself through the wholly joyless and uneducational grind of a ritualistic four-year university course solely in order to qualify for an *outside chance* of a graduate job, plus, perhaps the tenuous snob value of being able to put BA after his name. The clerkships, which such people now eventually settle down to (if they are lucky), will be available to them at the age of 16. And if the structure of

144/*The Diploma Disease*

the economy is such — as it is in a good many developing countries — that only 15 per cent, say, or 30 per cent of each age group reaching the age of 16, can reasonably hope to get *any kind of wage or salaried job at all,* then the other 85 per cent or 70 per cent will know at an early age that their future livelihood must lie in self-employment, and not have their hopes unrealistically raised, only to have them finally dashed — at great emotional and financial cost.

The morale of the technical school. A second major advantage is that it would cure the much-complained-of shortage of middle-level man-power. We have seen how the vocational secondary schools are blighted by their reputation of being the dumping ground for the 'failures' who could not qualify for academic secondary schools; technicians' courses are the low-morale repositories of those who have tried and failed to get into university engineering courses. Under the alternative dispensation the stultifying stigma of failure would be removed from these courses; even the brightest, destined for higher things, would go through them; every student in them could consider himself as having the engineer's slide-rule or the specialist consultant's bioscope in his knapsack. The transformation in morale could have important consequences.

More mature students. The third major advantage is that those who get into the tertiary institutes for professional training would be more mature; they would have some knowledge of the world outside school, they would have an idea of the *use* to which the knowledge they gain might be put, they would have their own clear purposes, their own criteria of the value of learning. At present the crucial decisions which determine career choices are made in total ignorance of what those careers mean in terms of work and life-style. I know a poet — or someone quite unmistakeably of the poetic cast of mind — who became an engineer simply because he was bright enough to become an engineer and in his country, where only engineers and doctors had secure employment prospects, no boy whose maths were good enough for the science stream was ever *allowed* by parents, teachers or friends to squander his life chances by choosing arts. He, fortunately, was able to retrieve his mistake eventually and became a radical sociologist (which is the closest one can come in most modern societies to leading the poetic life while still getting paid money for it) but the world is full of 'misfits' channelled into their occupations solely by virtue of the fortuitous circumstance that their position in an achievement-test mark hierarchy corresponded with a certain point in the hierarchy of jobs, as those jobs were ranked by scarcity, income, power and prestige.

Under the early recruitment system, however, those who embark on a professional engineering training would already have had several years in industry, long enough to convince themselves — and their selectors — that they do have some aptitude and commitment to the profession.

It is not only to developing countries that this applies. Consider, for instance, the thoughts of Lord Robbins, ruefully contemplating the state of British universities after eight years of 'Robbins expansionism'.

> It would be quite unrealistic to ignore the presence, in the enlarged higher education populations, of a number of young people who are there simply because friends or parents have given them to understand that it is the right thing to do, but who yet lack the motive to exploit the opportunity once they have arrived. . . . This sort of attitude is far less frequent among students of more mature years. The post-war generations, who had a period of military service between leaving school and coming to the universities did not exhibit these characteristics. They knew why they wanted to come to institutes of higher education; and they were determined to make the most of the opportunity. The same can certainly be said of the state of mind of students who come into such institutions for evening work or who are seconded from work in industry. . . .
>
> Why should we not . . . arrange an interval between leaving school and coming to the university during which the potential student may participate in the ordinary work of the world however humble, learn what ordinary people are like, and come to know whether he (or she) has a real vocation for advanced study.
>
> The rule I propose is that there should be no grants or advances for a fixed period after school leaving. (*Financial Times,* 21 August 1971.)

Quite apart from their commitment and greater seriousness of purpose there is another reason why students in a new kind of in-career higher education would be more likely to emerge genuinely educated and trained rather than merely formally qualified. They would not be so oppressed by the incubus of examinations. If their future careers were already reasonably well assured (presumably they would be expected to achieve a satisfactory level of performance in their courses, but a level which the vast majority of those selected for them could attain without much difficulty) they would be in a very different position from the students of many Third World universities today, who know that they must be placed in the upper quartile of their class if they are to have any chance of a job at all. They would be less anxiously concerned to cram for examinations, they would have the peace of mind and openness to curiosity which would enable them to be concerned with the actual substance of what they were taught, with its intrinsic interest and validity, with its future usefulness to them in helping them to do their job better as civil servant or manager or engineer.

Greater flexibility. A further, and not the least, advantage is that the present institutionalised concept of different 'levels' of courses would disappear as new, more purposeful students and their sponsoring organisations began to have greater influence on the content and design of in-career courses. Anyone who has observed the shifting sands of pomposity in which university teachers mire themselves when they discuss whether a certain course is to be considered a 'genuinely graduate-level course', or rather is only 'of undergraduate level', will know how wholly conventional these distinctions are. Once certificates cease to matter so that educational institutes can no longer impose *their* preconceptions that learning comes in standard two-year, three-year or four-year packages called diploma or degree courses, it is likely that there will develop a variety of 'learning modules' for particular purposes, each designed to be the length it has to be and no more. Then, the lines of division between polytechnic, undergraduate and graduate courses, between 'technician's knowledge' and 'technologist's knowledge', will become distinctly blurred.

That would be an excellent thing. The way in which organisations are currently stratified into clearly demarcated status groups — clerical, executive and administrative grades; craftsmen, technicians, technologists; orderlies, paramedicals, doctors — is yet another reflection of the scourge of the certificate. It mirrors the 'levels' of the educational system, *not* any intrinsic, functionally necessary division of labour. If one started without any preconceptions at all to design the most efficient division of labour to do what the organisation has to do, one would end up, depending on the tasks of the organisation, with a great variety of pyramids if jobs were ranked according to their degree of responsibility and difficulty. Some like this

this   or like this   or like this

but very few which would fit the three-discontinuous-status-groups pattern   into which many existing organisations are moulded, thanks to the success of the educational system in propagating the notion that there are basically three kinds of people: the primary educated, the secondary educated and the graduates.

Those conventional systems are not only socially divisive, splitting organisations into groups often divided by sharp us/them status antagonisms; they can also impair the actual efficiency with which organisations fulfil the function for which they are designed, as separate status groups organise to protect their own interests. Awareness of this in developing countries is greatest today in the health field. There is a growing conscensus that much more diagnostic and prescriptive responsibility can and should be given to 'paramedics', with a variety of forms of training a good deal shorter than conventional medical degree courses — but there is very considerable resistance to this from the organised graduate doctors.

Our discussion, here, of the early-recruitment-into-work system assumes that the present grading systems would by and large continue — that there would be an 'executive grade' for which people would be chosen for promotion and training from among the clerical workers, and an administrative grade drawn from the ranks of executive officers. That simplifies the discussion and probably is a realistic assessment of what would initially happen if such a restructuring were undertaken. But eventually things would probably change to produce more flexibly varied and functionally efficient organisations — an additional long-term gain.

Early recruitment into work: possible objections

If the early-recruitment-into work system has such enormous advantage, why is it not universally adopted? Partly, of course, because our present procedures are taken to embody the accumulated wisdom of the ages so that no one thinks of alternatives. Partly because many groups in society would have strong vested interests which would be threatened by such a change. But it must be admitted that there are also a number of objections which one might make on more objective grounds of social equity and efficacy. Some of them are weighty objections, but none of them such as to outweigh its advantages. I hope that in what follows I have anticipated all the important ones.

Loss of a dynamic spin-off? The first might be that it is all too neat and tidy. There are people who still believe that educated unemployment represents one of those beneficent imbalances celebrated by such economists as Albert Hirschman, imbalances which will give dynamism to the economy by somehow making their own backward and forward linkages. If you have a steel mill, somebody will find ways of using the steel; if you invest in men, somehow the men will find ways of making use of what they have learned. While the arguments for Hirschman-like strategies of economic development are, indeed, powerful in general terms, I trust that the reader will by now be convinced that they are grossly misapplied when used in the discussion of Third World education. Education *can* be an investment, in so far as it creates certain kinds of mental attitudes and aptitudes, but the sort of mental attitudes and aptitudes created by the ritualistic qualification-oriented schooling purveyed in most Third World secondary schools and universities are more likely to blight than to foster the chances of economic and social development.

The bureaucratisation of society? A second objection could be made precisely from the point of view of social development. The scheme proposed, it might be said, assumes a corporate structure of society; it assumes that all middle-level and professional careers are made within large organisations, that, for instance, the medical profession is organised as a centrally controlled bureaucratic structure of salaried employees, or that engineers are employed in large industrial firms. If training for higher-level occupations could only be gained through the sponsorship of employing organisations, there would be no freelance professionals or independent consultants, there would be little of the flexibility necessary for dynamic economies; individuals tied to particular organisations would not have the free openness of choice which they enjoy in a society where the professional qualification or the degree is a passport to a wide range of opportunities. And to those who place great value on individual freedom and see the growth of bureaucracy as a major threat to the good society, any scheme which helped to entrench Big Organisation's grip on the social structure could well be seen as inimical to genuine social development.

One can see the point, but there are several answers to this objection. The first is that the pass is already sold. In most developing countries the modern sector which employs the products of secondary schools and universities is already highly bureaucratised — a good deal more so than the economies of the industrial countries. Typically, in Africa and Asia at least, 80 or 90 per cent of university graduates who do get employment get it in the public sector, and most of the rest in large corporations; freelance professionals are rare exceptions. Moreover, in situations of acute unemployment for graduates, genuine freedom of choice does not exist; most people are happy to take what job they can get, and are likely to cling to the organisation which offers them security; job mobility is low, except for those with special skills in scarce supply.

A second answer to that objection is that the system need not operate too inflexibly. The one basic rule which it implies is that entry into further education and training should depend on certain kinds of appropriate work experience. It might be that support out of public funds for the cost of further education and training which prepares for, or confirms, a man's promotion to a new career grade would be dependent on the sponsorship of a public sector organisation which was prepared subsequently to employ him; but although the majority of those so sponsored would probably wish to return to that organisation, they need not necessarily be bonded to do so, or at least not for any long period (though bonding to work in the country rather than join the brain-drain, as exists now in many countries for the graduates of state universities, could well be maintained). The problems of small organisations if there was no bonding (the problem of losing the one man they trained every two years, say) would be eased if large organisations budgeted for a 5 or 10 per cent loss. (The risk that they might be 10 per cent overmanned would be a small price to pay in most Third World countries where bureaucracies are already of inflated size.) Outside the public sector, since the state now, anyway, bears most of the cost of training engineers and managers from private industry, it could continue to subsidise the training of those sponsored from private industry, again on a no-bonding basis. The courses could be open to the self-employed and to the prospective inheritors of family firms if they could afford it and had the requisite ability and work experience. The supply of freelance consultants and entrepreneurs who get their start in large organisations and set up on their own account when they have acquired experience and savings need not diminish. The sort of mid-career mature-entry provisions which now exist in most civil services could be maintained and generalised to permit movement between government and industry and the academic and other professions.

Objective and subjective criteria. A third and lesser objection relates to the last. Under the proposed scheme, selection for sponsorship on further training courses by an employing organisation (with the implied guarantee of a job in a higher grade on return) would, especially if work experience were to be taken into account, be extraordinarily difficult to manage without favouritism — or, just as damaging, the suspicion of favouritism. It is difficult enough in civil service organisations, for instance, to arrange promotion decisions *within* grades without suspicion of favouritism, which is one reason why the objective criterion of seniority is allowed to play such a large part. In this case the much more important allocation of people *between* grades would be at stake and seniority would be no help in choosing among a cohort of 20-year-old executive officers those to be promoted to the administrative rank. University degree qualifications do, at present, offer some kind of relatively corruption-proof objective criterion for allocating these all-important life-chances.

The objection is a valid one, and the answer can only be that having to face and live with this difficulty is the price to be paid for the other many advantages of the scheme. One would hope, in the first instance, that some valid and acceptable means of assessing work performance or aptitude within the work organisation could be devised. But one must recognise that many developing societies are so riddled with 'personalism' and patronage that this is a forlorn hope. In that case one would have to abandon the hope of placing much emphasis on work performance in selection, and rely instead on external agencies — most obviously the educational institutions which would provide the training courses — to do the selection by aptitude tests of their own devising.

Training and Education. A fourth objection might be as follows. One can see how the system might work well enough for vocational *training*, but how about *education*? If tertiary education was merely a matter of being sent on courses to become better at doing particular jobs, who would learn Amharic, who would study philosophy?

Such a system would, indeed, sound the death-knell of those higher-education institutions like the private universities in the Philippines or some of the state colleges in India which process large masses of students through ritualistic general arts or law degrees at teacher/student ratios of 1:100, solely to give them a tenuous chance of competing for a 'graduate job'. Their passing would be no loss. But universities which offer genuine education could continue to exist. If non-vocational courses cease to offer certificates which could be used for job-getting purposes, if they only, as Lord Ashby suggested in his discussion of British education quoted at the end of Chapter 2, do 'something which was common in Scottish universities in the nineteenth century: issue class certificates to those who have attended courses and done the required written work' (Ashby, 1972, p. 8) — simply a kind of *rite-de-passage* celebration of achievement and sentimental symbol of a bond between teacher and student — or fellow-learners — and if, as a consequence, these courses were attended only by those who wish to learn rather than by those who wish to obtain a job-entitling certificate, the quality of the education given and received could be vastly improved.

If such courses were thrown open to anyone, the numbers seeking education for its own sake might be sufficiently limited for it to be possible for the state and employing organisations to allow them to take leave from their jobs at little or no financial loss. For many professions a period of such education could become conventional, even required. Civil servants in the administrative grades, for example, need not just be sent for management training courses or to learn useful economics; it could be recognised that for those who are in the kind of job which makes their sanity and human sympathy and cultured thoughtfulness vital to the health of society, it is essential that they should spend some time studying and reflecting in a university on the nature of man and society and art and work and the physical universe and the purpose of human life. There would be no reason, of course, why these educational courses — or the training courses for that matter — should be concentrated in three- or four-year blocks in the earlier stages of a career like present higher education courses. There might well be the heaviest concentration in the early twenties (when mental appetites are most vigorous, salaries are lower, and the opportunity cost of a man's time is less) but also the possibility of taking several months or a year out later, in one's thirties or forties — on the lines of the recurrent education proposals now frequently made for industrial countries.

Too costly? The possible cost of such a scheme might constitute a fifth objection. Extending the period of education, having older and more mature people in full-time training, increases the social opportunity cost in production foregone; and if those who are sent for training in their twenties and thirties are to continue to receive their salaries while being educated or trained, the direct cost will be considerable. On the other hand, there would be two very important sorts of savings which in many societies would amply offset these increases in cost. The first is the reduction in the total amount of schooling required when it no longer becomes sensible to press on to ever higher levels of general education in order to get more certificates and slight improvements in job chances. Secondly, much more learning will be done 'on the job' so that the vocational courses which systematise practical knowledge and teach the theory behind it could be shortened. Moreover, once the idea is abandoned that all higher education has to come in two- or three- or four-year packages called degree or diploma courses, and it becomes easier to take specific 'learning modules' as suggested earlier, one could stop teaching a good deal of what is now taught in professional courses only because convention requires it — because that is the way academics have come to define the fundaments of 'the discipline' for historical reasons long since forgotten. There is also the possibility that many of the vocational/professional courses could be taught on a day-release basis which would in fact probably make for a lesser cost in production foregone than block-release. Technical institutes in many countries have, of course, a great deal of experience with sandwich courses and day-release courses to estimate the relative costs and benefits of different ways of combining work and study depending on the circumstances and on what has to be learned.

The cost of waiting? Another form of cost would be increased by the scheme. It would delay a man's arrival at full professional status until later in his life. The present system produces fully-trained engineers at the age of, say, 24. The average age at which men arrive at a comparable *theoretical* level of trained sophistication under the proposed scheme might be four or five years later.

This can be a serious cost for a country which still has an acute shortage of professional manpower with large numbers of expatriates in professional positions waiting to be replaced by local graduates. In such countries one can see why a four- or five-year lengthening of the maturation process for professionals might be alarming. The recipe might not work for a Papua-New Guinea or a Malawi — where, in any case, the base for expansion of the modern sector is so small and the percentage rate of expansion required consequently so great that it would be hard to get enough people into existing work organisations at the bottom in order to learn on the job. But for an India, or a Nigeria, a Pakistan or Malaysia, or even a Kenya, for any country, in fact, with a surplus of graduates, the situation is quite different. The four- or five-year hiatus in the supply of 'fully-trained' professionals which would occur at the time of switch-over to the new system would be a small price to pay for the advantages it brings. It may not even be a price. Many countries which started their modernisation drives in the last fifteen or twenty years are faced with serious promotion problems. All the top positions in their organisations are filled with young people from the first hastily-trained cohorts of the early years of independence. In order to open up promotion chances they are being forced to introduce retirement ages of 55 or even 50. Any delay in the recruitment process might be welcomed — and it need not lead to any real shortening of the working life. By the time the new-scheme generation approaches retirement, the retiring age could easily be put forward again for five years.

Besides which, one would expect that a society which got its managers and engineers and civil service administrators to full professional status at the age of 30 through a process of varied work experience and study would have far *better* 30-year-old managers and engineers and administrators than societies which keep them encapsulated in privileged educational institutions and launch them directly into privileged organisational positions without ever giving them a chance to find out how the world looks through the eye of a riveter or a file-clerk. They would be worth waiting for.

The specially gifted. One final objection to the early-recruitment-into-work scheme must be considered. Some talents require continuous cultivation, mature early and spoil early — the highest mathematical and musical talent, for instance. For musicians and artists there would presumably be no problem, since in those fields the distinction between training and work performance is blurred anyway. Anyone who has enough competence as a violinist at the age of 16 to want to make it his life work could already find a niche as a pupil-teacher, member of a youth orchestra or whatever. But to set a gifted mathematician at a work bench doing repetitive work for the good of his soul — even to give him a job as a junior demonstrator in a university — would be to waste the nation's stock of human talent. It should not be too difficult to make special exceptions to allow the exceptionally gifted in these fields to continue in full-time study. The more problematic question is how great would be the loss if the much larger numbers of those destined to become 'ordinary' scientists and technologists spent a good deal of their late adolescence in fairly routine work. Very probably, in those cumulative branches of study like mathematics in which each new step must be built on an understanding of the step that has gone before, lengthy gaps in the continuity of study might be serious (though in the course of a *Times* correspondence about the virtues of a work break before university, the dean of a London medical school reports a clear positive correlation between first-year academic performance and *not* coming to the university straight from A levels; *The Times,* 17 December 1974). If it does turn out to involve too much wasteful re-learning, however, it should not be beyond the wit of man to deal with the problem by providing day-release continuation classes for all those jobs which could lead to professional scientific work.

Selection Tests

The second part of our modest proposal is not an essential concomitant of the early-recruitment-into-work system, but it is one which could greatly enchance its effectiveness. Society still has to select. Some of the selection will be done within work organisations, but in societies where the modern-sector work organisations that everyone wants to get into — including teaching, the jobs of salaried co-operative secretaries and village clerks — can at best absorb only 20 per cent of each age group reaching the school leaving age, how is that 20 per cent to be selected?

And also, when? There are a number of developing countries which can already reasonably hope, as Sri Lanka does, to give every child a basic nine-year education lasting up to the job-recruitment age of 15 or 16, depending on whether schooling starts at 6 or 7. In most, however, it is hardly feasible to provide truly universal primary education for more than five or six years. Given that it would be unreasonable either to delay the start of schooling much beyond the age of 6, or (given the culture gap problem, too, between the modern and traditional sectors) to make the point of job recruitment earlier than 16, or at the most 15, this suggests a two-tier system— a universal and compulsory five or six years of primary schooling, followed by a selective secondary school for three or four years with (the only realistic assumption) most of the modern sector jobs being open only to secondary graduates. This would imply a double selection process: first for entry into secondary school, and secondly for entry into jobs.

These selection procedures, I suggested, should employ, not achievement tests, but instead tests which cannot be, or cannot much be, specifically coached and crammed for. The rationale for this suggestion should be obvious to those who have followed the argument so far. If the primary schools are to develop curricula which are genuinely helpful in preparing that majority of their students who are destined to spend the rest of their lives as self-employed farmers and craftsmen and fishermen and retailers, the schools have to be liberated from the 'backwash effect' of examinations which, as we saw when discussing Sri Lanka's experiments with pre-vocational courses, effectively prevent 'relevant' curricula either from being taken seriously, or else from being genuinely relevant (rather than additional intellectualised packages of knowledge made artificially examinable for selection purposes). If entry into secondary schools and later into jobs depended on aptitude tests, and if the nature of those tests were known, and if it were known that practice in the taking of those aptitude tests improved performance if continued for, say, about ten days but not thereafter, and if every child likely to take them was provided with that ten days' steady practice, the situation would be transformed. The brighter pupils, the 30—40 per cent who seem to have realistic chances of becoming one of the 20 per cent of their age group who eventually get the desirable jobs, would not feel that they were 'wasting' every minute spent on farming or other pre-vocational studies rather than on the 'hard' and serious examination subjects; teachers would not see their own performance as measured by the number of children who 'passed' into secondary schools or got into the civil service.

Freed of these pressures, one could hope that the schools could get on with *education* — with teaching all their children basic literacy and numeracy, with teaching those things about the nation's history and the working of its institutions that all its citizens need to know, the sort of elementary psychology that parents need to know, the sort of elementary economics and general science that farmers need to know, the elementary canons of ethics and of aesthetic enjoyment that human beings need as standards of judgement. And one would hope, too, that they would teach in unstreamed classes to maximise the learning chances of the dullest pupils, to make later selection tests as fair as possible and to help to breed a sense of social equality and mutual respect as a prophylactic against the élitist arrogance which might emerge from the unavoidable later selection processes. (An obvious point, but one which has to be stressed for a British reader, given the way in which much of the British educational establishment steadfastly refuses to believe it *possible* that Japan, Russia or the US keep children unstreamed until the age of 15.)

Aptitude Tests. What should the alternative form of test be? Aptitude tests are, of course, one possibility. The category is a wide one. Those conventionally used in selection either for further education or for occupational training have traditionally concentrated on the sort of tests of mental capacities that enter into the measurement of what is conventionally called intelligence — tests of verbal and non-verbal reasoning, memory, spatial perception, etc. — together with tests of psycho-motor skills, situational tests of executive skills (the leaderless group 'country house' type used for selecting administrators in some organisations) and various kinds of tests of emotional stability, maturity, etc.

There are deep-rooted resistances to the use of tests of this kind which presume to measure, not necessarily innate, but at least relatively unalterable-by-taking-thought characteristics, and some of these — usually unspoken — sources of resistance will be considered in the final chapter. The actual arguments used against aptitude tests, however, usually question their validity and rest on the charge that they do not predict educational or occupational performance as well as, or at least (the position most opponents retreat to) any better than, tests of achievement or interviews.

From the point of view adopted here, however, that is not a strong argument. Aptitude tests recommend themselves not because they would have better predictive validity than achievement tests, but because they would liberate the schools from the backwash effects of achievement tests. Provided that they are *no worse* than achievement tests in predicting performance, nothing would be lost and a great deal would be gained. Even if they were somewhat *less* valid as predictors, the loss might be more than compensated by the gains.

In fact, however, the balance of the evidence seems to be that for many purposes, even the relatively narrow range of tests which have been generally used are quite successful as predictors of subsequent performance. The Scholastic Aptitude Tests are widely used for college admission in the United States and similar tests are being developed in Canada (Traub and Elliott, 1973). Ghiselli's extensive review of the use of occupational aptitude tests in the United States did find correlations, though rather low ones, among the people in various occupations between various kinds of proficiency ratings and performance in various kinds of aptitude tests — and somewhat higher correlations between test scores and performance in training programmes for these occupations (Ghiselli, 1966, esp. pp. 62-3). This is what one would expect, given that some 'misfits' are weeded out in the course of training — notably through bad performance in the training programme — and the people tested in occupational groups were all people who have somehow or other been selected or selected themselves for that occupation, and had, perhaps, to some degree willy-nilly 'grown into' it. There would, therefore, be much greater homogeneity in the test populations (and hence lower validity coefficients) than if one were using tests in earnest on more heterogenous populations to discriminate between those who should and those who should not be advised to enter the occupations.

Another recent review, this time specifically of the use of occupational tests in developing countries (Ord, 1972), quotes many instances of aptitude tests being successfully adopted, proving better, that is, than achievement tests in predicting subsequent scholastic performance: in secondary schools in Zambia, in the university of Papua-New Guinea, in technical training institutes in India and for a variety of technical and clerical occupations in Nigeria (ibid., pp. 139, 150, 148, 140 respectively).

There is reason to suppose, too, that if there was a serious and widespread interest in using aptitude tests in critically important ways, new tests could be developed. Aptitude tests have generally been used as the sole test criteria only for selecting manual workers; at higher levels of scholastic attainment they have usually been used only to supplement educational records — to identify those curiously-named groups, the 'under-' and 'over-achievers'. The achievement tests have, therefore, taken care of the 'effort' part of the (IQ + effort = merit) equation, and there has been little work on the measurement, for instance, of persistence and application. A symposium on the use of tests in West Africa in 1960 noted the need for tests of motivation and personality (ibid., p. 160) but little had in fact been done. Nor have there been many attempts to apply all the work of the last decade on creativity and divergent intelligence to the practice of aptitude testing.

If there *were* a major effort in these directions, so that one could with confidence take personality traits also into account, one might well expect *better* occupational selection than results from present procedures. The following opinion of a *Times* leader writer about admissions to medical schools in Britain applies *a fortiori* to those developing countries where the competition for entry into medicine is made so much more intense by the fact that it is the one profession which still offers a certain job and high income.

In too many cases the procedure is essentially one of skimming off the academic cream. Preference is given to those with the highest examination results. This has the merit of simplicity, logic and apparent fairness. The only serious objection is that it is not likely to pick out the best potential doctors. Medicine has never been a profession where success is dependent simply upon intellectual merit. Still less is it one where all that is required is the mechanical application of certain scientific skills. The practice of good medicine is going to depend even more in the future than in the past on the ability to treat the 'whole man' and to take full account of psychological and social factors. (*The Times,* 5 May 1973.)

One other potential advantage: however chimerical may be the quest for genuinely 'culture free' or even 'culture fair' tests (see e.g. Pilliner, 1973), aptitude tests, as compared with scholastic achievement tests, give more weight to innate potential than to recent learning experiences — or rather, to put it more precisely, they give more weight to the way innate potential has been developed by the cumulation of learning experiences likely to be common to the majority of children in a society (especially the less socially-stratified developing societies) than to the way it has been developed by recent classroom learning experiences which may be more highly variable. Performance is therefore less affected by the sort of privileged educational opportunities that rich children have more of than poor children and urban children in developing countries than rural children.

. . . some years ago in Ghana . . . a perusal of the results of the secondary entrance examination showed clearly, every year, that the children who had been to certain fee-paying preparatory schools, largely staffed by native speakers of English, occupied most of the first two or three hundred places and so they were sure of entry into the élite schools where they would obtain an excellent (and subsidized) secondary education. (Deakin, 1973, p. 86.)

The use of aptitude tests should, therefore, make for greater equality of educational opportunity and be more effective in mobilising all available talent. By the same token, that is one reason why they would meet with a great deal of covert resistance. Let us not forget that the people who decide what tests to use are middle-class men and women (mostly men) whose children's chances of success in the rat-race are greatly enhanced by the quality of their family upbringing and by their parents' power to buy them the best coaching for achievement examinations. Aptitude tests threaten those privileges. A careful historian might well discover that the threat to the children of the middle classes had a lot to do with pushing the British 11-plus examination steadily and rapidly away from heavy IQ weightings to much greater reliance on achievement, interviews and teachers' reports from the 1950s onwards.

Other Tests. If aptitude tests are unacceptable, or not ready in time, there are alternatives. One is to change the range and type of achievement examinations. A common solution is to examine only two subjects: mathematics and a language. Singapore, for instance, recently cut down its secondary entrance examination from the whole range of primary subjects to maths and English. It had been discovered that the other subjects added nothing to the ability of the test to predict subsequent academic performance. Maths and language tests are much harder to cram for than history or geography or social studies or general science; they test the cumulative results of learning over a longer period rather than immediate efforts to memorise. They are, in short, closer to aptitude tests (particularly if they are so devised; maths papers, for instance, which test the ability to apply mathematical concepts to problems, rather than simply to do computations). The Scholastic Aptitude Tests used in the US are, in fact, tests in maths and English; there is no clear-cut division between an aptitude test and an achievement test; only a spectrum.

The problems with this solution are obvious. History, general science, social studies are freed from the pressures which now turn them into examination packages. But will they be taught at all? Will they not be squeezed out in favour of more and more maths and language — the serious and important subjects on which life-chances will really depend? And will the quality of learning in those basic subjects not be worsened by the even more intense examination pressures concentrated on them?

One answer to that is that although one cannot police what goes on in the classroom, it *is* easier to enforce rules about the overall apportionment of class time than it is to enforce rules about *how* a history syllabus, say, should be taught. Secondly, it might not be a bad thing, at the primary level, at least, if children did concentrate heavily on 'basic' mathematical and linguistic skills. That might, at least, minimise the proportions of children who leave school after four or five years without having secured enough of these minimum preconditions for further learning to remain literate and numerate five years later. And thirdly, these basic skills *do* require a great deal of disciplined drill to make them into automatic reflexes, so that the extrinsic motivation of examination preparation might not be so damaging, particularly if other parts of the curriculum did foster curiosity, the desire to discover and learn, and the ability to solve problems — as well as providing the opportunity to use the basic numerical and linguistic skills in a creative and interesting way which justified the labour of their acquisition.

The encapsulated achievement test. If, should aptitude tests be ruled out, a maths-and-language solution may be a second best solution for primary/secondary selection, a better alternative for later occupational selection might be special 'encapsulated' learning and testing courses. An example is a recent innovation of the Ceylon Institute of Chartered Accountants which gives applicants for articling a three-week course at the end of which they are tested on what they have learned. This was an achievement test; it tested the ability to learn; it tested it in a specifically relevant field, and it had no backwash effect on the school curriculum. (Except that, of course, entrance to the test course depended on general education requirements, which have climbed in a familiar manner from five O levels to four A levels in the course of a few years.)

Could one envisage every group of occupations organising similar, say, two-week courses every year, repeating them three times in succession so that each child could apply for three occupations? This would certainly succeed in insulating the schools from the backwash effect, though there is one obvious problem. Unless the courses could be varied widely each time they were run, there would be a great deal of anticipatory preparation which some children would be better able to get than others; enterprising publishers would very soon publish exhaustive guides to vocational selection courses which promised certain success. One possible solution would be for each occupation to produce its own guide to its courses and to give all children in their final year three or four periods a week of study time to pore over their chosen three.

That still leaves considerable logistic problems of organising the courses in a limited number of centres, getting the applicants to them and making sure that the teaching at different centres is of uniform quality. Another possibility might be to have a *general* occupational selection test which could be devised to be at least no worse than the present *general* scholastic achievements tests on which occupational selectors rely. It might work as follows. One week in the year is devoted to 'examination week'. On Monday morning the children arrive to find on their desks a one-week learning package dealing with some subject which does not normally figure in the school curriculum; it might be geology or the history of architecture, or circus management, or one of those things like symbolic logic which our starry-eyed proponents of new learning systems claim can be taught to any child of 6 — anything the subject matter of which provides exercise of the powers of memory, of verbal reasoning and calculation, and preferably, also, imagination and creativity. The subject would be a different one each year, of course, and until the Monday morning a closely guarded secret. The learning package should be complete in itself and teachers would be forbidden to do anything beyond administer words of comfort and keep order (though not prevent children helping each other — except in the tests); there might be topping-up radio broadcasts. On Saturday morning there would be an examination — a test of the ability to learn, the results of which could perhaps be designed to give a profile of the child's performance in the several different dimensions which are tested. This might have the advantage over aptitude tests that it does act as a measure of effort and the ability to learn and regurgitate under stress, both of which are features of achievement examinations the predictive efficacy of which prospective employers are said to value.

School Quotas. Another possibility, for the primary/secondary selection examination at least, is the use of school quotas. Each primary school is given a quota of places it may fill. It may be the highest scorers in a national or regional competitive examination who fill that quota, or, if it is one of those rare societies where favouritism would not be a problem, the matter may be decided by teachers' recommendations or internal tests. The method was developed to a fine art in the Thorne system of the West Riding of Yorkshire, with very complex methods for comparing the marginal students from each school to ensure equivalence of standards (Anon., 1961).

The ILO employment mission to Kenya recommended that a quota system should be used for secondary entrants there, with extra quota places for schools which distinguish themselves educationally in ways other than achievement test performances (ILO, 1973, p. 246). The main advantage, of course, is that it radically reduces the propensity of teachers to concentrate on examination preparation, since they can no longer improve their record by getting more examination 'successes'. On the pupils the effect may be nasty. It makes the competition internecine; no longer can all the children in the class see themselves as competing against the children of other schools or against a pass standard; they are competing against each other. This *might* provide an additional reason for teachers to make every effort to avoid drawing attention to the examination (unless they are the sort of teachers who are more concerned to harness motives of self-interest to make their children docile and diligent than about promoting co-operativeness and good social relations among them), and at the younger ages the teachers' influence might well succeed in altering the salience of the examinations in the pupils' minds. Among older pupils who are more aware of what is at stake, however, the net effect might be only to make the competition more socially damaging without any diminution in the preoccupation with cramming. Perhaps the worst situation would occur when the quota is in the form of a percentage. In one case where it was tried, 'the response of some students was to seek out the weaker brethren and encourage them not to drop out so that the proportion of failures could be maintained' (Anderson, 1973, p. 54).

Lotteries. A final device which also deserves looking at seriously is the lottery. This would certainly meet the equity criterion (though that also means that it would hardly be welcomed by the privileged whose children would go from an odds-on to an even-odds position), but hardly the efficiency criteria. One would hesitate to chose, say, entrants into medical training by a lottery among the population at large; society *does* need to put its brightest people in some of its more crucial occupations. If, however, the early-recruitment-into-work system is adopted, and initial recruitment into work organisations is to be for a broad span of occupations, with subsequent selection for different levels within the organisation, there would be a great deal to be said for using lotteries for the initial recruitment process, particularly in large organisations.

Consider, for example, the Sri Lanka situation where probably only 10 per cent of each age group will annually be able to get a modern-sector non-manual job — the 10 per cent who, under the new dispensation, are going to be permitted to proceed to senior secondary courses, having been the 10 per cent of top scorers in the national certificate exam. If, instead, the examination were to 'pass', say, 30 per cent of the age group and allocate the opportunities to one in three of them by lot, then:

1. The competition for that selection would be much less severe, the backwash effect of the examination on the curriculum much reduced. (A large segment of the class — the brightest pace-setters — would be sufficiently confident of their prospects of getting their one-in-three chance not to worry much about it, and it would not be such a desirable prize anyway.)

2. A large number of very bright people — including two-thirds of that brightest ½ per cent of the population who come out on a properly standardised Stanford-Binet scale with an IQ of 140 and above — would be chanelled into the traditional and self-employed sectors of the economy — with what could hardly be other than beneficial effects on the lopsided modern-sector-dominated development pattern.

3. The internal selection process which sorts out, within organisations, those who are to remain as clerks and those who are to be promoted to the managerial/administrative ranks, would be easier, and the fairness of the choices made would be more obvious, if there was a wider span of ability in the initial intake.

4. There is no reason to suppose that the lower-level clerical jobs would be much less well performed if a lot of those performing them were in the 30th rather than the 10th percentile of the ability distribution (after all, in many countries they are performed by people in the 60th and 70th percentile). It should not be forgotten that, in the typical IQ distribution, the 30th percentile is only 12 points lower than the 10th — about as far as the 10th is from the 3rd. At the other end of the scale, the surviving third of the top ½ per cent of the ability distribution would amount in Sri Lanka to about 500 people a year, which should be enough to run the commanding heights of the country's economy and society.

Some people may find the idea of using a lottery for such purposes slightly shocking. But lotteries have been used in Japan and Korea for distributing children among high schools, and in Holland for deciding who can and who cannot be admitted to universities.

Prospects for reform

The effects of conventional achievement examinations on school and society are widely deplored. A recent symposium on public examinations organised by the Commonwealth Secretariat showed plenty of evidence of such a concern. Examinations are 'the tail that wags the educational dog' said an Australian (Anderson, 1973, pp. 52-4). They have, said an Indian (Chari, 1973, p. 251), 'been the all-important motivating factor in education and relegated the true purpose of education to the background'. 'We teach what is tested rather than test what is taught'; 'the school's function to educate has been superseded by the demand that it qualify' — respectively a Ghanaian (Matys, 1973, pp. 239-41) and a Ceylonese (Premadasa, 1973, p. 149).

And yet, despite the frequency of such complaints, only one of the twenty or more contributions to the symposium seriously addressed itself to the possibility of radical alternatives of the kind suggested here. Most spoke of the need for better methods of evaluation, for gearing the tests more exactly to clearly specified curriculum objectives, for more use of continual assessments, or for decentralised systems of internal school assessment.

The main reason appears to be that the discussion took place, as is usual with such discussions, solely among educators. Educators tend to see the 'outside world' as none of their concern. They deplore the use that it makes of the tests and examinations they administer, and the effect that that use has on their educational efforts, but they see little they can do about it. For them the function of achievement tests is not to apportion life-chances. That is a use the outside world makes of them. The prime function of achievement tests — the reason they seem to teachers indispensable — is their internal function as an aid to instruction.

The pedagogical need for tests

And that they *do* have these important internal functions is undeniable. Frequent informal achievement tests, even occasional grander, more ritualised, stressful tests can be useful to both teacher and pupil when they do no more than give the teacher information about how successful his teaching efforts have been, and give the pupil short-term objectives to ease his long haul up the slope towards mastery, offer him some measure of his progress from which he can take satisfaction and encouragement, or receive a salutary jolt to his complacency, whichever he most needs. But *none* of our suggestions for alternatives to publicly-certified achievement tests need rule out the internal use of achievement tests for this purpose — provided only that the results are not made public in ways that allow the 'outside world' to use them as proxy measures of a man's position in the distribution of 'general ability'.

The second 'internal' use of achievement tests is rather more difficult to accommodate — their use by central educational administrations as a means of control over standards set in the school system. Thus, the report of a committee of the Ghanaian Ministry of Education and the West African Examination Council.

> In spite of inherent weaknesses external examinations are useful and necessary in many situations. In Ghana, for instance, some common measure is needed to provide objective norms and maintain a common standard owing to great disparities in staff, in training facilities, in libraries and the supply of textbooks etc.

To which the official quoting this conclusion adds the gloss: 'The point here then, is not to weigh the advantages and disadvantages of external examinations, nor to debate how much external examinations can affect classroom practice, for such argument or debate has limited value' (Matys, 1973, p. 241).

A fine *non sequitur*. If one wants to even up the supply of textbooks, one hardly needs to conduct examinations in order to find which schools are suffering from the lack of them. There do, indeed, need to be external controls to prevent schools from slipping unobserved into general lethargy or ritualism, but that is what inspectorates are for, and if something more objective than inspectors' impressions are needed, then it is perfectly possible to arrange *ad hoc* or even regular achievement tests which measure the performance of pupils in different schools without disclosing the performance of particular individuals.

The sources of resistance to reform

It is not, basically, for these reasons that conventional publicly-certifying achievement tests continue. A more fundamental reason is because no one has the responsibility of considering, together and in their mutual relationships, both the internal and external functions of educational certification. Educators, in their cosy little symposia, consider how to improve the internal functions, given that the occupational selectors will make use of certificates in the way *they* choose; and the occupational selectors doubtless have their symposia in which they consider what they can do, given what the schools are prepared to offer them. But education is too important to be left to educators, and occupational selection to the selectors. The fact that it is nobody's duty to oversee both — the fact that the Ministry of Education and the Civil Service Commission in most governmental systems have no co-ordinating power below the Cabinet — may explain why it is left to interfering sociologists, perhaps with more *hubris* than is good for them, to insist that the situation has reached such a pass that radical reform is needed, and that the reform must have a double-thrust, changing simultaneously both the system of occupational selection *and* the use of examinations in schools.

Resistance to such reforms would, of course, be deep-seated. Examinations 'have ritual significance', induce a 'sense of cohesion and belonging' (Anderson, 1973, p. 52) in the successful; they justify the power of those who would have to take the decision to abolish them. Teachers in particular have a strong stake in the system. Apart from not wanting to be assigned the rôle of mere testers, not creators of talent, the teachers of teenagers may well feel that life would become difficult if they were deprived of the prop of the diploma objective. If such extrinsic motives to learn were removed, teachers would not be able to coast along on the tide of their pupils' career ambitions. They would actually have to *teach,* to inspire their pupils with the desire to learn, to persuade their older pupils that what they want them to know is worth knowing, that the knowledge they have to offer is something necessary for their self-respect and efficiency as adults, as citizens, or as farmers or as doctors. And that would be a threatening challenge.

Teacher quality

And this brings us finally, as did Chapter 7, to the abilities of teachers as a crucial determinant of the quality of education. Would teachers have the capacity to respond to the challenge if the whole significance of examinations were altered? Would teachers — and there are many of them in Third World countries — who have achieved a bare competence in the recital of memorisable facts have the sophistication and confidence to open their children's eyes to the world about them? One cannot feel easily optimistic; as one critic of proposals such as these has remarked, 'inferior teacher training is not something that can be quickly remedied' (Blaug, 1973, p. 67, commenting on ILO, 1971, p. 139).

Not quickly remedied, indeed, but as long as the pressures of the examination system continue to make present practices viable, and indeed mandatory, there will be no incentive to *begin* the remedy. Beeby's view, in his well-known book on the quality of education in the Third World (Beeby, 1960), is that it is a matter of time; historical processes will take their course; the less-developed countries will slowly go through the progression which has transformed the fact-reciting Squeers of Victorian England into the imaginative primary school teachers of Leicester. But that is to ignore the late-development effect — the fact that Victorian England (at least after the ending of the payment-by-results system) had none of the examination pressures which serve in the developing countries to put a *premium* on fact-memorising, and to encourage the perpetuation of teacher training methods which produce efficient drill-masters rather than teachers.

A sharp change in the learning-incentive structure could catalyse the necessary changes in the objectives of teacher training. And, one hopes, there would (in line with the general rejection of the *finality* of pre-career diplomas) be a considerble diversion of resources to the continuous education and stimulation of serving teachers, to helping them to develop their own curricula — something which would become possible if the examination system's pressure towards centralised conformity were removed. The teachers who now derive extra income as markers for the central examination boards could be given equivalent 'special responsibility pay' to take an active part in this process. (Such 'judo tricks' —Jolly, 1973— to buy off those whose bread-and-butter interests are threatened by reform would in any case be a wise move on the part of its promoters. One additional point in favour of the 'encapsulated achievement test' alternative is that it would give a continued function to the many people who now find full-time employment in central examination boards.)

In short, the problem of teacher adaptation is a formidable one, but given the process of circular causation by which bad teaching and bad examinations perpetuate each other, it is a counsel of despair to say that the examination system should not be touched until teaching has improved, for the fact is that the examination system is the earth around which the whole Ptolemaic system of schooling resolves. Given the manifold forces which constrain professional educators to continue to turn in their accustomed musical spheres, the impetus for a Copernican shift which could re-centre the system on the sun of genuine education is unlikely to come from them. It is, however, precisely through the certification system that the outside world has a point of leverage. In many countries the public sector is so over-whelmingly the major employer of schooled manpower that *the single decision* by the Civil Service Commission to do all its recruiting at the age of 16 and to use its own specially devised aptitude tests would transform the whole picture.

The proposals summarised
It might be useful, if repetitive, to summarise the proposals made here in the words of what the special report on education and employment in ECAFE *Economic Survey of Asia and the Far East,* called a 'radical structural package' of reform.

Alter the public sector recruitment patterns to do all bottom-of-the ladder recruitment at 16—18, and give every incentive to the private sector to do likewise.

Higher education beyond that age to consist of three types.
  (i) In-service training, e.g. of future administrators to study politics, economics, public administration or sociology. Such training could be recurrent throughout life and in a variety of forms, not conventional degrees.
 (ii) Training for self-employment. Non-certifiable courses in carpentry, business management, accountancy, etc. (but certifiable when there is a need to protect the public, e.g. in the case of druggists).
(iii) In-career education: again non-certifiable courses, again not conventional university degree packages of knowledge, again not confined to the beginning of a career. They would be part-time or there could be a scheme of granting leave from work for these general education courses as much as for in-service training.

Use the resources released by the consequent natural shrinkage of tertiary-level education to make primary education as universal as possible, and extend the open-access span of universal schooling as long as possible.

Decisively shift the content of primary education to make it relevant to the work life of the community in which the school is situated.

All tests which serve to ration life chances, e.g. occupational recruit-ment tests, and selection in the educational system (in societies which cannot afford to keep all children in school until the age of 16 or 17 so that there has to be selective education at the secondary level), to be something other than achievement tests to avoid distorting the school curriculum.

In all fields, an encouragement of on-the-job learning, decisively shifting the balance of the society's learning from pre-career qualification to in-career preparation for a future career which one has already chosen, and for which one has already been chosen.

Chapter 14

Reform in China — and in Tanzania

The radical structural package of reform which the last chapter outlined *is* a radical one, a step into the unknown, with profound consequences, likely to lead to much anxiety and resistance. Perhaps only a society undergoing fundamental changes in other respects is likely to be able to face such an upheaval. And perhaps that is why the first country to reform its occupational selection process on these lines was China, as it emerged from the throes of the Cultural Revolution.

Or perhaps it is just that the Chinese are always ahead in these matters. It is, at any rate, fitting that the nation which first *invented* the device of choosing its civil servants according to the results of scholastic achievement tests, and fully institutionalised the system some 1,300 years before Western nations began to copy it, should also be the first to abandon it.

Since the whole thrust of the Cultural Revolution, at least as Mao originally seems to have promoted it, lay in restoring the purity of revolutionary motives, it is not surprising that a great deal of criticism should have been directed against the way in which the scourge of the certificate was turning the secondary schools and universities into hot-houses of place-seeking ambition. This was especially true of the élite secondary schools (some thirty of them) in Peking which, as a Red Guard newspaper later claimed, 'put intellectual cultivation in the first place and the results of the examinations in command. They fanatically pursue a high rate of promotion into higher schools for their students, so that their students may climb in to the privileged class through the channel of steady promotion into higher schools' (Ch'un Lei, 1967).

That Chairman Mao should have wished to subvert this sort of education is not, perhaps, surprising. He had already tried, in 1958, at the time of the Great Leap Forward, to give the school system a decisive push away from its central function as a hierarchical grading system for channelling the 'best talent' upwards to the commanding heights of society. There had been moves to decentralise curriculum control, to emphasise local initiative and local relevance, to involve the schools closely in productive work as half-work, half-study institutions, and to change the criteria for entry to higher education institutions, partly to

168

give more weight to qualities other than just academic achievement, partly to increase the proportion of workers' and peasants' children among students (Munro, 1971, pp. 267-8, 275). In the years after the failure of the Great Leap, these trends had been reversed. In the early sixties, in fact, there was a move to establish special hot-house 'forcing schools' — 'little treasure pagodas' — in each district to accelerate the academic progress of the brightest children (ibid., p. 278).

Already in 1964, Mao had made clear his dislike of some of these trends.

There is too much studying going on and this is exceedingly harmful. There are too many subjects at present and the burden is too heavy, it puts middle-school and university students in a state of constant tension. . . . It won't do for students just to read books all day, and not to go in for cultural pursuits, physical education, and swimming, not to be able to run around, or to read things outside their courses, etc. . . . Throughout history, very few of those who came first in the imperial examination have achieved great fame. The celebrated T'ang dynasty poets Li Po and Tu Fu were neither *chin-shih* nor *han lin*. . . . Only two of the emperors of the Ming dynasty did well, T'ai-tsu and Ch'eng-tsu. One was illiterate and the other only knew a few characters. Afterwards, in contrast, in the Chai-ch'ing reign, when the intellectuals had power, the country was in disorder. . . .

Our present method of conducting examinations is a method for dealing with the enemy, not a method for dealing with the people. It is a method of surprise attack, asking oblique or strange questions. . . . It should be changed completely. I am in favour of publishing the questions in advance and letting the students study them, and answer them with the aid of books. ('Remarks at the Spring Festival', February 1964, in Schram, 1974, pp. 203-4. This was the theme of a number of Mao's speeches that year. See Chūgoku Kenkyūjo, 1968, p. 282.)

As the ideals of 1958 were revived in the Cultural Revolution, the schools naturally became not only the source of Red Guard enthusiasm but also the objects of attack. It fell to the girls of Peking's No. 1 Middle School to claim the honour of dealing the death blow to the examination system in a much-publicised letter to the Central Committee in June 1966. I quote here from the more succinct restatement of the argument in the letter from the pupils of the 4th High School which followed five days later.

With the deepening of the great socialist revolution the reactionary nature of the present college entrance examination system has been increasingly and thoroughly revealed. Its poison has spread far and its effect has been wide in scope. For many years it was used by the exploiting classes as an instrument for fooling the people and grooming successors for the ruling classes. Today, under socialism, it has become a major means of training successors for the bourgeoisie and for bringing about the revisionist restoration.

It gravely violates the class line of the Party. It does not put politics in command but school marks in command; it does not bring up proletarian successors but bourgeois successors.

It puts vocation foremost and relegates politics to the background; it encourages students to 'make one's own way', to take the road of becoming 'white experts', i.e. bourgeois specialists, of seeking personal fame, gain and position and it gravely obstructs the revolutionization of the youth.

It is a new form of the imperial examination system: it hobbles the minds of revolutionary youths, and renders them incapable of following Chairman Mao's instructions to develop morally, intellectually and physically in a lively, vigorous way. (*Peking Review,* 24 June 1966, p. 21.)

The Central Committee gave a somewhat tempid endorsement to these resounding demands (ibid., p. 3) and suspended entrance examinations pending reform. The system which gradually emerged in the years which followed by and large conformed to what these student manifestos had suggested — more blending of work and study, abolition of entrance examinations, admission to higher educational institutions, by recommendation, of those who had got 'ideological diplomas' from the workers, soldiers and peasants for their work in the three struggles — the class struggle, the struggle for production and the struggle for scientific experimentation.

The roots of reform
Thus was Chu-Hsi, the great Confucian reformer of the Sung dynasty, finally vindicated more than six centuries after his death; for criticism of the examination system in China is about as old as the system itself. The Sung philosophers were especially critical: the imperial examinations, they complained, test only powers of memory, not the power to understand or to tackle problems. Secondly, they have a deplorable effect on character. Once, in the Golden Age of the Chou period, when officials were directly recommended rather than sorted out by examinations, 'men's minds were composed and they had no distracting desires. Night and day they were diligent, fearing only lest they be wanting in virtue, and not caring whether rank and salary came their way' (Nivison, 1963, p. 99, quoted in Munro, 1971, p. 294). By the

degenerate days of Sung they studied only for personal advantage. 'Study for fame and gain' is a phrase with a long history; it echoes through the reformist manifestos and educational philosophy of Tokugawa Japan, too (Dore, 1963, p. 62), before surfacing once again in the blood-curdling manifestos of the 5th class of the 3rd senior grade of the Peking Municipal No. 4 Middle School.

But, these historical roots in long-standing educational traditions apart, it is probably significant that these reforms came at a time when China, too, was beginning to face its own educated unemployed problems. By 1966 the number of middle school pupils was nearly fifteen times as great as at the time of the revolution. Around 20 per cent of the age group were then receiving what was — at least for the two-thirds of them in the ordinary academic streams — essentially a college-preparatory education. Yet only about 5 per cent of that 20 per cent (i.e. 1 per cent of the age group) could expect to get to a university (Munro, 1971, p. 286; Schram, 1974, p. 202), and there was undoubtedly a good deal of frustration and discontent among those whose education had raised their expectations of 'rank and salary' yet found themselves 'sent down' to work in humble manual jobs in rural areas — 'a serious political problem' in the judgement of one writer (Munro, 1971, p. 289).

The post-cultural-revolution pattern
Such expectations the post-cultural-revolution schools are less likely to foster. The primary school curriculum has been shortened from six to five years; the middle school from five to four, divided into a two-year junior and a two-year senior segment — a means of reducing the burden of only marginally useful learning and hastening the day when these basic nine years of education will be available to all. Primary education is getting close to universality in the cities and spreading rapidly in the countryside; junior middle provision is not far behind, but senior middle school is as yet available only to a minority. At the middle school level, in particular, the merging of study and work is taken much more seriously. At one middle school, for example, two of the ten months of the school year are spent working in a factory or on a farm commune, and part of the other eight months are spent in the school's own factory workshop where small electric motors are built for a local factory which supplies the (obsolescent) machines and materials and provides factory workers to supervise production (Dean, 1974, p. 20). A good deal of the instructional courses, too, are directly related to the work the students are doing.

But even in the towns, not all the children can expect a future in town jobs. In Canton, seventy-seven of the seventy-nine middle schools had by 1970 established their own rural branches — centres of agricultural study where teaching is combined with farming. Teachers and students take turns in 'going down' to these rural branches, some of which can accommodate up to 400 people. Both teachers and students are instructed to learn from the 'veteran peasants' who are among the part-time teachers at the centres (Unger, 1973).

There have also been changes in the organisation of the schools. Primary schools are now run, and financed, by production brigades, and most middle schools by brigades or communes, with locally-recruited teachers paid according to the same work-point system as the farmers.

There is, in general, much more discussion and self-questioning. Above all, in the middle schools which used to be most examination-dominated,

> ... the method of examination has been changed. Questions are now set before the exam and are discussed by the students ... Open-book exams are favoured and students are encoured to do research projects for their exams ('to use books and newspapers to make social investigations'). The objective of exams is no longer the individual student's mark or grade, but to help students learn to analyse and solve problems and to internalise what they have been taught. Hence, they are encouraged to express their own opinions, to be creative, to use their initiative, and to adopt a critical attitude (Dean, 1974, p. 22).

So, too, at the universities. At the end of the course no diploma awaits the student. Certificates may be given — practice varies widely — with written comments on the student by his teachers and some of his fellow-students (Terrill, 1972).

At the end of middle school all students go from part-time work to full-time work. It is through the schools, apparently, or through the pupils' parents' work organisations that jobs are arranged. Most students, even from city areas, can expect to start their careers on the land, for Communism cannot solve the developing country's unemployment problem by finding 'modern-sector' jobs for everybody any more than capitalism can. It just tries to make the modern sector less relatively privileged and attractive, though *how* much less attractive is still problematical; the job of a factory worker is much prized. Some of the youths will eventually get to factories after their stint in rural areas, though only the youngest child of a city family is likely to get such a job on leaving school; parents have a strong claim to having one of their children live close by to look after them in their old age.

The result seems to be a system of education which has been successfully integrated into the world of work.

The rural child's expectation, from the very start of his education is that he will remain within his community as an adult, and he therefore must perceive his education in terms of its contribution to his future rural life. For example, a Honan agricultural middle school writes that 'all students come from and return to the production teams'. Because the purpose is utilitarian, age does not matter, and some peasants in their 50s study alongside the younger students, acquiring specialised technical knowledge such as fruit-tree grafting, farm machinery techniques, etc. In this informal middle school 'short-term classes are not restricted by the schooling system. Students are sent to the school or taken back to their production teams whenever this is dictated by the needs of . . . production. Take an example. K'ueishi No. 7 production team required the services of a bookkeeper, and the school let a student graduate in advance and return to his production team to be a bookkeeper.' (*Hung Ch'i,* July 1970.) The reward for study is a worthwhile and respected role in the home village.

The effort to integrate work with study begins at the earliest years. Young first graders in the countryside carry baskets to and from school in which to collect whatever manure they might chance upon. Songs are sung in class glorifying work and labourers. The discontinuity between school and society, between aspirations and reality, is greatly reduced if not eliminated by gearing the schools toward the localities and toward a working life. (Unger, 1973.)

Recruiting the future élite

The chance of further education does not come until after two years' work — and depends on recommendation from the committee of one's work organisation. Some of the sponsored candidates are sent to learn things relevant to their work organisation's needs — the commune boys sent to teacher training colleges to train as a teacher for their commune school, for instance, or the technicians sent by a factory to an engineering college in the expectation that they will bring their skills back to the factory. Communes and factories are, apparently, given quotas of places at such institutions. Other students — and it is not clear if the same quota system applies here — are sent, on the sponsorship of their commune or factory, to study more general science or social science or humanities courses with more open-ended prospects; they will presumably become the cadres and members of the specialised professional services at the urban centres.

But who is likely to be selected? The boy, in the first place, who has used his middle-school experience to get practical skills and has got into a work organisation which is likely to require higher-level skills. Once in he will try to get the reputation of a good worker, quick to acquire new skills and to use his school knowledge, co-operative, a 'good sort'. Then he can apply. The committee prepares a shortlist, which is presented to a mass meeting for approval. Those on the shortlist are then seen by the university or college's touring selection team (perhaps in the provincial capital if it is a national university) which inquires into both their academic and political suitability.

What one would dearly love to know, and what visitors to China find it hard to get information on, is *how* the system works in detail; whether applications are prompted; how the local committees chose their shortlist when there are large numbers of applicants. They are supposed to take account of class origins — and there *are* reports that peasants' and workers' children made up 95 per cent of the students at Peking University, compared with 67 per cent in 1962 and 48 per cent in 1958 (Munro, 1969, p. 274). They are supposed to take account, too, of political commitment and character as well as aptitude for study.

And yet, and yet. . . . Surely there must be strong pressures to favour the chairman's son, strong undercurrents of resentfulness at the choices made? Almost certainly there are. In the second half of February 1974 the press was full of reports of conscience-stricken youngsters renouncing their places at universities and colleges because they had got in 'by the back door'. But it is significant that they were (though under what personal pressure one cannot know), conscience-stricken. The ideological indoctrination in the schools must have some effect in dampening personal ambition, and in building up moral pressures on local committees to act fairly. Very great emphasis, as one visitor to Chinese schools remarked, is given to

. . . selflessness and service. The heroes of stories, posters and text-books put the group ahead of their own interests; the only approved individualism is apparently the individualism of self-sacrifice. Even in the everyday world, evidence of personal success is muted. The slogan 'Friendship first competition second' is heard from Chinese of all ages (Kessen, 1974, p. 44).

One possible method of avoiding favouritism — the overt use of IQ or aptitude tests — is almost certainly ruled out. The very ideology of egalitarian group activity would forbid a system which utilised, drew attention to — even admitted to exist — significant differences of innate ability between individuals.

We spoke to one of our hosts about the absence of research on children, in comparison to the apparently sizeable investment in agricultural research. He replied, 'But we carry out research on plants because they are different; it is important for us to believe that children are all the same.' (ibid., p. 43.)

There is not a little sophistication in this view of society's need for useful fictions, but the teachers at higher education institutions who have to cope with the consequences may not think so. The abolition of standard entrance examinations has meant that students come to their courses with widely varying levels of preparation. When this first happened as the universities were re-opened in 1970 and 1971, teachers responded by trying to give remedial instruction in basic theory to the weaker members of their classes. It is symptomatic, perhaps, of the heady atmosphere which still prevailed in some institutions that they were soon denounced by the student body as unreconstructed revisionists still continuing their old practices of 'élitist education' and 'valuing theory above all'. Eventually it was acknowledged that there was a difference between the old 'valuing theory above all' which sought merely to perpetuate the hegemony of bourgeois culture isolated from the genuine revolutionary struggle, and on the other hand recognising the true importance of 'theory which was born out of practice and could be used to guide to better practice' (Chūgoku Kenkyūjo, 1971, p. 130). Such remedial and preparatory courses have become standard in many institutions — the Chungshan Medical College in Canton, for instance, has a regular six-month pre-enrolment course in basic chemistry and physics (Dean, 1974, p. 24) — but clearly they involve costs and some institutions have tried to re-impose selection examinations. A national argument was started in 1973 by a letter from a student on a Manchurian farm who complained that he was too busy getting in the harvest to spend enough time with his middle school notes cramming for the examinations. Clearly the admissions practices of the various institutions vary widely; a good number have formally instituted achievement-type selection tests; one imagines that there must be some which have devised their own informal aptitude tests, even if they are not acknowledged as such, and there is still a great deal of flux and experimentation. The principle that the educational institution has control over the selection process does, however, seem to be generally accepted.

How far, in the process of normalisation, some of the old practices have crept back, how far the current anti-Confucius campaign has altered matters, remains obscure. It does seem though that, unlike the more tentative reforms of the 1958-9 period, the educational system during the cultural revolution changed in a way that makes it seem likely to stay changed. The legitimacy, the social fairness, of the new pattern seems widely accepted. It may have efficiency costs — as was certainly believed by those who 'took the capitalist road' in the early sixties and undid the 1958-9 reforms, arguing that it was necessary to mobilise the nation's best intellectual talent (even if it did come from bourgeois families) in order to maximise the expertness of the 'red and expert' modern-sector élite. It will almost certainly, on the other hand, have efficiency gains in increasing the schools' contribution to, and improving the chances of economic growth in, traditional agriculture and the small-scale agro-based industrial sector growing within the rural commune structure. The educational reforms are both part of and a reflection of the Chinese strategy of moving forward by 'walking on two legs'. Their success or failure will be measured by the success or failure of the strategy as a whole.

Stop Press: Tanzania

As this chapter was being written, the *Daily News* of Dar es Salaam carried the following report of a decision by the National Executive Committee of TANU, the Tanzanian Government Party.

The National Executive Committee directed the Government to make all requisite arrangements to ensure that all school-age children in the country get places in primary schools beginning the school year 1977.

The NEC decision brings universal primary education to Tanzanians twelve years ahead of the 1989 target which had been set earlier.

After two days of deliberations, the Committee also directed that the University should no longer continue with direct intake system.

All students completing their secondary school education will be absorbed into the various walks of life including industry, office and village work.

On the basis of their performance in their places of work and depending on the requirements of the place or village, the Party branch in that area will recommend the worker or the peasant to be admitted to the University to acquire the skills required for the job he or she is doing.

The Party also called for far-reaching reorientation in education, including the watering down of the importance now attached to the final paper examinations.

A pupil's overall performance in all the fields in school throughout the duration he or she is in school will be the determining factor. All schools must engage in production which will result in their being fully self-reliant. (*Daily News,* 17 November 1974.)

Chapter 15

Afterthoughts: Equality and Diversity

Implicit in the modest proposals of Chapter 13 and in the actual reforms of the education system in China are some pretty fundamental assumptions about the nature of social life and about the range of human motivation which can be mobilised for collective purposes. For my part, I must confess that I share, as the reader will probably have guessed, a good deal of Chairman Mao's romantic Confucianism. Let me explain what I mean.

Some basic assumptions

In the first place, I believe that a love of learning is a noble thing, that curiosity is one of the best of human instincts, and that so also are what one might call productiveness, creativeness and craftsmanship — the urge and the ability to make two blades of grass grow where only one grew before, to write a novel, to harness the energy of a mountain stream, to solve a mathematical puzzle, or to raise the efficiency of a heat engine or a banking system by five per cent. I admire, in other words, a group of qualities for which a cultivated intelligence is a precondition.

One reason why I think these qualities desirable is because I believe they help to make societies richer. A difference in the diffusion of these qualities seems to me to go a long way towards explaining the difference in development patterns between, say, a Singapore and an Indonesia, or between a Punjab and a Bihar. And since poverty is a great inhibitor of human happiness, the cultivation and exercise of these qualities is correspondingly important.

But also, I admire these qualities for their own sake; they are virtues. And because they are virtues, they should be their own reward. I stress that because I think it necessary to distinguish between this particular set of intelligence-linked qualities: curiosity and creativeness and productiveness and craftsmanship — qualities expressed in self-fulfilling activities; and, on the other hand, other 'instrumental' qualities which are equally dependent on intelligence, like cunning and the ability to manipulate things and other people in order to acquire for oneself wealth or power or prestige. Let us, for the purposes of the subsequent discussion, label these two bundles of qualities — or manifestations of intelligence — respectively by the unashamedly moralistic terms 'productive self-fulfilment' and 'acquisitive achievement'. For me this is a crucial distinction, very largely glossed over in the literature on 'achievement motivation' (see e.g. McClelland, 1961).

So much for one of my value premises. Before I go on to others, let me set out a number of factual beliefs concerning the same phenomenon, 'intelligence'. I believe that in most populations intelligence — the potentiality for both productive self-fulfilment and acquisitive achievement — is rather unequally distributed. Some people are bright; others are not so bright. Like musical talent, or imagination or patience or perseverence, the capacity to reason and to remember and to perceive is not shared equally among men and women. In most populations the differences in endowment among the seventy or eighty per cent of the population who have something close to an average share of these qualities are not so marked that social arrangements need to be much affected by those differences. But the difference between the most well-endowed 2 or 3, or even 5, per cent and those who are below average in their endowment of intelligence is a good deal greater, and it makes a big difference to a society's efficiency, and power to grow in productiveness, and to its ability to live in relative harmony, if it is the former who empty the society's dustbins and the latter who take all the big decisions, or vice versa. (This last belief is nowadays called 'élitism' and is widely considered wicked.)

On the vexed question of how much a person's endowment of intelligence — around the age of 16, say, when the crucial choices about his work career are likely to be taken — depends on his genes or on his family and social environment I have no firm views. The controversy is passionate, the evidence not entirely consistent, and the mathematics involved in aggregating it very complex.[1] Nevertheless, as far as an outsider can judge, the weight of the evidence seems to support those who argue that heredity plays the dominant part. The most thorough-going reforms — even the elimination of the family and the rearing of all children in identical environments — would still leave a range of variation in abilities of substantial proportions (a variance in IQ scores, for instance, well over half that currently found in the British or American populations). It would still matter who became the station porters and who the traffic controllers on the railways.

[1] See, e.g. Herrnstein (1973), p. 117; Jencks (1972), Appx. A; Bodmer (1972), pp. 98-9; Jensen (1973), Appx.; Mittler (1971), Appx. B; Wiseman (1967), Part 5. Less informative but illustrative of some of the issues and most of the passions involved are: the papers by Rex, Swift, and Daniels and Houghton in Richardson and Spears (1972); Tort (1974); Merllié (1975); Muel (1975).

But the question in what proportions heredity and environment are responsible for determining whether intelligence is used for productive self-fulfilment or acquisitive achievement is a very different question. From the finding that personality variables have much lower heritability coefficients than mental ability variables (Mittler, 1971, p. 109) one can infer:

(a) that the extent to which this 'directionality' of intelligence is determined at birth is very small; environment is much more important;

(b) that school *can be* as important a determinant as the family, depending on all sorts of variables, but chiefly on the relative time spent in each environment and the explicitness of the character-moulding efforts in each (see p. 11 for the view that qualification-oriented schooling is bad precisely because it conduces to acquisitive self-regarding achievement, rather than to productive self-fulfilment);

(c) but that the possibility of changing this 'directionality' by environmental influences begins to diminish rapidly in the mid-teens. It is not likely to be much use, in other words, providing a genuinely mind-expanding and stimulating university education to people who have been conditioned by the previous twelve years of their schooling to learn only in order to earn.

Social development and the distribution of intelligence

So much, then, for some of the assumptions on which this discussion will be based. Now for a second batch of propositions concerning the way in which the distribution of intelligence is likely to vary in different types of society.

The first and rather obvious point is that the more technologically sophisticated the society and the greater the spread of education, the more visible the differences in men's capacities become. Differences in musical talent or in calculating ability are much less noticeable in those simpler societies where the only instrument is the human voice and the only use of numbers is to count sheep, than in a society run on computers and multivariate decision-models.

And concomitantly the more technologically complex a society becomes, the more its survival depends on getting its most talented members into the most intelligence-demanding jobs. And this has consequences for the status order and its legitimacy.

The division of labour in every society, as was long ago pointed out by Mencius, one of the best of Confucianists, automatically implies differences of power and prestige. Differences in the distribution of any kind of valued good, whether it is prestige or wealth or wives need to be made legitimate in some way or other if the society is to be stable (and that means that those who have most to lose are likely deliberately to seek some justifying rationale for their bigger shares in order not to lose them).

They do not have to try very hard — the legitimation takes place semi-automatically — when the unequally distributed qualities which are in fact most intrinsically admired in the society are those that get one to the top. If the society admires above all courage and aggressiveness, and the rules of the game permit the most ruthless baron to win, he may well keep his power without it being tested too often by challengers. A society which admires above all mystical poetical talents and heaps power and riches on its druidical bards may be equally stable.

The problem comes from the family. Once a status order gets itself established, men in the top ranks try to pass them on to their children; status becomes hereditary. That increases the legitimation problem because the baron's son may not be manly and courageous and a leader of men, nor need the bard's son turn out to have much poetic talent or mystical sensibility.

There are ways in which inegalitarian hereditary status societies can be kept stable, however. Pomp and circumstance can cover a lot of deficiencies in performance. Such divinity can be made to hedge a king that common people can touch the hem of his garment without ever noticing his feet of clay.

A second way of dealing with the problem is by education. The lower classes may contain many men of potentially superior talents, but if you confine the opportunity to learn Latin tags to those of high birth, you can effectively choke off any danger of upstarts developing pretensions to become statesmen. If the ploughmen's sons never have a chance to learn the mysteries of metre, they can reach their country churchyard graves mute and inglorious without ever knowing they have been cheated. And if at the same time you send merchants' sons to schools which teach them to be better merchants, and peasants' children to schools which teach them to be better — more diligent, loyal and obedient — peasants, the problem of stability is a long way towards solution.

That is what schools and universities used to be chiefly for in the traditional societies of Europe and East Asia. But as those societies began to industrialise, things had to change. New occupations requiring new knowledge were constantly being created. In a less routine, constantly changing society, government and administration required more new decisions in new situations. Inefficiency became more glaring: knowledge requirements escalated beyond the capacity of the less well-endowed of the hereditary upper classes to make themselves minimally competent. Class barriers became more fluid: first because lowly people found ways of making more money than those who had simply inherited their top positions, later because some of them who were well-endowed with native talent acquired knowledge and skills which gave them an undeniable claim to middle and top positions in society. Nations in competition with each other began to accelerate this process because their governments saw a need to 'mobilise the nation's talents'.

And these social changes led, simultaneously, through processes which remained mysterious even to those like Tocqueville who most ably charted the trend, to a growing egalitarianism — a growing tendency to question and to resent any inequality of power and prestige and wealth which was not justified by obvious differences in personal qualities or social functions.

Modern industrial societies, then, and societies which are seeking to become modern and industrial, have to do a difficult balancing act: somehow they have to reconcile three not easily compatible requirements:

(i) the need to get the most able people into the most demanding jobs, entailing (a) the need to identify those people and (b) the need to motivate them to train themselves for and do those jobs;
(ii) the demands of egalitarianism;
(iii) the unavoidable limitation on one form of equality, namely, that those who fill the more demanding jobs which entail the taking of decisions are bound to have a larger share of one valued good, namely, 'power' and also of the prestige which goes with power.

Sociologists are usually talking figuratively when they say 'society must ensure . . .', 'society must reconcile . . .', and they often get themselves a bad name by talking as if they assumed some kind of collective will whose existence they would hastily refute when challenged. But here we *are* talking of matters which are increasingly subject to collective decision. As market forces grow more attenuated in industrial societies — or fail to appear in developing ones — as the establishment of incomes policies comes to seem more and more like the inexorable logic of history, the balance between these three forces appears increasingly as a matter for central fought-over political decision. How should the decision go?

The sinful world and the Confucian utopia
Essentially, if one likes, the problem is to find an acceptable 're-definition of equality' — what Bell calls, surely rightly, 'the central value problem of the post-industrial society' (Bell, 1974, p. 425). It will help to clarify the discussion greatly to counterpose two alternative ideal-typical patterns, two methods of achieving resolution of these conflicting requirements. The first, the sinful world method, is roughly our present social system based on assumptions of Original Sin. The

second, the romantic confucian utopian method, is based on assumptions of Original Virtue.

The basic elements of the first, the sinful world system are:

(i) social selection partly through work performance but increasingly through tests of achievement in school;

(ii) the linking of other rewards with power so that by and large those who are in the most intelligence-demanding jobs also have more income and prestige as well as more power than others;

(iii) motivating people to compete for the top jobs by these differential distributions of wealth and prestige as well as power — hence directing intelligence towards acquisitive achievement rather than productive self-fulfilment;

(iv) meeting the demands of egalitarianism: first by making the opportunities to compete in the race for the top as equal as possible, secondly by justifying the superior rewards of the 'successful' by criteria which, while remaining ambiguous, place great emphasis on the effort they make to pass the selection hurdles ('. . . on the professional level at least, hard work is a necessary condition for success, and . . . if a rough equality of opportunity has allowed one man to go further than another, he has *earned* the unequal reward — income, status, authority — which goes with that success'; ibid., pp. 432-3), thirdly, by gradually reducing the role of inherited wealth and unearned income in shaping the income distribution, and fourthly — a precondition for the other egalitarian trends — by various forms of democratic control which institutionalise the concept of citizens' 'equality of condition' in the political and also in the industrial sphere and do subject the decision-makers, albeit in a roundabout way, to some control from the people whose lives their decisions affect.

By contrast the elements of the utopian system are:

(i) selection just as much through work performance, but in so far as that is insufficient (as in the initial distribution of career opportunities), by means like aptitude tests which explicitly recognise unequal endowments in intelligence and other desirable qualities as being, if not entirely inborn, at least ineluctable by the mid-teens when these initial processes of selection take place — which recognise, that is to say, that such relative differences are not much alterable by effort in short-term training courses, swotting for examinations, etc.;

(ii) the divorce of the rewards of power from other rewards — of wealth and prestige;

(iii) motivating people to take the difficult jobs by creating a social atmosphere in which the successful performance of these jobs is seen as its own reward, a social atmosphere which thereby channels intelligence into productive self-fulfilment and the performance of social duty rather than into self-regarding achievement;

(iv) meeting the demands of egalitarianism first in the way that other kinds of lottery meet it — by stressing the luck element in the distribution of talents, secondly and thirdly by the same elimination of inherited wealth and mechanisms of democratic control as in the 'sinful world' and fourthly, and most distinctively, by deliberately not allowing the distributions of power and prestige and wealth to coincide; by paying the dustmen more than professors or civil servants. This follows naturally from stressing the luck element in the distribution of talents. As Rawls points out: 'No-one *deserves* his greater natural capacity nor *merits* a more favourable starting place in society' (my italics) and consequently the social system should ensure 'that no-one gains or loses from his arbitrary place in the distribution of natural talents or his initial position in society without giving or receiving compensating advantages in return' (Rawls, 1971, p. 102). As Harry Johnson, whom few would suspect of being a romantic Confucian, once put it rather more directly: 'if poverty and inequality are considered problems, one should recognize that the poorest among us, and the one most deserving of help from his fellow men, is the one whom nature forgot to endow with brains — and that the way to make it up to him is . . . to give him money in lieu of the brains he lacks' (Johnson, 1972, p. 289).

If the main universal driving force of the first kind of society is self-interest, the second seeks to mobilise, among those who have the most important social tasks at least, a different motive force — one which may be described as a modern and somewhat more modest version of *noblesse oblige,* or of the Confucian virtue awkwardly translated by the terms 'Goodness' or 'Benevolence'. It is not, however, the luck of being born in certain status positions which is thought to entail obligations, but the luck of being born with the right package of genes and the sort of stimulating family background which enables one to make the most of them. Those who reach top positions are not encouraged to claim privileges on the grounds that they *deserve* them, that they have earned them by their efforts; they should, rather, feel humbly grateful that fate has 'called' them to interesting and worthwhile jobs.

There are several reasons why I would prefer the second to the first kind of society. In the first place it follows from what I have said already about admiring 'productive self-fulfilment' as opposed to 'acquisitive achievement'. A society in which people try to do a job well because they would not be satisfied with themselves if they did it badly seems to me likely to be a better society than one in which people work only for extrinsic rewards. We generally recognise this at the extreme by our horror stories of the American doctors who check up on a patient's financial means before they will consent to do emergency operations, and yet most of our social arrangements are based on the assumption that it is only the incentives of money or power or prestige which can make people use their talents for the benefit of society.

Secondly, a society based on these principles is likely to have a school system which provides a genuine education rather than a competitive exercise in qualification hurdle-jumping — and that seems to me in itself a mark of a good society, quite apart from its ramifying consequences.

Thirdly, it seems to me a more just sort of society. I have confessed my admiration for certain qualities linked with intelligence. But I also admire the qualities of compassion which make patient and loving social workers and teachers of backward children, the creativity of the artist and the musician, the conscientiousness and craftsmanship of those who do simple jobs well, the courage of the soldier or of the pacifist defending his minority conviction against a hostile society. It does not seem that the pattern of monetary rewards which prevails in most societies corresponds to any acceptable criterion of fairness. The jobs which are counted as most important and are the best paid are also, for the most part, the most interesting jobs, the jobs which offer the greatest opportunity for self-fulfilment. Why should people who were lucky enough in the lottery of talents and opportunities to get the most interesting jobs — a lot of which also by their very nature give them a good deal of power — also expect, in addition, to have riches added unto them?

And fourthly, both because such a society would do less to cultivate selfishness, and because the variety of valued rewards would be distributed more equally, it would I think (though there are contrary considerations: see below) have a greater chance of achieving the third of the French revolution's ideals, fraternity. It should be a more co-operative and less divided society, while permitting, because it explicitly recognises the diversity of human endowments, that diversity of tastes and life-styles which the opponents of egalitarianism (in all the debates about comprehensive schooling, for example) claim would be sacrificed by any concessions to its advocates.

How viable the sinful world?

All these moral evaluations apart, it can reasonably be argued that we shall be forced into adopting social arrangements of the Confucian utopian type because the alternative — our present conventional system of allocating jobs and motivating and rewarding work — is becoming increasingly unworkable as a result of three, seemingly inexorable forces in modern industrial societies: corporatism, increasing affluence and egalitarianism.

Let us first take corporatism, by which I mean a structural trend rather than an ideology, and a trend towards what Harris (1972) would call pluralistic rather than etatist corporatism — the increasing tendency for both economy and polity to be shaped by the bargains struck by powerful corporate groups rather than by the cumulative weight of the decisions of individuals in market places and polling booths. Perhaps the older name for the process, bureaucratisation, is still a better choice.

The assumption of the classical political economists and of their neo-classical successors has always been that the social good is well served by encouraging acquisitive achievement; through the invisible hand of the market the self-seeking efforts of the individual are directed to the common good, and the greater the productive achievement of the individual, the greater both his reward and his contribution to the welfare of society. This discipline of the market still works for the hairdresser and small restaurant owner; perhaps, indirectly, on those who work in business firms producing for a competitive market. But an increasingly high proportion of jobs in modern society are not subject to such discipline. More and more people work in government services, in education, in nationalised medicine, and in large, bureaucratically organised, oligopolistic business firms.

There can be, of course, equivalent mechanisms within such organisations which harness individualistic self-seeking to the purposes of the organisation — systems of material incentives and disincentives. The search for 'systems so perfect that nobody needs to be good' has been endless: from the Legalist opponents of the Confucians in classical China who prized Law, not Morality (Waley, 1956, p. 155) to those who wished to 'take the capitalist road' in opposition to Chairman Mao; from the Taylorite scientific managers to the Soviet designers of material incentive schemes and the McKinsey management doctrine of accountable profit centres. But ultimately the effectiveness of such systems depends on somebody genuinely caring. There must be enough people within the organisation who are 'good', who can work for productive self-fulfilment or a sense of duty rather than acquisitive self-regarding achievement. Otherwise, the rules of the incentive schemes will be stretched; 'goal displacement' will turn the organisation into a mere conspiracy for pursuing the individual short-term interests of its members. The best civil services exist in countries where these conscientious and responsible attitudes towards work are more prevalent, not in countries where the incentive systems are designed with the most meticulous ingenuity. They, by and large, are the countries of Europe and of the Confucian cultural sphere where the older educational traditions which value knowledge for its own sake or for its practical use still have some strength and still uphold the ideals of work for productive self-fulfilment.

But the paradox of the process of bureaucratisation is this: the very trend towards bureaucracy which, by weakening the discipline of the market, makes these 'inner-directed' attitudes an increasingly necessary pre-condition for social efficiency, increases also the importance of school qualifications, turns the schools imperceptibly away from genuine education and towards qualification-getting ritualism, orients men more and more towards the self-regarding pursuit of place (towards gaining the certificates necessary to *get* jobs rather than the knowledge necessary to *do* them) and thus breeds men more and more for acquisitive self-regarding achievement rather than for productive self-fulfilment. And, as Chapter 6 argued, the developing countries whose poverty gives them the greatest need for efficient and devoted civil servants and managers are for a variety of reasons already farther along this road; their schools even more wholly dedicated to qualification-getting, their civil services and state corporations even more likely to be staffed by self-regarding achievers, enjoying their prebendal rights at the ·expense of the community without much trouble from their consciences.

If corporatism has significance for the work motivation chiefly of managers and professionals, the second trend, greater affluence, affects the work motivation of the larger mass of those in subordinate routine jobs. Greater affluence, combined with the growth in egalitarianism and state collectivism, leads to the establishment of full employment policies and welfare minima; the fear of the sack, of poverty and hunger, loses its effectiveness as a means of evoking effort. So, too, do positive material incentives when they mean the difference between getting one's new television set this year or next, not whether one has a joint of beef at the weekend or makes do with bread and dripping. In consequence, a much larger proportion of the working force moves up the scale of Maslow's hierarchy of needs, and can afford to concern itself with the intrinsic satisfactions of its work, with respect and belongingness and opportunity for self-fulfilment. The attempts in automobile factories in Sweden and America to respond to these new needs, by redesigning assembly lines, by sacrificing Tayloristic efficiency in order to give men greater opportunities to get satisfaction out of the job itself, are straws in the wind, indications that the assumption that a society can run simply on acquisitive self-regarding achievement can no longer be accepted.

And egalitarianism, thirdly, attacks both the structure of differential rewards which the system was always thought to require, and the authority structure which goes with it. The explanation of the growth of egalitarianism is difficult. Bouglé was probably on the right track (Bouglé, 1901) when he saw it as the consequence of the increased differentiation of social organisation and social rôles, and the growing diversity of status rankings in modern societies as compared with more monolithic ranking systems in traditional societies which are better able to enforce and legitimate the overall divisions between rulers and ruled. But whatever the explanation the trend itself is hard to deny. Even if one would hesitate to join Tocqueville in seeing it as 'an unquestionable sign of God's will' (Tocqueville, 1954, p. 7), it is hard to challenge his thesis of its inexorable 'fated' nature. Can it be wise, he asked, 'to imagine that a social movement the causes of which lie so far back can be checked by the efforts of one generation, can it be believed that the democracy which has overthrown the feudal system and vanquished kings will retreat before tradesmen and capitalists?' (ibid., p. 6). Or, indeed, one might add, before the high-salaried meritocrats?

In this century, indeed, as egalitarianism has gathered strength, with the guilty egalitarianism of those-who-have increasingly helping to swell the tide of the envious egalitarianism of those-who-have-not, its attack has shifted from the 'capitalists', from concentration on the inequalities of wealth, to other forms of inequality once accepted without question. As an increasing proportion of personal income is neither unearned income nor profit, and differentials in wages and salaries become an increasingly important source of income inequalities, the demand has grown for the compression of these differentials, a demand which organised labour is increasingly capable of enforcing. How far this trend has gone is a matter of much dispute; how far it will go is problematical, but the long-term trend runs fairly clear. And there are even good grounds for expecting it to accelerate.

As disparities have increased, as democracy has become more tangible, the expectations of equality have increased even faster, and people make more invidious comparisons ('people may suffer less but their sensibility is exacerbated'), a phenomenon now commonly known as the 'Tocqueville effect'. The revolution of rising expectations is also the revolution in rising *ressentiment* (Bell, 1974, p. 451).

The important implication for the sinful world is this: as earned-income differentials narrow, the material incentives which are supposed to motivate people to train for and to perform the more difficult jobs which require higher levels of intelligence and other scarce qualities have become, and are likely to become, less effective; acquisitive self-regarding achievement is just not likely to work any more as an effective motivator in the way that it used to.

Another part of the egalitarian trend is the increasing unwillingness to accept authority without question. If one compares the Britain of 1975 with the Britain of 1925, in all spheres of society — in industry, in politics, in the army, in universities and schools, in the family — the weight of authority carried by those in superior status positions has weakened; automatic obedience can less often be expected (and, of course, the change in the training institutions, family and school, reinforces the change in other spheres). Management in industry is forced increasingly to shift from modes of divine right management to constitutional management. Those in positions of authority must increasingly explain and consult, if their decisions are to command the consent of their subordinates. That consent is harder to obtain when there is a general assumption that the dominant motive for work is acquisitive self-regarding achievement; however much the manager demonstrates his superior technical competence, the suspicion is likely to remain that the decision is tailored to his own personal ends, not to the shared goals of the organisation. Only where there is a general assumption that those with the interesting and responsible jobs do in fact have a responsible attitude, are keen to 'do a good job' as an end in itself, is it likely to be possible to create what Fox has recently called a 'high-trust' situation (Fox, 1974), in which demonstrated technical competence is accepted on its merits and the decisions of those who have that competence treated without great suspicion.

Two Other Utopianisms

There are *some* reasons, then, for thinking that the romantic Confucian utopia is not, or will prove in the future not to be, too unrealistic. It can at least lay claim to a greater realism than two other forms of romantic utopianism which have more widespread currency.

The first is the post-industrial paradise romanticism, the belief that somehow or other 'the production problem will be solved'. We shall all opt for zero growth; R&D will cease; the machines will churn out abundance; everyone can practise self-fulfilment *without regard to* any social requirements for keeping the system ticking over; government, education, heart surgery can all be reduced to a matter of routine chores, the burden of which can be shared out more or less equally and at random. The need invidiously to rank and select people, to match talents to social functions, will disappear. We shall be able, as Marx predicted in the *German Ideology,* 'to hunt in the morning, fish in the afternoon, rear cattle in the evening, criticise after dinner, in accordance with . . . inclination, without ever becoming hunter, fisherman, shepherd or critic'.

This vision is reflected in UNESCO's *Learning To Be,* the great educational manifesto which was supposed to help mankind gird up its loins and march head high into the twenty-first century. After deploring in terms which one can only applaud the educational and social evils of meritocratic methods of dividing superior sheep and inferior goats, it goes on: 'It remains true that it is usually in society's interest to select its most capable members for performing difficult or responsible tasks', and this principle, it grants, is most valid in the developing countries with the most 'urgent needs for trained executives in the economy and administration'; nevertheless 'this narrow conception of human capacities and of the relationship between the individual and society can, must — and, at any rate will — be superceded' (Faure, 1972, p. 76).

Can, must and *will;* it is a strong prediction. The economic structure of this future ideal society remains, alas, unexplained.

The second kind of romanticism is today much more common — that particular form of egalitarian romanticism which denies the importance of inborn human differences. Again, *Learning To Be* proposing its solution for the examination rat-race — recurrent education, *education permanente*:

> Once education becomes continual, ideas as to what constitutes success and failure will change. An individual who fails at a given age and level in the course of his educational career will have other opportunities. He will no longer be relegated for life to the ghetto of his own failure. (ibid., p. 77.)

No one, in short, is so dumb that he cannot be a doctor or a nuclear physicist if he goes on trying. As a similarly kindly old polyanna of an educator said, making the same point in eighteenth-century Japan, some people can walk from Edo to Kyoto in fifteen days; some take forty and some even longer, but everyone can get there in the end. In British society today, the discussion of differences in intelligence becomes increasingly difficult. Words like 'pool of ability' can hardly be uttered except with derision or in apologetic quotation marks. It is a subject avoided except by men like Keith Joseph who are proud to bear a 'right-wing' label, or men like Eysenck, who cannot forebear to 'épater les naifs'. And when one observes the comfortable double-think of those middle-class egalitarians who sublimate a guilty sense of not deserving their middle-class privileges into a generous indignation against the iniquities of the class and social system, but for which *everybody* could be comfortably middle-class like them, then one is rather glad that there is an Eysenck around to tease them. They are, of course, not without reason on their side. If, as in Israeli kibbutzim, the family were eventually abolished and children brought up in public institutions the situation would be different, but (see above p. 178), not so much different that the question of *who* empties the dustbins and *who* builds the nuclear power stations would lose its importance.

So, among the various forms of romantic utopianism, I consider what I have called my Confucian one (and would, I suppose, have called a Platonic one, if I had had the benefit of a Western, rather than a Chinese, classical education) to be better than most. Confucian is not quite right, of course, because those moralistic Confucians who wanted society to be run on goodness by people who worked for self-fulfilment and from a sense of social duty were not particularly explicit (less so than Plato, in fact) in their demands for income equality, nor were they very precise about where 'superior men' came from or how they emerged. It was left to the earnest, pure, middle-class daughters of 'revolutionary' cadres in the fourth class of the third senior year of the Peking No. 1 Girls Middle School to take their ideas further. Wracked with guilt at their privileges, hating their parents for not being authentic workers-peasants-or-soldiers, and burning with the urge to join the production struggle, shoulder to shoulder with the peasants in the rice fields (and doubtless inspired by prior assurance of the approval of the Great Helmsman), they up-dated the doctrine and breathed into it the authentic, radical, egalitarian fire. The problem with the modern Chinese version of the doctrine, however, is precisely the romantic nature of its egalitarianism which enormously complicates the business of social selection. The relevance of innate ability differences is overtly denied, so that explicit aptitude tests are ruled out, and judgements of intellectual potential have to be made *sub rosa*. The only avowed principles of selection are, first the ascriptive, privilege-stood-on-its-head one of birth in a peasants'-workers'-soldiers' family, and secondly revolutionary purity. Defining the latter is an obvious problem. For China's sake, one *hopes* it means how well one gets on with the job and proves oneself by one's deeds to be a useful member of the community. One *fears* it may all too often be measured by the sanctimoniousness and glibness with which one denounces error and proclaims virtue.

The pitfalls of the Confucian utopia

But it is time to consider the obvious objections to the Confucian utopia. The most obvious one is also the most fundamental: no social order based on the assumption of Original Virtue will work, because man just is not originally virtuous. Among the major ideologies of our time the common premise of both Marxism and neo-classical economics is the assumption that overwhelmingly the strongest motive for human action, in all known historical societies, has been pursuit of material self-interest; to which the neo-classicals, if not the Marxists, would add that it always must be so. Likewise, the functionalist theory of social stratification holds that a social hierarchy in which there is a coincidence of the rankings of power and prestige and income is a universal feature of all societies; only thus can society motivate those who are capable of doing the difficult and responsible jobs to undertake the costly task of training themselves to accept them. The experience of communist societies is often cited as decisive: one recent survey concludes that the 'early policies which aimed at levelling out incomes generally have not been long-lasting because the constraints of economic and technical efficiency have required wider differentials' (Lane, 1971, p. 132; see also Bell, 1974, p. 450).

Economists insist that the growth of bureaucracy has only slightly constrained, not fundamentally altered, the forces which shape the rewards for work. Relative scarcities will always remain the overwhelmingly important determinant. Given an equally strong demand from society, those jobs which require talents which only a tiny minority possess will always command higher salaries than jobs which almost anyone can be trained to do. Only when the *willingness* to empty dustbins becomes as scarce (*relative to society's need for dustmen*) as the ability to teach sociology (relative to society's need to learn sociology) will dustmen earn as much as sociologists.

These are arguments one is entitled to be suspicious of. Material interest will be a dominant motive in societies whose institutions are based on the assumption that it is so. There is no such thing as Original Man capable of being virtuous or sinful. Actual men, in actual societies, are shaped by the culture of their society, a culture which is bound in large measure to snuggle up to the institutional structure which makes that particular society work. To be sure, human nature sets limits to the range of possible cultures; it is harder (requires a good deal more vigilant coercion) to run a social system which requires life-long celibacy of half its members than one which permits free marriage. But the evidence is not conclusive that Marx was wrong in thinking the potentiality of human nature to be, with respect to work motivation, rather wide — sufficiently so for one to expect that when decent standards of living could be assured for all it would be possible to create a society freed from alienating exploitation and class antagonism, in which men and women could learn to work for self-fulfilment rather than for self-enrichment. And if *that* sounds a bit too good to be true, at least it is easier to believe that in the mixture of actual motivations for work — money, self-expression, a sense of duty, and what modern communist régimes call the 'moral incentives' of being praised and given medals — the balance could be shifted decisively away from money. Even in our society with its predominantly materialistic ideology, it is not always clear where the balance lies. Let the reader ask his professional friends how much more a brick-layer would have to be earning than themselves before they would want to give up their jobs to lay bricks.

In any case, the functionalists' argument from the universal characteristics of stratification in all societies to the ineluctable functional necessity of such stratification systems is not a valid one. Wrong's alternative explanation (Wrong, 1959) of the universal nature of stratification will equally fit the facts — namely, that in all societies those who have the power, the people who take the allocative decisions, simply make sure that they have more than the average share of material rewards. Djilas' analysis of the origin of the privileged new class in communist societies accords better with that explanation than with the theory of functional prerequisites for social order and efficiency.

That argument, too, of course, can be a powerful challenge to the Confucian utopia. Why should the 'natural aristocracy' of tested talent be any more abstemious than other aristocracies have been? If they reach the controlling positions, why should they ever refrain from taking advantage of their control over the allocation of income? There are two possible answers to that, two reasons why it might possibly 'be different this time'. The first is that the ideology resulting from the selection process which gives them their greater power would provide a constraint on their power which previous élites have not be subjected to. They might genuinely see themselves as the lucky ones who should pay for their good fortune in having power and interesting jobs by serving society, rather than as the winners in a competitive struggle who deserve all they can get. The second is that one postulates, by definition, a modern society in which egalitarianism is a stronger force than it has ever been in previous phases of history. The democratic controls which are one product of that egalitarianism could and would be used by the powerless to ensure that the powerful lived up to their pretensions and that the compensatory principle of paying more to those with the boring jobs was, in fact, enforced.

For these reasons, it is hard to accept the argument from original sin as being decisive. There are, though, at least three other problems inherent in the Confucian utopia, which are very serious indeed.

The first is the difficulty of institutionalising a system which determines people's future quite explicitly according to their inborn, or at least by the time the judgement is made largely unalterable, qualities. To be told that one has failed an ability test is, in some ways, more emotionally devastating than to be told that one has failed an achievement test. Failure in an achievement test says to a man: not a very good performance; buck your ideas up; try again next year. Failure in an ability test says to a man: sorry chum; you're not in this class; horses for courses. It is not just the definitiveness of the judgement, though that is clearly part of it; achievement tests 'cool out' the failure more gradually; hopes have time slowly to adjust to prospects; few people can approach their fourth shot at O level maths with the same expectations as the first. But that is not all there is to it. It also has something to do with where people feel the core of Peer Gynt's onion to be; the essential irreducible self. A failure of will, the failure to try hard enough, is something one can forgive oneself, something a little less intrinsic to one's sense of selfhood than 'not having the ability' to do something. In one of the few experiments that bear on these matters, a psychologist has shown that as children grow up they become less apt, when judging others, merely to condemn failure and praise success, and are more likely to make moral judgements on the basis of effort — of 'try' rather than 'can'. There is a hint, though, that the process is later reversed and 'can' becomes more important in adulthood — at least American adulthood (Weiner, 1973). In any case, moral judgement and admiration (like guilt and shame, that other pair of concepts which psychologists tie themselves in knots trying to disentangle) are by no means the same. We all express disapproval of the lazy brilliant man and praise the dull plodding trier. But which would we rather be? The whole thing is curious, since there is no reason why the power to persevere should not be seen as just as much a matter of genetic luck as intelligence, but the fact is that a distinction is made.

And for that reason, there is likely to be a good deal of social resistance to the use of aptitude tests — because of the same trend towards a greater 'respect for people' as marks the difference between a Britain in which men were hanged for stealing sheep and a Britain which has abolished capital punishment. It is probably not without significance that a broad-ranging survey of the use of aptitude tests for job selection in the developing world (Ord, 1973) finds most of its examples of the fully institutionalised use of intelligence-type tests in Southern Africa or in New Guinea — places where it is an almost exclusively white expatriate group who do the testing and blacks who are 'culled' by the process. Intelligence tests are all right used *de haut en bas*, less so amongst one's own kind. They used to be quite acceptable for grammar school entry in Britain in the thirties when the middle class was doing the selection among the working class. With the abolition of fee-paying in local grammar schools after 1944, however, as the middle class began to have to sort out its own children by this method, their acceptability rapidly diminished.

What one cannot tell, however, is how far this situation would change if there were a change in the stratification system — if those who were being selected by the tests for the more difficult, interesting and responsible jobs ceased, at the same time, to be promised higher incomes. Would the prestige attaching to the possession of those particular sets of abilities, conventionally called intelligence or leadership, be so much reduced thereby that less mortifying shame would be entailed in being told that one does not possess them?

However much a change in the reward system might obviate *that* difficulty, there is a second problem implied in basing social selection explicitly on the luck of the gene distribution which no change in the income/occupation relationship could cure. Generally speaking, that which is rewarded is valued. When effort is rewarded, effort will be a virtue. A society which institutionally devalues effort, which does not reward the 'over-achiever' may well have problems in persuading its members that effort remains a social virtue.

The third problem implicit in my utopia is the problem of many utopias and anti-utopias from Plato's Republic to 1984 — the problem of social divisiveness — of the division of society into the alphas and the betas and the gammas; the people of gold, of silver and of brass. One aspect of that problem, brilliantly forecast in Michael Young's *Rise of the Meritocracy,* is perhaps inherent in either type of society — both the sinful world and the Confucian utopia. Whether selection is by the indirect method of ability-testing through achievement examinations or by explicit ability tests, over the generations (particularly as with the liberation of women, more marriages are made in universities and work places rather than in family drawing rooms, so that mating becomes more assortative with respect to intelligence rather than merely to social class), the disparities in average intelligence between different occupational groups will increase, social mobility will diminish, and a new caste system will emerge, more deeply entrenched, by virtue of its biological base, than any caste system in history.

But the process *is* likely to be different in the Confucian utopia. The experience of Czechoslovakia during the 1950s when it had what was probably the most egalitarian income distribution in Europe is instructive (Gellner, 1974, p. 167). Working-class parents became much less concerned to urge their children to study hard in order to get into the gymnasiums that led to administrative and professional jobs. They were happy that they should work in a factory if they could thereby earn as much — or even more — money. Middle-class parents, on the other hand, still wanted their children to go into the more responsible, more intrinsically satisfying, and in their eyes more prestigeful, middle-class occupations — even though the financial advantages were small — or negative. Social mobility declined.

Something similar is likely to happen in any society which moved towards utopia. What was called earlier the 'directionality' of intelligence — whether people are motivated to use it for self-expressive activity or as a means of gaining extrinsic rewards — is largely a matter of the values which prevail in the family, and in most societies there are obvious differences; work is more likely to be seen as self-fulfilment in the families of the middle class who have interesting jobs, and as a means of getting money by children whose fathers have the boring jobs which no one in his right mind would choose to do for their own sake (though there are differences between societies in this regard: Japanese in quite humble jobs are much more likely to express apparently genuine pride in the way in which they 'serve society' through their work than their English counterparts; Dore, 1973, p. 246; 1967, p. 143).

These initial differences might, then, be perpetuated in any newly-fledged utopia: not all children whom the tests designate as 'lucky enough' to have the interesting and difficult and responsible — but ill-paid — jobs would want to take them. This would, at least, slow down the process of biological selection and delay the onset of Michael Young's meritocratic state. The trade unions would be likely to have intelligent leadership — which they are decreasingly less likely to have in England as it is now constituted. The working class would perhaps be better able to defend the new income distribution against all attempts of the decision-makers to erode it. But still it would be likely to be a divided society, with a good deal more hereditary continuity of classes than is compatible with most people's view of the good society — or it would be, at least, in countries like Britain or France with quite sharply differentiated class cultures; much less so in more culturally homogeneous societies like Japan.

This leads on to a final problem inherent in the Confucian utopia. What *would* be the effects on social equality if one divorced the distribution of power from that of income? One must assume a level of egalitarianism and sophistication in the society sufficient to ensure that wealth is no longer a *necessary* reinforcer of authority. One must assume that it has become counter-productive for a managing director to keep a Rolls in addition to his everyday Mini especially for going down to the factory — 'so that the men will respect you' (see Unger, 1974, pp. 52-4). Otherwise the Confucian utopia just would not be viable. But if one is going to try to run the society on Goodness, on *noblesse oblige,* what will be the self-perceptions of those who hold power? Will they always be conscious of their luck in having the interesting jobs and awed by their sense of their good fortune into a suitable modesty, or will they somehow feel (as bright people are apt to feel) that 'they' — those essential selves of theirs — can claim the credit for being bright and that they really are rather morally upright people in taking their duties so seriously as to give their all to their mandarin jobs with so little expectation of material reward? Will they be just so insufferably moral and arrogant that people will want the Stuarts back? Might society not find in the end that it needs to give them an expense account Rolls just so that a tinge of guilt at their special privileges can give an edge of modesty to their exercise of power?

And, the other side of the coin, what will be the self-perceptions of those whom the talent-lottery has destined for the high-income, and low-interest, low-responsibility jobs? Will they find their higher incomes *real* compensation for their low-power low-intrinsic-satisfaction job? Or, will we discover that in our society now the possession of a second house and a boat only confer prestige, not for themselves, but because they are seen as symbols of earning power, and that when that connection is broken, the prestige ceases to attach to the consumption symbols themselves and remains firmly linked to the occupational positions — in other words, that those in the low-interest low-responsibility jobs will be deprived not only of power and the opportunity for self-fulfilment, but also of social respect, to a degree that material satisfactions cannot compensate for. Rawls, who would base his socially just society on the talent-equals-luck, compensate-to-equalise principle of the Confucian utopia, believes that that would indeed be the case. Different dimensions of inequality cannot be made to compensate for each other; true equality can only be obtained if there is equality in each dimension separately, particularly in the most fundamental dimension of all — that of self-respect. For this reason Rawls, following his principle through to its logical conclusion, concludes that a just society would have to give up the ambition to maximise the use of native talent; justice will have to be pursued at the *expense* of greater affluence, of emphasis on social efficiency and technocratic values (Rawls, 1971, p. 101).

He is probably right. One can try to retrieve the position, following Runciman and Bell, by insisting that there is a difference between basic 'respect' which can be accorded to all by virtue of their humanity, and 'praise' which is differentially accorded by virtue of performance (Bell, 1974, pp. 456-8). But it is hard to sustain. It is true that societies differ widely in the basic minimum of respect accorded to all — as they differ widely in their welfare minima on the income dimension of difference. Tocqueville was overwhelmed by the sense of that difference when he first took his French perceptions of society to America. But, just as there is no 'absolute' welfare minimum, only socially relative ones, so too it is impossible to attach any absolute sense to Toqueville's 'basic equality of condition'. An income which provides the basic necessities is not different *in kind* from the income received by the chairman of ICI, nor is the respect minimum which one receives *qua* British citizen different in kind from the respect accorded a doctor or an actor — at least it is not subjectively perceived as different — and that is what counts.

The viability of compromise
I have, in the course of this exploration, talked myself out of my
enthusiasm for the Confucian utopia. But it has, I think, been a useful
way of exploring the issues. When one moves from black and white
ideal types and thinks of the complexities of human motivation —
reflects, for instance, on the occasions when one has eagerly seized the
opportunity to give a lecture for the genuinely altruistic reason that one
wishes to propogate a certain point of view, but has not been *entirely*
unaware of the size of the fee that was offered, or on the way in which
people who say that they are 'only in it for the money' nevertheless seem
often to do jobs with a devotion that can only be explained by the urge
to self-fulfilment or a sense of social duty — when one realises these
complexities of motivation one realises too that all modern socially
mobile societies are bound to be some form of compromise between the
sinful world and the Confucian utopia.

In other words, the modest proposals of Chapter 13 can still stand as
modest proposals — all, that is, except the shift in recruitment
patterns. That particular change, substituting more in-career selection
and training for pre-career selection and training, has got to be a sharp
break — as it has been in the two societies, China and Tanzania, which
have tried it. But the other changes can be more-or-less changes; the
instruments of selection can shift from the 'pure' achievement test pole
towards the 'pure' ability test pole; the social rationalisation of success
can subtly move from overwhelming emphasis on the *efforts* of those
who thereby *earn* and *deserve* their superior positions and are entitled
to all they can get, towards a greater recognition of the luck of those
who are privileged by the gift of scarce abilities and should feel suitably
grateful and humble about it; the income rewards for occupying the
'higher' decision-making jobs can be gradually reduced — and perhaps,
if inflation and powerful trade unions work at it long enough,
eventually be taken past the point at which conventional differentials
get reversed.

I am not sure, though, that there is any happy and stable point of
compromise between the sinful world and the Confucian utopia. The
closer one sticks to the sinful world the more likely one is to be caught
up in the dilemmas which increasing corporatism, affluence and
egalitarianism bring in their wake, and the less viable the system
becomes. The closer one gets to the Confucian utopia, the more
apparent the dangers of divisiveness and moral arrogance and the
fundamental maiming of the individual self-respect of a large part of
the population.

The sad fact is that the claims of equality, of individual dignity, are
not easily reconciled with the diversity of human talent and with the
increasing need — as society becomes more technologically complex, or

begins a late twentieth-century development drive as in the Third World — to take account of that diversity in deciding who does what. A number of species in the history of this planet have disappeared because they have developed characteristics which, in changed environmental circumstances, became incompatible. Diplodocus' long tube of a neck and his crude digestive apparatus were a not impossible combination when he lived half in the water in swamps; they proved rather unfunctional when the swamps dried up.

And so natural historians of the future might judge the fate of Man. It does seem a blunder on somebody's part to have created a species with our capacity for envy, for *ressentiment*, and with our need to clothe some core essential self with dignity, which at the same time was so biologically constructed as to permit such a wide diversity of individual capacities. It did not matter so much when the organisationally most important dimension of differential capacity — as now among baboons — was strength of will and muscle. Things worked out because those most endowed with the strength could enforce a social order on the others. And if cleverness played the same simple rôle in modern technological societies that brawn and strength of will played in primitive ones, we might reach a similarly viable resolution of the problems; the clever ones could simply outwit the rest. But that is not the way it works, if only because the clever ones are not *that* clever, nor the rest of us so dull; abilities vary across a spectrum with most of us clustered around the average. And so the tension between equality and diversity becomes increasingly apparent.

If Man does follow Diplodocus and disappear from the face of this globe, his failure to reconcile the desire for equality with the diversity of potentialities is likely to have a lot to do with it.

Bibliography

Abbott (1966): F. Abbot, 'Traditional and Religious Barriers; the Makateb of Bahawapur', in Hanson and Brembeck (1966).

Ajia Chōsakai (1974): Ajia Chōsakai, *Chūgoku Sōran* (1975).

Alexander and Simmons (1975): L. Alexander and J. Simmons. *The Determinants of School Achievement in Developing Countries; The educational production function,* IBRD Staff Working Paper No. 201 (1975).

Allen (1962): G. C. Allen, *A Short Economic History of Japan* (1962).

Ames (1967): M. M. Ames, 'The Impact of Western Education on Religion and Society in Ceylon', *Pacific Affairs,* **40,** i and ii, (Spring and Summer 1967).

Anderson (1961): C. A. Anderson, 'A Skeptical Note on Education and Mobility', *American Journal of Sociology,* **66,** ii (May 1961). Reprinted in A. H. Halsey *et al.* (1961).

Anderson (1965): C. A. Anderson, 'Literacy and Schooling on the Development Threshold', in Anderson and Bowman (1965).

Anderson (1973): D. S. Anderson, 'The Social Context of Examinations', in Commonwealth Secretariat (1973).

Anderson and Bowman (1965): C. A. Anderson and M. J. Bowman, eds, *Education and Economic Development* (1965).

Anon (1961): Anon., 'The Thorne Experiment', *Education* (10 February 1961).

Arrow (1974): K. Arrow, 'Higher Education as a Filter', in Lumsden (1974).

Ashby (1961): E. Ashby, 'On Universities and the Scientific Revolution' (reprinted from his *Technology and the Academics*), in Halsey *et al.* (1961).

Ashby (1972): E. Ashby, *'The Structure of Higher Education: A world view',* paper for Lancaster Conference on Higher Education, mimeo (September 1972).

Asō (1968): M. Asō, *Eriito to Kvoku,* Tokyo (1968).

Azumi (1968): K. Azumi, *Higher Education and Business Recruitment in Japan* (1968).

Balogh and Streeten (1964): T. Balogh and P. Streeten, 'The Coefficient of Ignorance', *Bulletin of the Oxford Institute of Statistics,* **25,** ii (1963), reprinted in Blaug (1968).

Baghwati (1973): J. Bhagwati, 'Education, Class Structure and Income Equality', *World Development,* **1,** v (May 1973).

Beeby (1966): C. E. Beeby, *The Quality of Education in Developing Areas* (1966).

Bell (1974): D. Bell, *The Coming of Post Industrial Society* (1974).

Bennett (1973): N. Bennett, *A Scheme for Improving the Quality of Rural Life through Community Centred Education,* mimeo, CIDOC, Cuernavaca, Mexico (1973).

Berg (1973): Ivar Berg, *Education and Jobs; The great training robbery* (1973).

Bienefeld (1972): M. A. Bienefeld, 'Planning People', in Uchumi Editorial Board (1972).

Blaug (1968): M. Blaug (ed.), *Economics of Education,* Vol. 1 (1968).

Blaug, Layard and Woodhall (1969): M. Blaug, R. Layard and M. Woodhall, *Causes of Graduate Unemployment in India* (1969).

Blaug (1970): M. Blaug, *An Introduction to the Economics of Education* (1970).

Blaug (1972a): M. Blaug, 'Educational Planning and the Economics of Education', in Rockefeller (1972).

199

Blaug (1972b): M. Blaug, 'The Correlation between Education and Earnings: What does it signify?', *Higher Education,* **1,** i (1972).

Blaug (1973): M. Blaug, *Education and the Employment Problems in Developing Countries,* ILO, Geneva (1973).

Blaug (1974): M. Blaug, 'An Economic Analysis of Personal Earnings in Thailand,' *Economic Development and Cultural Change,* **23,** i (October 1974).

Bodmer (1972): W. F. Bodmer, 'Race and IQ: The genetic background', in Richardson and Spears (1972).

Bouglé (1901): C. Bouglé, *Les Idées égalitaires* (1901).

Bowles (1971a): S. Bowles, 'Cuban Education and the Revolutionary Ideology', *Harvard Educational Review,* **41,** iv (November 1971).

Bowles (1971b): S. Bowles, 'Unequal Education and the Reproduction of the Social Division of Labour', *Review of Radical Political Economics,* **3,** iv (Fall/Winter 1971).

Bowles (1973): S. Bowles, 'Education, Class Conflict and Uneven Development', in Simmons (1973).

Bowman and Anderson (1974): M. J. Bowman and C. A. Anderson, *Mass Higher Education: Some perspectives from experience in the United States,* Paris, OECD Conference on Future Structure of Post-secondary Education (1974).

Bowman (1965): M. J. Bowman, 'From Guilds to Infant Training Industries', in Anderson and Bowman (1965).

Briggs (1973): A. Briggs, 'Are Your A-levels Really Necessary?', *Sunday Times Magazine* (30 September 1973).

Britain: Advisory Committee (1925): Government of Great Britain, Advisory Committee on Native Education in British Tropical Africa Dependencies, *Education Policy in British Tropical Africa* (1925).

Britain: Education (1950): *Education 1900-1950, Report of the Ministry of Education and Statistics of Public Education for England and Wales,* (1950).

Bryce Commission (1895): Royal Commission on Secondary Education, *Report* (1895).

Burns and Saul (1967): T. Burns and S. B. Saul (eds), *Social Theory and Economic Change* (1967).

Burrage (1972): M. Burrage, 'Democracy and the Mystery of the Crafts: Observations on work relationships in America and Britain', *Daedalus* (Fall 1972).

Cameron and Dodd (1970): J. Cameron and W. A. Dodd, *Society Schools and Progress in Tanzania* (1970).

Carter and Carnoy (1974): M. A. Carter and M. Carnoy, *Theories of Labour Markets and Worker Productivity,* discussion paper, 74-4 mimeo (August 1974), Portola Institute, Menlo Park, California.

Ceylon (1966): Government of Ceylon, *Proposals for Reform in General and Technical Education* (1966).

Ceylon: Commissioner (1971): Ceylon, Commissioner of Examinations, *Administration Report for the Year 1968-69* (1971).

Ceylon: Education (1973): Ceylon, Ministry of Education, *Medium-term Plan for the Development of Education, 1973-77* (March 1973).

Chari (1973): S. M. Chari, 'Public Examinations and the Curriculum', in Commonwealth Secretariat (1973).

Chūgoku Kenkyūjo (1968): Chūgoku Kenkyūjo (ed.), *Shin Chūgoku Nenkan,* Tokyo (1968, annual).

Ch'un Lei (1967): *Ch'un Lei* (13 April 1967) article extracted in *Survey of the Chinese Mainland Press* No. 3940.

Clements (1958): R. V. Clements, *Managers, a Study of Their Careers in Industry* (1958).

Colclough and Hallak (1975): C. Colclough and J. Hallak, *Rural Education and Employment,* IDS, University of Sussex, mimeo (1975).

Collins (1971): R. Collins, 'Functional and Conflict Theories of Stratification', *American Sociological Review*, **36**, 1002-19 (1971).

Coombs and Ahmed (1974): P. H. Coombs and M. Ahmed, *Attacking Rural Poverty: How non-formal education can help*, Baltimore, Johns Hopkins U.P. (1974).

Commonwealth Secretariat (1973): Commonwealth Secretariat, *Public Examinations, Report of the Commonwealth Planning Seminar. Accra, March 1973*, (*Education in the Commonwealth No. 8*) (1973).

Curle (1966): A. Curle, *Planning for Education in Pakistan* (1966).

Davies (1967): D. Davies, 'Education for a Technological Society: A scarce resource called curiosity', in *The Listener* (4 May 1967).

Deakin (1973): J. Deakin, 'Trends and Problems', in Commonwealth Secretariat (1973).

Dean (1974): G. Dean, 'Report on a Visit to People's Republic of China', mimeo, East-West Centre, Hawaii, East-West Technology and Development Institute (1974).

Deane (1962): P. Deane and W. A. Cole, *British Economic Growth 1688-1959* (1962).

Denison (1962): E. F. Denison, *The Sources of Economic Growth in the U.S. and the Alternatives Before Us*, Supplementary Paper No. 13, New York, Committee for Economic Development (1962).

Doeringer and Piore (1971): P. B. Doeringer and M. J. Piore, *Internal Labour Markets and Manpower Analysis* (1971).

Dore (1963): R. P. Dore, *Education in Tokugawa Japan* (1963).

Dore (1964): R. P. Dore, 'Education', in R. E. Ward and D. Rustow, *Political Modernization in Japan and Turkey* (1964).

Dore (1967): R. P. Dore, 'Mobility, Equality and Individuation', in R. P. Dore (ed.), *Aspects of Social Change in Modern Japan* (1967).

Dore (1972): R. P. Dore, *False Prophets: The Cuernavaca Critique of School*, IDS Discussion Paper, No. 12, IDS, University of Sussex, mimeo (1972).

Dore (1973): R. P. Dore, *British Factory—Japanese Factory* (1973).

Dore (1976): R. P. Dore, 'Human Capital Theory, the Diversity of societies, and the Problem of Quality in Education', *Higher Education* **6**, i (1976).

Dyer (1904): Henry Dyer, *Dai Nippon: The Britain of the East* (1904).

ECAFE (1974): Economic Commission for Asia and the Far East, *Economic Survey of Asia and the Far East, 1973, Part One: Education and Employment*, mimeo (January 1974).

Edwards (forthcoming): R. C. Edwards, *Alienation and Inequality: Capitalist relations of production in bureaucratic enterprises* (forthcoming).

Faure (1974): Edgar Faure *et al.*, *Learning To Be*, UNESCO (1972).

Flinn (1967): M. W. Flinn, 'Social Theory and the Industrial Revolution', in Burns and Saul (1967).

Foster (1963): P. J. Foster, 'The Vocational School Fallacy in Development Planning', in Anderson and Bowman (1965).

Fox (1974): A. Fox, *Beyond Contract: Work, power and trust relations* (1974).

Gellner (1974): E. A. Gellner, *Contemporary thought and politics*, (1974).

Gerschenkron (1965): A. Gerschenkron, *Economic Backwardness in Historical Perspective* (1965).

Ghiselli (1966): E. E. Ghiselli, *The Validity of Occupational Aptitude Tests* (1966).

Gillette (1972): A. Gillette, *Cuba's Educational Revolution*, Fabian research series 302, London Fabian Society (1972).

Gintis (1971): H. Gintis, 'Education, Technology and the Characteristics of Worker Productivity, *American Economic Review*, **61**, ii (May 1971).

Glass (1961): D. V. Glass, 'Education and Social Change in Modern England', in Halsey *et al.* (1961).

Goldstone (1972): L. Goldstone, 'A Summary Statistical Review of Education in the World', in Rockefeller (1972).

Halsey *et al.* (1966): A. W. Halsey, J. Floud and C. A. Anderson (eds), *Education, Economy and Society* (1961).

Hanson and Brembeck (1966): J. W. Hanson and C. S. Brembeck, *Education and the Development of Nations* (1966).

Harker (1974): B. R. Harker, 'The Contribution of Schooling to Agricultural Modernization: An empirical analysis', in P. Foster and J. Sheffield (eds), *World Yearbook of Education 1974,* London (1973).

Harris (1972): N. Harris, *Competition and the Corporate Society* (1972).

Herrnstein (1973): R. J. Herrnstein, *I.Q. in the Meritocracy* (1973).

Hill (1965): C. Hill, *Intellectual Origins of The English Revolution* (1965).

Hurt (1972): J. Hurt, *Education in Evolution* (1972).

Illich (1971): I. Illich, *Deschooling Society* (1971).

ILO (1971): ILO, *Matching Employment Opportunities and Expectations: A programme of action for Ceylon* (1971).

ILO (1972): ILO, *Employment, Incomes and Equality: A strategy for increasing productive employment in Kenya* (1972).

ILO (1974): ILO, *Sharing in Development: A programme of employment, equity and growth for the Philippines* (1974).

Jackson and Marsden (1966): B. Jackson and D. Marsden, *Education and the Working Class* (1966).

Japan: Education (1964): Mombushō, *Gakusei Kyūjūnenshi* (1964).

Japan: Education (1965): Ministry of Education, *Japan's Growth and Education in the Social and Economic Development of Japan,* Tokyo (1966).

Japan: Unesco (1966): Japanese National Commission for UNESCO, *The Role of Education in the Social and Economic Development of Japan,* Tokyo (1966).

Jayawardena (1972): V. K. Jayawardena, *The Rise of the Labor Movement in Ceylon* (1972).

Jayasuriya (1969): J. E. Jayasuriya, *Education in Ceylon Before and After Independence 1939-1968,* Colombo (1969).

Jencks (1972): C. Jencks *et al., Inequality: A reassessment of the effect of family and schooling on America* (1972).

Jensen (1973): A. R. Jensen, *Educability and Group Differences* (1973).

Johnson (1972): H. G. Johnson, 'The Alternatives Before Us', *Journal of Political Economy,* **80,** iii, part 2 (May/June 1972).

Jolly (1971): A. R. Jolly, 'Contrasts in Cuban and African Educational Strategies', in J. Lowe (1971).

Jolly (1973): A. R. Jolly, 'The Judo Trick: A plea for less concern with what to do in education and more experiments (and research) on how to do it', Paper for Rockefeller (1973).

Kahn (1965): A. Kahn, 'Russian Scholars and Statesmen on Education as an Investment', in Anderson and Bowman (1965).

Kessen (1974): W. Kessen, 'An American Glimpse of the Children of China, Report of a Visit', *SSRC ITEMS,* **28,** iii (September 1975).

Keynes (1936): J. M. Keynes, *The General Theory of Employment Interest and Money* (1936).

King (1973): K. King, *Skill Aquisition in the Informal Sector of an African Economy, the Kenya Case,* mimeo (1973), Centre for African Studies, Univ. of Edinburgh.

Kinyanjui (1973): P. K. Kinyanjui, 'Education, Training and Employment of Secondary School Leavers in Kenya', in *Manpower and Employment Research in Africa,* Centre for Developing Area Studies, MacGill, **6,** ii (1973).

Lane (1971): D. Lane, *The End of Inequality?* (1971).

Lewis (1969): O. Lewis, *Pedro Martinez* (1969).

Lindbeck (1971): J. Lindbeck (ed.), *China: Management of a revolutionary society* (1971).

Little and Oxenham (1975): A. Little and J. Oxenham, *Credentialism: Speculations on careers handbooks and newspaper cuttings,* Paper for Lancaster Conference on Higher Education, mimeo (1975).

Lowe (1971): J. Lowe (ed.), *Education and Nation Building in the Third World,* Edinburgh (1971).

Lumsden (1974): K. G. Lumsden (ed.), *Efficiency in the Universities,* Amsterdam, Elsevier (1975).

McClelland (1961): D. C. McClelland, *The Achieving Society* (1961).

McClelland and Steele (1973): D. C. McClelland and R. S. Steele, *Human Motivation: A book of readings* (1973).

McNamara (1973): R. S. McNamara, *One Hundred Countries; Two Billion People,* New York, Praeger (1973).

Malaysia (1972): Malaysia, Ministry of Education Planning and Research Division, *Preliminary Report on a Study of Opinions about Education and Society* (1972).

Maslow (1973): A. Maslow, 'Deficiency Motivation and Growth Motivation', in McClelland and Steel (1973).

Matys (1973): G. J. Matys, 'Tests and Measurement Procedures, Review and Evaluation', in Commonwealth Secretariat (1973).

Mazumdar (1972): V. Mazumdar, *Education and Social Change,* Simla, Indian Institute for Advanced Study (1972).

Merllié (1975): D. Merllié, 'Psychologie et mobilité sociale', *Actes de la Recherche en Sciences Sociales,* **3,** (May 1975).

Meyer (1973): John W. Meyer, *National Economic Growth, 1950-1965: Educational and political factors,* mimeo, Paper for Seadag Seminar on Education and National Development, Singapore (September 1973).

Miller (1969): S. M. Miller, *Strategies for Reducing Credentialism,* mimeo (1969).

Mittler (1971): P. Mittler, *The Study of Twins* (1971).

Muel (1975): F. Muel, 'L'Ecole obligatoire et l'invention de l'enfance anormale', *Actes de la Recherche en Sciences Sociales,* **1,** (January 1975).

Munro (1971): D. J. Munro, 'Egalitarian Ideal and Educational Fact in Communist China', in Lindbeck (1971).

Nagai (1971): M. Nagai, *Higher Education in Japan: Its take-off and crash,* University of Tokyo Press (1971).

Naipaul (1961): V. S. Naipaul, *A House for Mr Biswas* (1961).

Nyerere (1967): J. K. Nyerere, *Education for Self-reliance,* Dar es Salaam, Government Printer (1967).

Obeysekere (1974): G. Obeysekere, 'Some Comments on the Social Backgrounds of the April 1971 Insurgents in Sri Lanka', *Journal of Asian Studies,* **33,** iii (May 1974).

O'Connell and Beckett (1975): J. O'Connell and P. A. Beckett, 'Social Characteristics of an Elite-in-formation: The case of Nigeria University Students', *British Journal of Sociology,* **26,** iii (September 1975).

OECD (1971a): OECD, *Reviews of National Policies for Education: Japan* (1971).

OECD (1971b): OECD, *Occupational and Educational Structures of the Labour Force and Levels of Economic Development* (1971).

Ord (1972): I. G. Ord, 'Testing for Educational and Occupational Selection in Developing Countries — A review', *Occupational Psychology,* **46,** iii (1972).

Passin (1965): H. Passin, *Society and Education in Japan* (1965).

Pieris (1964): R. Pieris, 'Universities, Politics and Public Opinion in Ceylon', *Minerva,* **2** (1964).

Pilliner (1973): A. E. G. Pilliner, 'Testing with Educationally Disadvantaged Children', in Commonwealth Secretariat (1973).

Premadasa (1973): B. Premadasa, 'The Examination Scene in Sri Lanka (Ceylon)', in Commonwealth Secretariat (1973).

Psachoropoulos (1973): G. Psachoropoulos, *Returns to Education: An international comparison,* Amsterdam, Elsevier (1973).

Rawls (1971): J. Rawls, *A Theory of Justice* (1971).

Reimer (1971): E. Reimer, *School Is Dead: Alternatives in Education: An indictment of the system and a strategy of revolution* (1971).

Richardson and Spears (1972): K. Richardson and D. Spears (eds), *Race, Culture and Intelligence,* Penguin (1972).

Rockefeller (1972): Rockefeller Foundation and Ford Foundation, *Education and Development Reconsidered,* Conference at Bellagio (May 1972), 2 vols, mimeo.

Rockefeller (1973): Rockefeller Foundation and Ford Foundation, *Education and Development,* Conference at Bellagio (June 1973).

Rudolph and Rudolph (1972): L. Rudolph and S. Rudolph (eds), *Education and Politics in India: Studies in organisation, society and policy* (1972).

Sato (1972): K. Sato, *A Definition of the problem: A pre-requisite for identifying educational strategy for employment promotion,* mimeo, Seminar on Employment Strategy, UN Asian Institute for Economic Development and Planning (November 1972).

Schram (1974): S. Schram (ed.), *Mao Tse-Tung Unrehearsed* (1974).

Shimizu (1957): Y. Shimizu, *Shiken* (1957).

Simon (1960): B. Simon, *Studies in the History of Education 1780-1870* (1960).

Simmons (1973): J. Simmons, *Investment in Education: Radical strategies,* mimeo, IBRD (September 1973).

Smith (1937): A. Smith, *The Wealth of Nations* Random House edition (1937).

Somerset (1973): H. C. A. Somerset, 'Educational Aspirations of Fourth Form Pupils in Kenya', in *Manpower and Employment Research in Africa,* Center for Developing Area Research in Africa, McGill, **6,** ii (1973).

Sri Lanka (1971): Sri Lanka, Ministry of Planning and Employment, *Five Year Plan* (1971).

Sri Lanka (1972): Sri Lanka, Ministry of Education, *Comprehensive Plan for Educational Development,* mimeo (1972).

Sri Lanka (1974): Sri Lanka, Planning Division, Ministry of Education, *Educational Reforms in Sri Lanka (Draft),* mimeo (August 1974).

Tanzania (1967): United Republic of Tanzania, Ministry of Education, *Annual Report 1967,* Dar es Salaam, Government Printer (1972).

Tanzania (1967): United Republic of Tanzania, *Tanzania Second Five Year Plan for Economic and Social Development,* Vol. IV, Dar es Salaam, Government Printer (1969).

Taubman and Wales (1973): P. J. Taubman and T. Wales, 'Higher Education, Mental Ability and Screening', *Journal of Political Economy,* **81,** i (January/February 1973).

Taunton Commission (1868): Schools Inquiry Commission, *Report* (1868).

Terrill (1972): R. Terrill, 'Tomorrow's China', *Observer* (9 January 1972).

Tocqueville (1954): A. de Tocqueville, *Democracy in America,* Vintage paperback edn (1954).

Tort (1974): M. Tort, *Le Quotient intellectuel* (1974).

Traub and Elliott (1973): R. E. Traub and H. A. Elliott, 'Development of the Canadian Scholastic Aptitude Tests', in Commonwealth Secretariat (1973).

Uchumi Editorial Board (1972): Uchumi Editorial Board (ed.), *Towards Socialist Planning, Tanzanian Studies, No. 1,* Dar es Salaam, Tanzania Publishing House (1972).

UNESCO (1963, etc.): UNESCO, *Statistical Yearbook* (1963 etc.).

UNESCO (1971b): Third Regional Conference of Ministers of Education and Those Responsible for Economic Planning in Asia, *Final Report* Paris, UNESCO (1971).

Unger (1973): J. Unger, *Rural Education in Post-Cultural Revolution China,* mimeo, IDS, University of Sussex (1973).

Unger (1974): J. Unger, *Politics of Wages in the Socialist States,* IDS Discussion Paper No. 59, IDS, University of Sussex (1974).

Vaizey and Debeauvais (1961): J. Vaizey and M. Debeauvais, 'Economic Aspects of Educational Development', in Halsey *et al.* (1961).

Waley (1956): A. Waley, *Three Ways of Thought in Ancient China,* Doubleday Anchor edn (1956).

Weiner (1973): B. Weiner, 'From Each According to His Abilities: The role of effort in a moral society', *Human Development,* **16,** i, pp. 53-60 (1973).

Wickwar (1949): H. and M. Wickwar, *The Social Services* (1949).

Wijemanne and Sinclair (1972): E. J. Wijemanne and M. E. Sinclair, 'General Education: Some developments in the sixties and prospects for the seventies' *Marga,* **1,** iv (1972).

Wiles (1974): P. J. Wiles, 'The Correlation Between Education and Earnings: The external-test-not-content-hypothesis' *Higher Education,* **3,** i (1974).

Wilkinson (1964): R. Wilkinson, *The Prefects: British leadership and the public school tradition* (1964).

Williams (1974): P. Williams, 'Lending for Learning: An experiment in Ghana', *Minerva,* **12,** iii (July 1974).

Wiseman (1967): S. Wiseman (ed.), *Intelligence and Ability,* Penguin (1967).

Wrong (1959): D. H. Wrong, 'The Functional Theory of Stratification: Some neglected considerations', *American Sociological Review,* **24,** vi (December 1959).

Young (1958): M. Young, *The Rise of the Meritocracy* (1958).

Index

Abbot, F., 17
abilities, differential, 93, 95, 139, 142, 162, 174, 178, 179, 189-90
ability tests, 28-30, 34, 192
academic bias, 124
academic profession, 149
accountancy, 20, 23, 73, 143, 159
achievement motivation, 9, 138, 139, 178
achievement tests, *see also* examination orientation, 94, 154, 163
acquisitive achievement, 178-99
administrative skills, 143
aesthetics, 124
affluence, 186, 197
agricultural improvement, *see also* rural development, 2
agriculture — in curriculum, 11
Ahmed, M., 105
Alexander, L., 96
ambition, 170
Ames, M., 55
Anderson, C., 14, 16, 86
Anderson, D., 161, 162, 164
apprenticeship, x, 15, 18, 22, 27-42, 133-4
aptitude tests, x, 154-8, 174, 175, 182, 192, 193
architecture, 20, 143
aristocracy, in Japan, 38
arithmetic, 59, 62
army, 44, 188; recruitment into, 20, 30
army training — for industry, 30
Arnold, T., 16, 52
Arrow, K., 94
artists, 153
arts/science specialisation, 56, 60, 101, 123, 144
Arusha declaration, 112
ascription, 190
Ashby, E., 14, 19, 33, 150
Asian immigration in East Africa, 74
Asian Manpower Plan (UNESCO), 98
aspirations, 125
astrology, 130
authoritarianism, 110-11
authority, 195; acceptance of, 188

baboons, 198
backwash, *see* examination orientation
Baghwati, J., 94
Balogh, T., 92
Bank of England, 29

BBC, 32
Beckett, P., 79
Beeby, C., 7, 165
belongingness, 186
Bell, D., 181, 182, 187, 196
benevolence, 183
Bennett, N., 105
Berg, I., 94
Besant, Annie, 55
Bienefeld, M., 116
biology, 127
Blaug, M., 86, 88, 89, 91, 94, 104, 165
boarding schools, 109, 114
Bodmer, W., 178
Bolivia, 132
bonding, 149
bookishness, 82, 129
Bouglé, C., 187
Bowles, S., 95, 107, 108, 109, 110
Bowman, M., 17, 86
brain-drain, 59, 149
Brazil, 136
bridge-head strategy, *see* dualistic development
Briggs, A., 26, 27
Britain, x, 14-34, 85, 155
Bryce Commission (1895), 76
Buddhism, 37, 55, 128
Buganda, 79
Bukoba, 118
bureaucracy, ix, 81, 94, 146-7, 148, 185, 186, 191; *see also* corporations, large
Burghers, 52
Burrage, M., 28

calling, 183
Cameron, J., 113
Canton, 175
capital aid, 1
capitalism, 172
career guides, 22
Carnoy, M., 95
Carter, M., 95
caste, 58
Castro, F., 107
Catholicism, 52
centralisation of educational administration, 78
certificates, as celebration, 150
'character', and man-management, 30, 54, 70-1, 118

207

traditional sector, *see* dualistic development
training and education, 150
training mystique, xi
translation, 51
Traub, R., 155
Trevelyan, G. M., 19
tribalism, 115
Trotsky, L., 8
trust, 188
Tu Fu, 169
Turkey, 90
two legs, walking on, 172, 176

Uganda, 3
Ujamaa, 13
unemployment, 61, 122, 133; *see also* educated unemployment
UNESCO, 103, 104, 188; Addis Ababa conference, 1, 99; Asian Manpower Plan, 98; Karachi conference, 1, 99
Unger, J., 172, 173, 195
UNICEF, 104
United States, 21, 33, 131, 132, 135, 136, 137, 155, 158, 186
universities, 18, 19, 21, 33, 188; enrolments, 46, 48, 78; entrance examinations, 45, 59, 90, 124, 125, 145, 170, 173-5, 176 (*see also* selection tests); length of courses, 146, 151; social function of, 29, 36
university education: and business management, 30, 43, 44; returns to, 90
utopias, 194

Vaizey, J., 2

village crafts, 127
vocational aptitude, 24
vocational education, 11, 62, 87, 101-3, 109, 115, 124, 151, 154

wage determination, 191
Wales, T., 94
Waley, A., 185
Waseda university, 46
Weber, M., 74
Weiner, B., 193
welfare minimum, 196
West Riding, 160
Westernisation, in Japan, 40
white-collar employment, 122
Wickwar, H., 18
Wijemanne, E., 123
Wiles, P., 94
Wilkinson, R., 17
Wiseman, S., 178
work, 12
work ethic, and education, 50
work motivation, 65, 109, 121, 141, 146, 185-8, 191
work/study schools, 109-10, 114-16, 133, 151, 168, 171
World Bank, 91, 102, 104
Wrong, D., 192

year of education (Cuba), 107
Young, M., 194, 195
youth revolt, US, 135

Zambia, 156
zero growth, 188